Studies in the Political Economy of Public Policy

Studies in the Political Economy of Public Policy presents cutting edge research on the origins and impacts of public policy. The series takes as its starting point the recognition that public policy and its outcomes are shaped by and shape the political-economic context within which they exist. It accepts that conflicts and cooperation between public and private interests and how they are reconciled are crucial determinants of public policy and its impact on society. Titles in the series will focus on the competitive and cooperative dynamics operating in increasingly complex policy spaces in a range of diverse settings. The series will launch with a set of books on emerging and frontier markets, failed states, and crisis-afflicted developed countries. Fundamentally pluralist and interdisciplinary in nature, the setting is designed to attract high quality original research of both a theoretical and empirical nature that make sense of contemporary public policies as well as their determinants and impacts in novel and relevant ways.

Series editors:

Toby Carroll, Senior Research Fellow, Centre on Asia and Globalisation, Lee Kuan Yew School of Public Policy, National University of Singapore

M. Ramesh, Chair Professor of Governance and Public Policy, Hong Kong Institute of Education

Darryl Jarvis, Associate Dean, Faculty of Liberal Arts and Social Sciences, Hong Kong Institute of Education

Paul Cammack, Professor, Department of Asian and International Relations Studies, City University of Hong Kong

International Advisory Board:

Michael Howlett, Simon Fraser University, Canada

John Hobson, University of Sheffield, UK

Stuart Shields, University of Manchester, UK

Lee Jones, Queen Mary, University of London, UK

Kanishka Jayasuriya, University of Adelaide, Australia

Shaun Breslin, University of Warwick, UK

Kevin Hewison, Murdoch University, Australia

Richard Stubbs, McMaster University, Canada

Dick Bryan, University of Sydney, Australia

Kun-chin Lin, University of Cambridge, UK

Apiwat Ratanawaraha, Chulalongkorn University, Thailand

Wil Hout, Institute of Social Studies, Erasmus University, The Netherlands

Penny Griffin, University of New South Wales, Australia

Philippe Zittoun, Sciences Po, Grenoble, France

Heng Yee Kuang, National University of Singapore

Heloise Weber, University of Queensland, Australia

Max Lane, Victoria University, Australia

Titles include:

Toby Carroll and Darryl S.L. Jarvis
THE POLITICS OF MARKETISING ASIA

Daniel Novotny and Clara Portela (*editors*)
EU-ASEAN RELATIONS IN THE 21ST CENTURY
Towards a Stronger Partnership

Philippe Zittoun
THE POLITICAL PROCESS OF POLICYMAKING
A Pragmatic Approach to Public Policy

Forthcoming titles include:

Pascale Hatcher
THE WORLD BANK AND NEW MINING REGIMES IN ASIA

Studies in the Political Economy of Public Policy
Series Standing Order ISBN 978–113–700–1498 hardback
978–113–700–1504 paperback

You can receive future titles in this series as they are published by placing a standing order. Please contact your bookseller or, in case of difficulty, write to us at the address below with your name and address, the title of the series and the ISBN quoted above.

Customer Services Department, Macmillan Distribution Ltd, Houndmills, Basingstoke, Hampshire RG21 6XS, England

The Political Process of Policymaking

A Pragmatic Approach to Public Policy

Philippe Zittoun
Research Professor, LET-ENTPE, University of Lyon, France

First published 2014 by
PALGRAVE MACMILLAN

Palgrave Macmillan in the UK is an imprint of Macmillan Publishers Limited, registered in England, company number 785998, of Houndmills, Basingstoke, Hampshire RG21 6XS.

Palgrave Macmillan in the US is a division of St Martin's Press LLC, 175 Fifth Avenue, New York, NY 10010.

Palgrave Macmillan is the global academic imprint of the above companies and has companies and representatives throughout the world.

Palgrave® and Macmillan® are registered trademarks in the United States, the United Kingdom, Europe and other countries.

ISBN: 978–1–137–34765–7

This book is printed on paper suitable for recycling and made from fully managed and sustained forest sources. Logging, pulping and manufacturing processes are expected to conform to the environmental regulations of the country of origin.

A catalogue record for this book is available from the British Library.

A catalog record for this book is available from the Library of Congress.

Contents

1
Introduction: The Political Process of Policymaking

Machiavelli's advice to Lorenzo de' Medici goes beyond the most conservative and traditional issues in political philosophy (Machiavelli, 2005)*. He does not restrict his reflections, unlike many authors who preceded and succeeded him, to the nature of Power or the forms that government must take. Nor does he indulge in what State or society should ideally be.

On the contrary, he addresses the issue of Power by starting from a simple, original and specific question: what must a Prince do to remain in Power? Rather than focusing on how to access the ultimate status and making this the key of his legitimacy, Machiavelli suggests that this legitimacy stems essentially from the Prince's actions.[1] According to him, the stability of a state is therefore linked, first and foremost, to the capacity of its governments to act, its *virtù* to handle *fortuna*, the multiple unpredictable events which disrupt society.

By pinning the legitimacy of the power on governmental action, Machiavelli points the way towards new reflections on public policy, no longer simply understood as simple governmental practices that must resolve problems but also, and perhaps essentially, as where the stability of a Power is determined and where a politician's identity is forged. From this perspective, Machiavelli, who is among the first "advisers" to edit these recommendations (Radin, 2000), occupies what Hannah Arendt referred to as a "unique position" in the history of political thought (Arendt, 2006).

Machiavelli therefore highlights the complex and inextricable link that connects public policy to political action. It is not about generating a simple causal link which makes it possible to grasp public policy merely through the cynicism of political actors seeking to remain in power, neither is it a matter of assuming that political action is always

1

linked to a public policy as there are other kinds of action such as votes, manifestations, or partisans' actions which are also political (Walzer and Miller, 2007). First and foremost, it involves recognising public policy as a political action where for each decision taken, the Prince calls into question, or even endangers, his identity and legitimacy.

Machiavelli's intuition which designates policymaking as a vital political activity is at the heart of the issues discussed in this book. In an entirely different context, his intuition is in line with issues raised by other authors such as Walter Lippmann (1922, 1925) and Harold Lasswell (1942a, 1942b) who, while also seeking to advise government on public policy, placed emphasis on the strong link that connects a government's actions to its legitimacy. To combat the democratic disenchantment that he noted after the First World War, Walter Lippmann proposed specialised services to advise governments in order to improve their public policy and reinforce their legitimacy. In the midst of the Second World War, Harold Lasswell argued that ensuring the stability of a democratic system in Europe after the conflict required the implementation of a public policy institute able to produce expert advice.

Admittedly, Machiavelli's advice is intended for a Prince forced to operate in a non-democratic context of violence, instability, war, overthrow risk, crime, and assassination where he risks not only his crown but his life as well. On the contrary, Lasswell's advice is intended for an American government against the background of war and the overthrow of democratic European regimes. Nevertheless, by declining to narrow a government's legitimacy to how it acquires its position, be it by divine right or by democratic election, these authors enable us to address wider issues concerning both these crisis situations, as well as the more peaceful contexts of our contemporary democracies.

Is public policymaking fundamentally political or not? Far from being a mere definitional issue, this question that has already been formulated by authors such as Machiavelli, Lasswell, and Lippmann is at the core of our work. Existing positivist literature on public policy has often limited its inquiry to defining new cognitive ways to solve problems, analysing public policy, or understanding policy change processes by identifying the numerous constraints that governments encounter. Although interesting, this inquiry generally considers public policy as a "neutral" object that researchers can define by themselves, thereby grasping its dynamic in the same way as physicists follow the movement of objects (Bevir and Rhodes, 2003). While some authors still consider values in public policy, this remains illusory. Indeed, they end up generally reducing these values to data that they can distinguish from "neutral" policy instruments. Thus, these researchers take an interest in these valueless objects, that is, tools, and analyse them as other authors have done.

Questioning the political character of public policy is an approach that differs from the one generally used by policy analysts. This innovative questioning makes it possible to place public policy studies back to the centre of political science issues with regard to the transformation of politics, Power and society. To question the political character of policymaking is therefore to consider that the activities carried out by the stakeholders to shape public policy are core processes not only in understanding the forms that public policy eventually takes but also in understanding the unfolding forms of politicisation and the modes of legitimacy used by those who govern.

Interrogating the political character of public policy therefore allows us to grasp its significance within the policy process and to better understand how contemporary government legitimises itself through this dimension. It allows us to contemplate policymaking not only as a process to solve social problems but also as a means through which to build legitimacy. By this, we do not imply that problem solving does not legitimise governments but rather, we wish to take into account the fact that even if governments try to solve problems, they are always confronted by the growing complexity of society, the desperately insoluble character of major social problems, the weight of stagnation, or the imbroglio of multiple actors eager to act. In other words, if policymaking contributes to legitimising governments, why does their incapacity to resolve major issues such as unemployment or inequality not endanger our democracies?

To respond to these questions, we posit that the political character of public policy lies less in the direct outcome of implementation (Merriam, 1925; Easton, 1965a) than in the outcome resulting from the policymaking activity itself, an activity which consists of defining, formulating, propagating, and imposing a policy proposal. In other words, it means observing a policy proposal as a succession of primarily political actions rather than as a desperate process marked by a few rare successes in the midst of numerous failures, both heroic and surprising, that are genuine markers of the persistence of politicians' claims to govern our societies. These actions contribute to the legitimisation process that is both fragile and resistant.

Before we present our approach in greater detail and show that public policymaking can indeed be considered as a political activity, we need to return to what we refer to as "public policy" on the one hand, and "political activity" on the other.

1.1   Definitional activities in public policy

Despite the attempt by a large number of authors to define the concept of policy, no one has managed to impose one specific definition. In his preliminary studies on policy sciences, Lasswell uses the term "policy" to designate an "important" decision. This context enables the author to define a possible scope for researcher intervention that distances itself from both partisan issues and politics (Lerner and Lasswell, 1951).

Gradually, Lasswell both refines and renders his definition more complex by considering policy first as a programme composed of objectives, values, and practices (Lasswell and Kaplan, 1952). This complexity is confirmed a few years later in *A preview of policy science*. Here, the author does not hesitate to conceive policy as the grouping of values, stakes, "instruments", and "outcome practices" (Lasswell, 1971, p. 57).

The tendency to complexify the concept and its definition is especially true among numerous authors specialised in the study of public policy. On one hand, the definitional processes carried out by the authors are primarily based on a series of reductions and deconstructions. Public policy is therefore considered as a group of elementary objects and concepts that are multiple and varied. Notably, there are objectives, instruments, alternatives (Simon, 1945), technical means (Dahl, 1949), decisions, outputs and outcomes (Easton, 1965a), policy actions and courses of action (Jones, 1970; Friedrich, 1963; Rose, 1969), policy demands, and policy statements (Anderson, 1975). On the other hand, this study consists in coupling these different elements together in order to show that public policy consists of more than just one element. It is therefore defined as a more or less complex association of problems, objectives, values, instruments, actions, consequences, etc.

Faced with the plethora of definitions, some authors have chosen to abandon this issue or to avoid it. Counting more than forty different definitions in 1972, Thomas Dye concluded that only a relatively non-discriminatory broad definition would be satisfactory, which he summarises as follows: "whatever governments choose to do or not to do" (Dye, 1972). Rather than attempt to characterise content, Dye avoids this definitional task by focusing on its producer.

Although interesting, this approach circumvents the definitional process and remains limited with regard to what these same authors practice when defining a problem. Indeed, when they study problem agenda setting, they are less interested in defining the problem than in understanding how the participants themselves carry out this definitional task. An author such as Kingdon, for instance, does not hesitate to

reject all problem definitions and to highlight the importance of prob-
lematising situations carried out by the actors themselves (Kingdon,
1995). In this way, the author does not only acknowledge the cognitive skills of each of these actors but also the importance of a definitional framework in agenda setting. This differential treatment between
"problem" and "public policy" probably results from the influence of
pragmatic studies which have largely influenced the study of problems
since the studies carried out by John Dewey (1927).

Rather than embarking on a never ending search for a definition, we
have chosen to follow the path traced by pragmatic studies on problems
by applying them to solutions as well. Consequently, we will focus on
the numerous discursive practices which enable actors to transform a
set of fragmented public policies into a coherent public policy, and to
attach objectives, problems to be solved, values, consequences, and a
public to this public policy.

Grasping the definitional framework that practitioners develop thus
makes it possible to better understand its significance in policymaking.
Far from being insignificant or purely semantic, this definitional framework restores participants' skills by seriously taking into account their
ability to define and analyse public policies. The issue is therefore not
in knowing if their analyses are true or not, nor if the researcher can
conduct significantly better analyses, but rather in questioning the
conditions of emergence, diffusion, evaluation, and use of these analyses by practitioners.

1.2   Exploring the political question

The key assumption of this book is not only to consider that the definitional framework plays a major role in policymaking but also to show
that this activity is first and foremost a political activity.

To achieve this, we must first define what we mean by "political
activity" and understand what policymaking activities have to do with
politics. This is far from evident. There exists what Pierre Favre refers to
as "already given"[2] political activities (Favre, 2007). These are socially-
constructed activities that often have visible materiality and a political
character which is not an object of debate. Analysing voting or the activities of a political party does not necessarily evoke debate with regard
to the political dimension. When dealing with an activity in which
the political attribute seems evident, debate on the political nature of
the activity diminishes. This is the case when analysing politicians, for
instance.

This situation is more complex when it refers to objects such as public policies. Admittedly, we can assume that as the State, which is the principal policymaker, practices ontological politics, then policy is politics. The studies that rediscovered institutions, therefore, posit that to understand society, the State in its specificity must be taken into account. Is this not why Theda Skocpol developed the assumption that to understand the presence or absence of revolution within a country (Skocpol, 1979), emphasis must be placed on the role of State in society? Did Peter Hall and Paul Pierson not insist on the importance of institutional constraints progressively forged within the State and which subsequently reduce decision-making possibilities (Hall, 1986; Pierson, 2000)?

However, all these analyses shift political issues from participant intention and behaviour to institutions and the constraints that these impose. Consequently, actors have limited influence on public policy, and this also renders obsolete the issue of legitimacy. Consequently, what is political is no longer the policymaking or transformational act, but rather the governing public organisation.

The first casualty of this shift is the politician himself who researchers keep dispossessing of his ability to produce or to influence policies, and more generally, to do politics. Subsequently, his only solution is his capacity to produce discourse that has no effect on public policy itself. Numerous studies have highlighted the illusory nature of such discourse in order to lift the veil on appearances more effectively and show the "real" actor practices that make a difference. Faced with political discourse which highlights a proactive "decision-maker", capable of resolving problems by reforming policies, researchers highlight the key role that stakeholders such as experts, bureaucrats, and social and professional partners play from "behind the scenes" (Gilbert and Henry, 2009). In this silent world that researchers disclose, the politician disappears often in favour of alternative and apolitical causalities such as knowledge, experts, networks, or even institutions.

However, if the administration and institutional routines play a significantly larger role than politicians with regard to public policy, how can we analyse the link between policy and politics other than through this ontological evidence which sees the State as politics? Do institutions alone raise political issues or do actors also generate politics? Put differently, how else can we analyse the political issues which make it possible to place the actor and his proactivity back to the centre of the political debate?

And here we enter into a study based primarily on the concepts and objects that "are not already given" (Favre, 2007). Politics therefore becomes an intangible concept that the researcher must define and then illustrate through empirical studies. To achieve this, he must equip himself, that is make and/or use observation tools comprising methods, concepts, or paradigms that enable him to glimpse beyond the empirical reality.

It is from this particular moment that analysing public policy becomes complex. After demonstrating that political discourse does not reflect reality, and that politicians have only a minor influence on policy, researchers find themselves relatively unprepared to identify the political issues in what they have observed.

To overcome this difficulty, we must reconsider the very definition of the concept of "politics" by examining it slightly differently. This is a particularly perilous exercise considering the polysemy of the term and how it is used. Rather than get into an endless debate on the exhaustive list of definitions of politics, we have selected two contradictory definitions in existing literature. These make it possible to characterise activities as "political" as they echo empirical activities that one comes across in policymaking.

The first definition defines "politics" as all activities that seek to order, govern, resolve social conflict, and re-establish order within society. According to Max Weber, for instance, politics is first, the leadership of a State: "We wish to understand by politics only the leadership, or the influencing of the leadership, of a political association, hence today, of a state" (Weber, 2000, p. 112). Here we find Plato's idea that politics is, above all else, the "science of commanding". Governing is therefore taking decisions to end conflicts, establishing common principles to punish the behaviour of those who endanger society (Favre, 2005, p. 266).

On the contrary, the second definition considers that "politics" are activities of contestation, opposition, conflict, partisan competition, and more broadly of social disorder. For instance, according to Leca and Grawitz, a political activity is primarily an activity of competition among groups – irrespective of how they are constituted – in order to support or contest policy decisions and their authors (Grawitz and Leca, 1985). Jacques Lagroye argues that political activities are based primarily on the infringement of rules and established orders as well as the ability to exceed limits (Lagroye, 2003). Political action therefore amounts to disputing the social orders that ensure a society's stability.

While these two definitions appear to be opposed in every respect, we would like to consider them in their necessary complementarity or, to take up the hypothesis developed by Julien Freund, in their "antinomian dialectics" (Freund, 1986). This implies that a political activity is always nourished by disorder that it cannot eliminate, but also that disorganisation is based on opposing orders which attempt to impose themselves in vain. Political activity therefore resembles the incessant and paradoxical development of order and disorder which, similar to Yin and Yang, feed off each other from their opposition.

Julien Freund's reflections echo those of Hannah Arendt who also insisted on this paradoxical tension between the preservation of the irreducible diversity of man and the production of order necessary to live together.[3] She argued that politics exist simply because this diversity is presupposed, and they seek to establish order or organisation. Consequently, political order cannot eliminate this diversity from which it derives its legitimacy; what really matters is the coexistence of diversity and order.

Although in a different register, that of political anthropology, Georges Balandier also highlights how order and disorder feed off each other. He therefore stresses the importance of the sacralisation of order to ward off disorder and chaos which would be the "realisation of its [a society's] own death" (Balandier, 1967, p. 119). Among a number of societies that he studies, the sacred and the political are intertwined and are both grounded in the necessity to import order from nature and to ward off provocative forces which bring about disorder. It is the king who, on one hand, opposes the witch to establish order and, on the other, feeds off her presence to legitimise his position. Balandier thus reminds us of a Chinese proverb that states "the prince is yang, the multitude yin".

To illustrate this, Balandier cites the case of the Agni of Ndenye in the Ivory Coast among whom periods of interregnum following the death of a king impose chaos. The royal seat is occupied, behaviour turns outrageous, captives act as free men, and the most sacred commandments are violated. Through these acts, the members of the tribe stress that a power vacuum generates disorder. Once the new king is appointed, each member returns to his place and order is restored: "They show in a certain sense that there is no alternative to the established social order but derision and the threat of chaos" (...) Each subject and each thing resumes its rank and place and the new sovereign can assume the direction of an ordered society and an organised universe. Contestation in ritual form belongs therefore to the strategy that enables power to periodically give itself a new vigour" (Balandier, 1967, p. 137).

With a focus on ordering, Balandier therefore shows the dialectic of order and of disorder, of power and of challenges, of action and of chaos. "What men revere through the guardians of the sacred and the depositaries of power is the possibility of constituting an organised totality, a culture and a society" (Balandier, 1967, p. 129). In a more recent study, Balandier (1992) takes a particular interest in the myth of heroes and the importance of theatrics when observing daily political activity.

The authors that we have cited tackle, each in their own way, the complementarity of these two facets of political activity. They enable us to understand this double movement of order and disorder that is complex, contradictory, and paradoxical, in which political activity is forged. They equip us to examine differently the activities that contribute to policymaking and thus analyse their relationship to order, disorder, and to the antinomian dialectics that this makes possible.

1.3   An activity that is essentially political

Equipped with a political activity approach and a specific understanding of policymaking, we can now revert to the principal assumption of our book. Demonstrating that policymaking is essentially a political activity highlights that a definitional process is an activity, the specificity of which is to enable antinomian dialectics between political order and disorder. To achieve this, we have developed a concept and three assumptions around which the principal chapters of this book are organised.

The concept is that of a public policy statement. By this we designate all discourse, ideas, analyses, and categories stabilised around a particular public policy and which give it meaning. The statement is therefore an essentially heuristic concept that seeks to grasp the development and stabilisation processes of the interpretations that we would like to describe. It can equally be applied to a specific measure such as VAT or to a wider public policy, for instance, a taxation policy in which it is embedded. It can also be applied to an existent public policy that needs to be redefined, defended, or criticised, as well as to proposed change, transformation, or innovation that needs to be recommended or contested. A statement is therefore stabilised discourse that wholly depends on how stakeholders organise it in order to grasp and act on their object.

A problem statement is undoubtedly what has been analysed most in public policy literature. The first chapter, which is dedicated to problem statements, presents a synthesis of the studies which have focused on the development of problem statements dating back to Dewey's pragmatic studies. This is therefore about demonstrating that the development of a problem statement is based on definitional processes made up of both struggles and agreements, which make it possible to make a situation unacceptable. This process contributes to social disorder.

The second chapter of this book focuses on the shaping of this statement. While the definition of issues is essentially based on a definitional process that transforms a phenomenon into an "unacceptable" issue, we would like to show that the definitional framework of a proposed public policy is based on a double process of coupling; the proposal is coupled with a problem whose solution it facilitates on one hand, and with a public policy that it seeks to transform, on the other. The shaping of such a statement, which in any case is our first assumption, is based on redefining the problem to make it "treatable", the public policy to make it "reformable", and the solution itself in order to "associate" it to the problem. It is precisely this coupling and shaping which contribute to restoring order from the disorder created by the problem agenda-setting.

The third chapter primarily focuses on the propagation of the statement that we can analyse by observing interactions, and which contributes to gluing the couple. We will show that it is the persuasion and conviction of actors who interact at the forefront and behind the scenes which enables this propagation. More specifically we will show that this discussion tests both the argument and identity through which a proposed public policy transforms itself to enable the aggregation of actors who become the "co-owners". Discursive practices in general, and notably persuasion practices, therefore, make it possible to stabilise the proposal statement by gluing the solution to the problem to be resolved and to the underlying coalition. This is our second assumption.

The last chapter alludes to the power issue, an issue that is all the more delicate as the majority of studies that seriously consider the power of arguments do not address actors' power and vice versa. By enlarging our area of study to both upstream and downstream processes with regard to persuasion, we would like to propose an approach that reconciles them and shows that the success of a coupling procedure is based on its capacity to cement the proposal statement by defining unequal positions and by imposing a "decision-making" figure. This process simultaneously involves analysing the strategies behind the choice of interlocutors by those who endorse an action as well as by the manner in which these actors redefine their proposal in order to legitimise the actors who have become the "decision-makers".

While John Kingdon has already shown the significance of coupling between a problem and a solution in the policy change process, he has given no attention to "gluing" or "cementing" processes. These processes enable couples to resist, consolidate, and propagate themselves in order to impose themselves or, on the contrary, disappear should they not resist the onslaught of the arguments they encounter.

These three assumptions help us grasp the policymaking process by analysing both language games which give meaning to a policy proposal by transforming it into a "solution", games of actors which construct "co-owner" coalitions around this solution, and power games which impose these actions and forge "decision-makers". Through these three assumptions, we would therefore like to better understand the policy-making process as well as its highly "political" character.

Indeed, making a policy statement can be considered a political activity in the sense that not only does it lead to order, but it also contributes to making disorder both visible and possible. By acknowledging that the problem cannot remain unresolved and by showing who is responsible for restoring order, a policy statement reinforces problem visibility. By offering a solution to an ever-insoluble problem, it makes possible contention and differentiation. Georges Burdeau goes even further with this train of thought. He argues that not only does "the problem implicate authority (...) Its intervention therefore appears as destined to compensate the absence of a solution," and especially, "as authorities are not a miraculous power capable of solving the issues that are unsolvable, its intervention consists, not in removing the obstacles, but in enabling society to live with them" (Burdeau, 1979, p. 29). In his opinion, it is therefore an issue of making authority desirable, and this desire emanates from necessity: "the only basis we can assign to political authority is its necessity".

Without defending this point of view which sees politics as an activity in which myths embodying human groups "which uphold society" (ibid., p. 29) are created, we share the author's notion that "politics is an activity which consists in defining an authority and exercising the prerogatives" (ibid., p. 22). Among these activities, those that consist in policymaking are crucial, as they share their capacity to solve public issues.

While fundamental public issues such as social inequality remain generally insoluble, continuously renewed activities show that some solutions can contribute to resolving them, even partially, and are not only at the centre of political activity, but assemble what holds society together: politics.

2
Creating Social Disorder: Constructing, Propagating and Policitising Social Problems

Before we discuss solution-making processes, we would like to begin by addressing problem agenda setting. We focus on agenda setting not only for what we learn concerning the problems stage, but also for what is revealed with regard to the pragmatic approaches used by sociologists and political scientists to understand how problems emerge. For this reason, we have chosen to begin this first chapter by discussing John Dewey's influential work on pragmatic approaches to problems, *The Public and its Problems* (1927), before engaging in a brief synthesis of pragmatic studies on problem construction and problem agenda setting.

We would like to pay particular attention to the politicisation of problems even though numerous syntheses on this issue already exist. The politicisation of problems has been dealt with in two largely different ways. First, from a pluralist perspective, politicisation is understood essentially through the definitional mechanism of transforming a given situation into a social problem. The authors suggest using the struggle between social groups to better grasp the different discursive politicisation processes. The pragmatic and pluralist legacy given impetus by John Dewey's work is fundamental here. Indeed, he is one of the first authors to have stressed the importance of the phenomenon of defining problems, of identifying a public, and of ensuring accountability from public authorities. We will largely incorporate Dewey's studies to show how a social issue is politicised and transformed into a societal problem (Dewey, 1927).

The second dimension of politicisation was primarily developed by the critics of pluralist theories to underscore the importance of propagation which accompanies the definitional process. Their objective is to show

how difficult it is for a problem to become important, and to highlight the unequal distribution of group resources which support or hinder all forms of problem propagation. Here we find principally the studies of Schattschneider on the bias that problems face and the importance of politicisation as a process of domination (Schattschneider, 1975).

Far from being contradictory, these two dimensions have ended up being complementary to highlight the complex phenomenon of "agenda setting". On one hand, studies such as those developed by Joseph Gusfield or Murray Edelman highlight that the definitional process is itself a political phenomenon which can establish or reinforce the hegemony of a group over other groups (Edelman, 1988; Gusfield, 1981). On the other hand, propagation phenomena are sometimes conceived as competitive mechanisms which help us to better understand the chaotic aspect of agenda.

However, while questions on competition/hegemony remain controversial, a common understanding of agenda setting processes as subjective constructions has imposed itself in the field of public policy studies since the 1970s. All contemporary manuals and studies conjointly emphasise the importance of understanding the phases of definition, perception, and mobilisation that encompass the phenomenon (Jones, 1970). They associate politicisation phenomena to how the problem is defined as well as to how it becomes public, and designate the authority responsible in the propagation of the problem, the amount of support it gets, its mediatisation, and how it is taken into account by public authorities.

2.1 A pragmatic approach to public problems

Written in 1927, John Dewey's book, *The Public and its Problems*, was initially intended as a critical response to the assumptions developed by Walter Lippmann in a book published two years earlier titled *The Public Phantom* (Lippmann, 1925). Opposed to the dominant philosophers of his day (Ross, 1991) and having developed original ideas dating back to 1880 (Coughlan, 1975), John Dewey published only one book on this theme and took a particular interest in issues such as knowledge, culture, and education. Nevertheless, this book is considered to be fundamental by numerous authors working on public policy analysis such as Lasswell (1971), Anderson (1975), and even Simon (1959) (Bernstein, 1992).[1] Dewey's influence results from how he has been able to, following William James (1890) and Charles Peirce (1878) (Tiercelin, 1993), consolidate the pragmatic approach, as well as address problems in an innovative way.

Pragmatic philosophy, a consequence-based approach

To understand this book, we must first immerse ourselves in pragmatic philosophy which was ignored for many years in the United States. Eclipsed by the development of multiple forms of positivism within the different disciplines which it had nonetheless paradoxically boosted and scorned in Europe (Tiercelin, 1993), it is only over the last 20 years that pragmatic philosophy has been rediscovered in France (Debaise, 2007) and in the United States as well (Bernstein, 1992). Richard Rorty thus explains that the American philosophy has been marked by a gradual "pragmatisation" of the original tenets of logical positivism which had eclipsed this movement (Rorty, 1982).

Pragmatism is a philosophical movement initiated by Charles Sander Peirce (1839–1914), adopted and popularised by William James (1842–1910) and then by John Dewey (1859–1952). The three are all considered founders of a similar movement, although, in reality, there are many subtle differences among them, so much so that as from 1905, Charles Peirce used the term "Pragmaticism" to differentiate himself from the pragmatism promoted by William James.

In spite of their differences, these authors all advocated for the rejection of the Kantian distinction between thought and action and the construction of the meaning of concepts from the practical consequences that one could expect from them. In 1868, Charles S. Peirce published a series of articles (Peirce, 1868a, 1868b) in which he formalised a concerted attack against "nominalist platonism" (Tiercelin, 1993). The author thus contested the Cartesian method according to which the point of departure for all knowledge is intuition deprived of a few fundamental principles, and whose point of arrival is all the resulting deductions. He rejected the notion of a point of departure, of a "principle of principles", and the Cartesian intuition of an interior universe separated from an exterior universe; similarly, he rejected Kant's distinction between understanding and reason.

According to Charles Peirce, pragmatism is primarily a method that clarifies concepts. He therefore proposes a "pragmatic maxim" based on the expected practical effects: "Consider what effects, that might conceivably have practical bearings, we conceive the object of our conception to have. Then, our conception of these effects is the whole of our conception of the object" (Peirce, 1878, p. 286). Consequently, Peirce argues that the concept "hard" in "a diamond is hard" suggests a specific practice, that of scratching a diamond against other substances in order to materialise this hardness by observing the effects of this scratching. In other words, according to Peirce, the meaning of a concept can only be measured by its uses and the identification of its practical consequences. This method is therefore less interested in defining truth than in proposing the conditions for its validity. This means that we should avoid considering concepts as having their own internal meaning to which we can gain access through intuition, but rather, identify a series of operations with practical results. As Stéphane Maldérieux summarises, no idea is clear in itself and by itself, but it becomes clear if we develop it taking into account its practical effects (James, 1995).

From this perspective, pragmatists oppose metaphysics and sciences, which have established a method that makes it possible to translate a concept into an experimental protocol. They would like philosophy to follow the same path as experimental sciences by testing concepts. It is here that positivism and pragmatism meet through their desire to take interest only in what is verifiable.

William James positioned pragmatism as a new avenue which made it possible to move away from the then dominant debate opposing empiricism and rationalism. While empiricism is only interested in facts, rationalism takes an interest in the logic of reason. For the former, religion is inconceivable while for the latter, all thought presupposes an initial and transcending concept. For James, the pragmatist method makes it possible to overcome this opposition which he qualifies as sterile. To do this, he suggests implementing a method which makes it possible to distinguish between concepts based on their practical consequences on reality. Seen in this light, religion is conceivable because it clearly has practical consequences within society (James, 1995).

According to James, pragmatism is, first and foremost, a method that avoids philosophical categories of thought and turns towards the observation of consequences. This pragmatic approach by consequences is essential provided that it is clearly distinguished from a pragmatic approach by outcomes. Roberto Frega (Frega, 2006) differentiates pragmatic action which involves an action carried out depending on known and predictable outcomes, from the pragmatist action which involves determining the meaning of actions based on consequences which are unknown and which are not specified solely by intentions.

Far from the traditional method of normative philosophy, pragmatism is therefore, first and foremost, a specific method that seeks to define concepts. It is a method of analysis which does not consider that philosophy is a discipline that is better than others, capable of producing concepts uniquely through thought. Nevertheless, this method associates philosophy with the different sciences by making implementation the essential mode of knowledge production. The importance accorded by Peirce, James, and Dewey to the methods of analysis and the issue of logic clearly reveals this.

Alongside Peirce's pragmatic method, William James went further by proposing a "genetic theory of truth". In a certain way, "it's ideas that work": "our thoughts become true in proportion as they successfully exert their go-between function" (James, 1995). This "theory of truth" is less interested in the intrinsic value of truth than in the consequences of what individuals consider as truth. This shows that "truths can grow petrified by antiquity" and that "a pragmatist talks about truths in the plural" (Ibid., p. 129).

The studies undertaken by William James on this issue received heavy criticism, including from Peirce for whom, as a method of thought, these studies were no longer pragmatic. Indeed, a changeover is clearly visible. Pragmatism is no longer simply a method recommended to those who would like to have "clear ideas", to employ the words used by Peirce. It is also an epistemology which does not intend to define concepts but to observe their concrete use (James, 1995).

According to James, the issue is not in knowing whether truth exists, an issue that is impossible to prove and which constitutes a never ending philosophical debate, but rather, to take an interest in how individuals assimilate themselves to it, develop it, conform their actions to it. For him, truth is inextricably linked to what is useful and used. The issue is therefore not in knowing whether God exists but the very fact that he is useful and has consequences on social life is enough to consider him as "true": "On pragmatist principles, if the hypothesis of God works satisfactorily in the widest sense of the word, it is 'true'" (Ibid., p. 134).

As a result, difficulty or even confusion has emerged when distinguishing the definition of a concept such as truth and implementing a pragmatic method to define it. From this perspective, John Dewey's approach differs from that of William James and is closer to that of Peirce. For Dewey, it is only through inquiry that one can produce knowledge; therefore, one cannot start from intuitive knowledge and simply analyse its consequences. He refuses to start from an already given proposal such as "God exists" in order to observe the consequences: "The object of knowledge is eventual; that is, it is the outcome of directed experimental operations, instead of something in sufficient existence before the act of knowing" (Dewey, 1938, p. 64).

According to Dewey, whereas doubt and incertitude exist at the beginning, knowledge and belief are attained only when inquiry is accomplished: "Doubt is uneasy; it is tension that finds expression and outlet in the processes of inquiry. Inquiry terminates in reaching that which is settled. This settled condition is a demarcating characteristic of genuine belief. In so far, belief is an appropriate name for the *end* of *inquiry"* (Dewey, 1938, p. 63). It is therefore primarily through inquiry that knowledge is generated.

Beyond these differences, pragmatic philosophy has bridged the gap between philosophy and social sciences by refraining from distinguishing thought from action. It has rendered absurd the existence of philosophy that builds concepts without preoccupying itself with their real use. It has paved the way for an epistemological foundation of social sciences which analyses uses but does not always know what to do with thought. Pragmatic philosophy opens up a complex avenue that Dewey used to propose a method for tackling public problems that was different from that elaborated by Walter Lippmann.

A public shaped by problems: pragmatic consequences of uncontrolled human interactions

John Dewey wrote *The Public and its Problems* in 1927 as a response to a book published two years earlier by another American author, Walter Lippmann, entitled *The Public Phantom* (Dewey, 1927; Lippmann, 1925). In this book, Lippmann studied the democratic crisis. Following this, Dewey proposed an in-depth analysis of Lippman's arguments on the illusory character of the Public. He also proposed a different, original, and pragmatic conception of the Public. From this perspective, Dewey's book is no longer a simple response but a book in its own right which has subsequently inspired many authors.

Lippmann and Dewey's books are close and, in reality, share many common points. They both explore the dilemmas of a representative democracy confronted with declining vote participation, with difficulties in reconciling political activity and public policy, and with its citizens' limited skills. They both consider that political action necessitates increased technical skills and expertise but both reject the idea of an enlightened government.

Nevertheless, in contrast to Lippmann, John Dewey considers first of all that far from being a phantom, the Public exists and is merely in eclipse. For Lippmann, the Public is simply a disinterested and alienated group of "spectators" who watch a few "actors" incapable of resolving their problems interact. For Dewey, the Public appears only when consequences of actions affect citizens who have not participated to this action. Indeed, Dewey argues that a public does not really exist until a negative externality resulting from the consequences of an action calls it into being. The pragmatic inspiration discernible through the strong allusion to consequences is, from this point of view, central; the consequences give meaning to the actions and construct or consolidate the concepts.

Unlike Lippmann, Dewey considers that the public is not the direct output of interaction. The protagonists of the interaction cannot become a Public. A Public is then called into existence when there are individuals concerned by a problem without soliciting for it. These individuals are not applicants, actors or spectators but only victims. They are affected by an inter-action external to them.

While the presence of victims of an interaction is a necessary condition in determining how a Public comes into being, Dewey argues that this is far from sufficient. Indeed, while these consequences are necessary, they are insufficient in producing a public. According to him, two other conditions are essential. The first one involves acknowledging these consequences. In other words, generating consequences is insufficient; interactions must also carry out specific inquiry to identify the victims based on the consequences. Hence, this specific task of acknowledgement is based primarily on generating knowledge which identifies and brings victims together in order to transform them into a "Public". We can therefore evoke the indispensable Public making.

The second condition is the attempt to control this Public and actions through legislation. This second condition must first be understood through the pragmatic prism of the relationship between action/experimentation and knowledge. Control and regulatory mechanisms are central to how a Public can come into being and be distinguished from what is private. It is by identifying "public buildings" and distinguishing them from "private buildings" that a Public emerges. Specific processes distinguishing public schools from private schools are at the heart of how these concepts come about. In other words, it is the actors, seen as active individuals, who construct knowledge. It is for this reason that, for Dewey, a civil servant is an ideal example of the existence of this Public. A public therefore exists through all the human or non-human mechanisms whose duty it is to watch over it.

Dewey proposes to go beyond the opposition among those who consider the State and the Public as detached concepts involved in causal theories and those who reduce the State to private individuals who represent it and attempt to underscore the specific interests which it is subject to. While Dewey argues that we can only grasp State and the Public through the individuals and the devices that keep it alive, he rejects the idea that these individuals are private beings, or operate as such: "the lasting, extensive and serious consequences of associated activity bring into existence a public. In itself it is unorganised and form-less. By means of officials and their special powers it becomes a state. A public articulated and operating through representative officers is the state; there is no state without a government, but also there is none without the public. The officers (of the state) are still singular beings but they exercise new and special powers" (Dewey [1927], 1991, p. 67).

It is an individual's position within a State that structures his behav-iour and transforms him into a public actor. The State, civil servants, and the public are thus inseparable. One cannot exist without the others. The singularity of a civil servant is therefore his grappling with all the interactions in which he finds himself intertwined and which condition his behaviour.

Exploring problems and the Public differently, between intentionality and unexpected consequences

Dewey's book broaches a series of reflections that are both innovative and fundamental for the social and political sciences. To achieve this, he breaks away from both classical philosophy and the emerging soci-ology. He first sets the foundation for a scientific approach which is not based on the causes but on the consequences of social activity. Social activities are marked by both intentions and unexpected consequences. Most of the challenges that the social sciences have encountered have been linked to analysing the stated intentions by observing outcomes. As outcomes rarely correspond to intentions, it has been concluded that rather than focusing on intentions, rationalities should be reconstructed *a posteriori*.

By distinctively analysing intentionality and consequences, Dewey paves the way to an interesting avenue. For him, one should not lose self in adjustments which end up twisting intentions in order to make them correspond to outcomes. He therefore argues that social sciences can take into account relationships between social phenomena without enclosing society in causal determinism.

His study also shows that in order to observe reality and act on it, we cannot separate ourselves from knowledge devices. This is especially true for actors who grasp reality based on a set of knowledge devices that are always reductive and distorted. It is equally true for the researcher who must also use these devices to observe the world. It is this principle that makes it possible to overcome the opposition between object and subject, realist and relativist.

Finally, Dewey rejects the separation between thought and action and, in this way, breaks away from traditional philosophy. He considers that knowledge is made within action and is tested through experience. As a consequence, an individual does not reason independently of action but rather by reflecting in and through action. According to him, it is only "ideas in action" that exist.

Moreover, by refusing to distinguish the individual from the society, Dewey also goes against traditional sociology. While the latter considers that the tension between individual/society is a central issue, Dewey argues that an individual is a social being who acts in relation to others with whom he is in permanent interaction. It is therefore wrong to think of him as isolated. On the contrary, an individual can be considered as a participant within multiple networks, each one capable of compartmentalising his behaviour. Consequently, "one of the obstructions in the path is the seemingly engrained notion that the first and last problem which must be solved is the relation of the individual and the social (...). In fact, both words, individual and social are hopelessly ambiguous (...) even that seemingly 'individual' tree must live in soil and be fed by water, air, and light, which are in turn the by-products of processes of other living things. (...) so the human being which we fasten upon as individual *par excellence* is moved and regulated by his associations with others; what he does and what the consequences of his behaviour are, what his experience consists of, cannot even be described, much less accounted for, in isolation" (Dewey, 1927, pp. 183–184).

When we combine these two ideas – rendering indivisible thought/action and individual/social – it becomes clear that Dewey is not interested in the traditional question of power as such but in the manner in which democracy finds its legitimacy in action, the only means for the Public and its problems to exist. From this perspective, Lippmann and Dewey are relatively comparable, even though their recommendations on how democracy can be reinforced differ.

Rather than define State as has generally been done in political philosophy and observe the reality that is generally considered to be inconsistent, Dewey proposes to first analyse the State through its actors and its actions in order to understand it. Instead of analysing the Public and its problems, he takes an interest in the means that make them identifiable and recognisable, through which his analysis can be carried out. Here, Dewey is more interested in the recognition and instrumentation of public problems rather than in their resolution. It is no longer an issue of analysing the confrontation between competing interests; it is an issue of understanding the existence of an autonomous legitimisation process of the State. This approach, which is, according to Dewey, the only one capable of explaining the plurality of State and the diversity of historical paths, is characteristic of what Raymond Aron terms a sociological intention (Aron, 1967). It is at the core of the logic that consists of analysing public policies known as "the State in action" in order to understand the State, politics, and democracy.

2.2 Definitional struggles around unacceptable problems

Inspired by John Dewey's book on public problems, multiple studies have sought to highlight the manner in which problems are formed and put on the agenda. Numerous sociologists have hence tackled this thematic issue by taking a particular interest in the elaboration of knowledge devices which render definable and visible a public of victims. They have taken an interest as well in the labelling phenomenon which contributes in naming, designating and qualifying their situation into a "problem". Finally, they have taken an interest in the complex set of definitional practices which give meaning to a situation and transform it into an "unacceptable problem".

Influenced by Dewey's studies as well as by a pluralist heritage, political scientists have also shown interest in definitional processes. In particular, they have focused on the definitional struggles between concurrent problems, and on the political strategies of propagation to enable or prevent their enrolment on the governmental agenda. We would like to outline here the different stages of the definitional process and the different strategies of propagation that these key sociologists and political scientists have identified.

The different conceptions of problem construction

Two sociological conceptions of the construction of social problems

In the 1970s, Spector and Kitsuse proposed an overall classification of sociological studies on problems around two distinct conceptions (Spector and Kitsuse, 1977). The first conception focused on the idea that there are objective and latent problems in society which are generally in the dark. To make them visible, individuals must build and mobilise some concepts and knowledge devices. This conception met even greater success not only for its relevance in understanding reality but also in justifying the critical role of sociologists who seek to highlight these problems using this type of concept. From racial issues to those on inequality, from social reproduction to ghettoisation, not forgetting criminality, sociology studies proposing to construct, collect, and interpret data in order to make reality and its "latent" problems visible are not lacking.

The second conception which also emerged in the 1970s rejected the distinction between an objective situation and a subjective perception in order to underscore that one cannot grasp reality without a knowledge device. Moreover, it argued that there are always competing devices which reflect different realities. Based on specific knowledge devices, every problem is both partial, because no theory can claim to be alone in possessing the only reality, and prejudiced, because each device always deforms the reality that it wants to reflect.

Consequently, it is less the quality or performance of knowledge devices than the mobilisation of actors which enable researchers to understand the construction of problems. Hence, Herbert Blumer developed a model for each stage where problems are more a collective definition built by the actors, than a result of the objective situation.

A few years later, Spector and Kitsuse went even further in questioning this frontier by considering that a researcher should first and foremost focus on how actors create the conditions of emergence of a complex problem. After carrying out a review of the literature in sociology and concluding that there was no pertinent definition of social problems, the two authors proposed that sociologists must primarily focus on the activities through which groups identify problems and qualify them as offensive, unacceptable, or harmful. The consequence of such an approach is acknowledging that a social problem does not result from objective conditions but rather from a claims-making activity between interacting individuals who organise themselves to designate a situation and declare that it is a "problem". As a consequence, the authors propose concentrating on this definitional process, which consists in actors defining a "problem" from a situation by themselves.

A shared political framework in constructing public problems

Although this distinction is particularly strong and cleaving for sociologists, it is less pronounced among researchers interested in public policy. While the latter often evokes the notion of "latent" problems, it is less interested in their existence or their validity, but rather in the processes which transform a complex situation into a public problem.

Particularly attentive to the stage following their emergence, authors have been primarily interested in describing the different definitional stages which transform a social situation into a public problem that public authorities decide to take charge of. While these stages differ in terms of their form, qualification, and number, their heuristic deconstruction into comprehensible definitional activities is relatively similar.

Accordingly, David Easton (1965b) proposes to grasp the process which enables a "desire" or an "expectation" within society to become a real "input" which the political system takes charge of. The author also identifies two definitional stages which transform a "desire", that is, "what men want from society", into a "demand", that is, what they expect the government to do. According to the author, this requires discursive clarification – while desire can be latent, demand is always an explicit discourse – as well as the designation of an authority charged with responding to these demands, in this case, the political system.

Similarly, Charles Jones (1970) distinguishes four stages which make it possible to pass from a complex issue to a problem. While the point of departure is the existence of a perceived issue, the author insists on the definitional process which transforms this simple perception into a collective demand addressed to the public authorities empowered to act. Taking the example of those who sleep in the streets, the author proposes that researchers should focus on the activity of the actors who label the problem "homelessness", and turn towards public authorities to ask them to act. The author therefore shows that far from observing a natural or evident phenomenon, this research reveals a complex process where significant sorting and selection is carried out; consequently, only a few complex situations are transformed into public problems.

Kingdon also distinguishes a complex situation from a public problem and insists not only on the importance of value judgement but also on the process which transforms a public issue into a treatable problem (Kingdon, 1995). The author takes the example of poverty. For this to become a problem, actors must not only judge it as an unacceptable issue but must also consider it as treatable.

Authors interested in public policy therefore focus their attention on the definitional process driven by actors who contribute to transforming a situation into a problem. As Gusfield (1981) argues, this must first be understood as ordering and making coherent an incoherent and fragmented reality. Moreover, it is a process through which actors name, judge, describe, and attribute causalities and responsibilities.

Murray Edelman (1988) even suggests that rhetoric on the problem-signifies those,

> are virtuous and useful and who are dangerous and inadequate, which actions will be rewarded and which penalised. They constitute people as subjects with particular kinds of aspirations, self-concepts, and fears, and they create beliefs about the relative importance of

events and objects. They are critical in determining who exercises authority and who accepts it. They construct areas of immunity from concern because those areas are not seen as problems. Like leaders and enemies, they define the contours of the social world, not in the same way for everyone, but in the light of the diverse situations from which people respond to the political spectacle. (p. 37)

The process that Edelman highlights makes it possible to better understand the importance of the statement enclosing a problem. The statement, that is, the discourse of actors in relation to a problem, is what enables them not only to analyse a situation and designate it as a "problem" but also to politicise it by integrating it within a more global vision of a society in disorder.

The five stages in the problem definition process

To understand problem agenda setting, we would like to present a general overview of the definitional process that actors use to transform a situation into a public problem. Easton and Kingdon described two stages. Felstiner, Abel, and Sarat (1980) evoked the significance of the triad "naming, blaming, claiming" in the agenda setting process.

We can evoke five definitional stages to explain how some actors transform a situation into a public problem. By proposing five stages, we not only want to be more precise in the description but also to be more attentive to the politicisation process where actors create disorder and make the society unacceptable.

The first stage: labelling a situation and qualifying it as a problem

To transform a situation into a public problem, actors generally start by attributing a name by attaching a label to the situation that makes it possible to describe it as problematic. This first phase must therefore be understood as a practice that is discursive, normative and taxonomic. It enables actors to describe the social disorder that such a situation reveals.

The labelling theory was highlighted in the 1960s by Howard Becker (1985) while studying "deviant" individuals. The author renewed how this issue was tackled by viewing it less as the result of the psychological trajectory of individuals who have transgressed an agreed upon rule. He argued that deviance should be understood from the social practice of labelling in which the social group not only identifies the deviant practice and names the deviant but also constructs or reinforces the social norm transgressed by him.

Inspired by Becker's studies, many authors have shown that labelling is largely present in transforming a given situation into a social problem. Citing legal dispute procedures, Felstiner et al. (1980) illustrate to what extent "naming", that is, the labelling of a situation, is essential in raising the awareness of individuals to transform a problem into a grievance. The authors give the example of individuals displaying cancer symptoms but who perceive the existence of a problem only from when they are able to name their symptoms, relate them together, and give them meaning. "Naming" is therefore a discursive practice which provides the wording to a problem.

Choosing a name is neither neutral nor objective and is a genuine normative practice. It generally refers to a social norm in order to better highlight the existence of a gap, which is the source of the problem. Labelling a situation in order to describe it as a problem means first establishing the existing gap between what is – the problem – and what should be the normal situation. According to Gusfield (1981), labelling road accidents as an alcohol problem, for example, means attributing a value judgement on the drinking-driver by characterising him as guilty, thus exonerating other potential perpetrators such as alcohol vendors. In the same way, evoking the "right to abortion" or "the right to life" is making a different value judgement of the abortion practice itself (Padioleau, 1982) by defining what is normal and what is not. The struggle over the naming of AIDS between "gay cancer" and AIDS also reveals the issues in labelling. In our own studies involving the homeless, we observed substantial differences between actors and/or cities to label people as "homeless" (Chebbah-Malicet et al., 2005). Some were quick to evoke "the housing problem" while others preferred the term "homeless" or "destitute". We were also able to witness a debate which was then rife among sheltered housing centres: are "asylum seekers", who possess no housing, homeless? Far from insignificant, the choice of name can open or close the doors of these centres.

In public policy, this labelling process develops from a discursive practice which often involves adding the term "problem" as well as a term designating a particular object. Consequently, actors rapidly transform suburbia or housing into a problem by evoking, in a relatively tautological manner "the problem of suburbia" or the "the housing problem". Sometimes, a category can even be constructed as a problem that does away with the term "problem", as in the case of unemployment, for instance, where "unemployment" and the "the unemployment problem" appear to be equivalent, but cases such as these remain rare.

This discursive process that consists in attaching the term "problem" to a situation therefore enables actors to describe and to qualify the situation, that is, to judge it as far from the norm. For instance, evoking "the housing problem" means considering that the housing situation is not what it should be. Labelling a situation as a problem therefore means referring to a norm, to the normal situation, and in parallel, judging a situation that goes against the norm.

In the housing domain in which our studies were focused, when actors sought to evoke a problem, they used labels such as "the housing problem", "the problem of homelessness", "the problem of student housing in large cities", and "the rent problem". In other words, all themes could be transformed into problems under the condition that the actors added the term "problem".

The advantage of such labelling is that it prevents its authors from defining a problem in precise terms, thereby maintaining vagueness. Consequently, when the actors evoke the "problem of suburbia" or the "the housing problem", they do not have to define, to determine the boundaries, or to justify the complex character. The term "problem" therefore functions as a form of self-reference which proves the existence of the problem stated.

A discursive and normative practice, labelling is also a taxonomic practice which makes it possible to exchange views between specific situations and more general problems. When a range of cars burn, labelling these situations as a "problem of surburbia" enables them to lose their singularity and draw a comparison with other similar situations. The "problem of surburbia" becomes a category with a label under which a wide range of situations can be classified.

Admittedly, each situation can lead to different interpretations and labels. Labelling is therefore a taxonomic practice which is far from evident and which leads to conflict between actors bearing a label and how this is tested. Faced with a financial problem, the farmer from Corsica, Northern Ireland, or the State of Alabama can associate his situation to the "agricultural problem". In this way, he transforms his situation into a public problem and reinforces the validity of the problem by associating it to a concrete situation. He can equally classify his situation as a geographical problem. By explaining that his problem is a Corsica, Northern Ireland, or Alabama problem, he mobilises other forms of politicisation (Jobert and Muller, 1987). Thus, it is this complex dialectic between a concrete situation and general conceptualisation that is important and that constitutes a specific phase in qualifying a situation as a public problem.

To withdraw a given situation from its singularity, actors can use various types of processes. We would like to highlight two of these processes that we consider to be particularly common. The first process involves showing that an event can be linked to other similar events. As a consequence, it loses its singularity status. A classic example is that of an air disaster which, taken in isolation, is considered to be an unfortunate occurrence but not necessarily a problem. Associated to other disasters, it can become a public problem. Should the disasters share a common point such as period, obsolescence or airplanes belonging to poor countries, then the problem takes on a whole different meaning. A road accident that occurs at an intersection is a singular event but, associated to other accidents that have occurred at the same location, it loses its singular character and becomes a public problem. A burning car is a singular phenomenon but cars burning in the same neighbourhood can be labelled as a public problem. This calls for a specific heuristic construction of equivalence between varying complex situations. If a situation is equivalent to others, then the problem experienced in this given situation can be reproduced in other situations.

A second way to withdraw from the singularity of a particular problem is to associate it to a much broader social problem that is recognised as such. To some extent, this implies "classifying" the problem within a problematised category that is large and already stabilised. As a result, the situation appears to reveal a problem or serves as an example of an already existent problem. It is this dialectic between a singular situation and a general problem evoked earlier that is of interest to us here.

In these two ways, labelling works as a means through which some actors point out the presence of an important problem within society. These actors, that we can call problem-makers, contribute to developing discourse not only to alert the world on the existence of disorder but to shape it as well.

The second stage: categorising society by identifying a Public of victims

In the process that leads to the transformation of a situation into a public problem, problem naming is generally insufficient. Problem-makers typically accompany it by specifically identifying a social group of victims. They thus present a fragmented view of the Public and underscore the idea of a world in disorder.

This process of constructing a Public of victims first begins by identifying a group of individuals whose situation is qualified, by themselves or others, as complex. Using the term "victim" here makes it possible to stress the idea developed by Dewey where this description first assumes that the individual is not responsible for his own problem, but rather is a victim of the unexpected consequences resulting from the interaction between others.

Associating the term "Public" to "victims" involves identifying a group which is not simply the sum of victims, but is also a social group labelled as a collective autonomous actor, and which forms a real social division. It is this complex relationship between society, the whole Public, and the Publics of victims that we focus on.

To understand how a Public of victims is constructed, it is therefore necessary to centre on how problem-makers produce knowledge devices and the discursive labels which reveal it. It no longer simply involves labelling a situation as a "problem" as in the previous phase. Here, the problem-makers need to complexify their labelling activity by shaping the social group with regard to social norms.

As concerns the "housing problem" previously discussed, labelling remains relatively vague in relation to the social groups of the victims concerned. Identifying specific victims contributes to completing the definitional process of the problem by defining its contours. This implies that actors must identify a particular group of victims, be they the "homeless", the "poorly-housed", "students", or "handicapped persons".

In certain cases such as those that deal with the "homeless" or the "poorly housed", it is the existence of a group which is problematic. It is important to stress that in such cases, the problem leads to the creation of the social group. The "homeless" or the "poorly housed" exist as a social group only because of the existence of housing problems, and they remind us of the existence of a norm, that of decent housing. "Having a roof over one's head" is seen as a norm for society as a whole and the contrary is therefore seen as a problem illustrating a complex social structure.

From this perspective, knowledge devices which highlight these problematic groups fix the frontier that distinguishes a norm from its deviance. When actors seek to highlight the existence of a "poorly housed" group, they begin by defining the norms of "decent housing" by establishing, for example, standard sanitary equipment, the standard number of inhabitants per room, the safety standards, etc. It is only through this process of co-constructing the norm and its deviance that they can indicate, for example, the number of houses labelled as overpopulated.

In other cases, that of "students" or of "handicapped persons", it is not the group of victims in itself that constitutes a problem. Rather, the problem comes from the alignment between the social group of victims and the social group. In other words, while the cutting of the group is not directly responsible, it is, once again, the manner in which the problem cuts society in puzzling groups which is questionable.

Whatever the case, identifying a group of victims is therefore based first on the need to mobilise the normative devices of knowledge to cut society into different groups. However, this process is insufficient. The individuals must be identified as the victims of others and not of themselves.

Through his study on road accidents, Gusfield offers a particularly relevant example of this distinction between a group of individuals faced with a problem and their transformation into a Public of victims. Indeed, the author argued that while the number of road deaths had been high over a long period, victims had often been considered as victims of themselves. This had therefore not led to a public reaction. It was therefore necessary to take a distance from this image of a responsible driver in order to change how the phenomenon was understood (Gusfield, 1981).

The problem definitional process is therefore not only based on identifying a specific definition of society and of how it is cut in puzzling parts by the problem but is also influenced by the dissociation between the group of victims and the group of the guilty.

The third stage: designating causes, authorities, and the group of the guilty

In transforming a situation into a public problem, the third phase that is generally identifiable after the labelling of the problem and the identification of a Public of victims is the designation of causes. This process that is driven by problem-makers must be understood as a discursive process not only to identify those responsible and to designate the group of culprits, but also to shift the problem to another problem; in this shifting process that still generates disorder, the terms of the problem have changed.

Designating causes also results from the labelling process via actors who establish a social phenomenon as the "cause" of the problem. The cause presents itself as a statement which designates a social phenomenon distinct from, but associated to, the problem itself. This association is both temporal, as it implies showing that the situation in question indeed preceded the problem, and causal, which means that the actors are able to show that it does not imply a simple correlation, but that the label "cause" can indeed be attributed to it. To achieve this, problem-makers must notably be able to make this temporal sequencing between the cause and the problem lose its singularity, by showing that all identical situations give rise to similar problems (Boudon, 1995).

Associating the cause to the problem is therefore a complex process which assumes a specific argumentation to attest its generalisation. Here, we distance ourselves from the simple task of naming or defining that is structured around a normative process of equivalence and enter into the more complex process of demonstration. Each time an actor highlights a correlation and wishes to qualify it as a "cause", he may be required to prove, in other words, to provide arguments showing that it does not imply a simple correlation of two distinct situations. Demonstration is at this point complex as it can only be partial and uncertain, giving way to contestation and controversy (Perelman, 1958).

Let's take an example from the current French political debate. Is the reduction in working hours partly responsible for the unemployment problem? This debate begins with the identification of a problem, unemployment, whose description as "the unemployment problem" remains vague. Actors then need to debate on it in order to determine whether the working duration is the cause, even partially, of this problem. Starting from a real or even assumed theoretical correlation, the reduction in working hours took place at the end of the 1990s just before rising unemployment over subsequent years. Problem-makers have attempted to demonstrate that a cause and effect relationship exists, and have been put to the test in the face of contradictory arguments, or when their own arguments have been contested.

However, these causal relationships are not demonstrable, that is, they cannot give rise to any incontestable demonstration. As Perelman (1958) reminds us in his treatise on the New Rhetoric, as soon as we leave the world of mathematics, rigorous and rational "demonstrations" become impossible and are replaced by "arguments" destined to show the "plausible" character of such a link. This is verified even further as it involves particularly complex social phenomena. Owing to the fact that there is nothing that makes it possible to demonstrate incontestably the existence of a causal relationship between these two phenomena, there is always room for contradictory statements or for arguments challenging the solidity of the relationship. This controversy around the causes is as important as the controversy surrounding the name or identification of victims.

It must be noted that identifying a cause is undoubtedly not without implications on the problem itself. For the problem-makers, it allows them to modify the terms of the debate by replacing the problem by its cause. Making 35 hours the cause, even partially, of the problem of unemployment, means shifting the unemployment debate towards the 35 hours debate. With this shift, the 35 hours policy is transformed into a problem. The definitional process relative to the causes of the problem is equivalent to shifting debate from a problem towards another problem, translating it somewhat into a new language.

Let's take another example from the housing issue. Our studies clearly showed that for a significant number of actors, the "housing problem" was primarily a result of "the insufficient number of new housing built each year". Based on this, the problem-makers redefined the terms of debate by replacing "the housing problem" with the "problem of the number of houses built each year". Subsequently, debate on the cause shifted once again due to the fact that another problem that substituted the previous one emerged. The actors therefore shifted once again by evoking the market and its inability to self-regulate in order to respond to the offer.

Actors always dispose of a registry of arguments, proofs, precisions, definitions, etc., which contribute in constructing a causal chain thereby linking several complex phenomena. Consequently, to show that there is a relationship between the housing problem and the problem of the insufficient number of new housing each year, the actors use arguments by mobilising figures and statistics often constructed for the occasion such as the gap between the evolution of demand and that of offer.

Numerous actors have contested these causal chains with equal argumentative vigour. They argue that the insufficient number of new housing is not the cause of the housing problem and that the market is not a culprit but a victim of excessive regulations. They too advance arguments to show that the homeless and the "housing problem" existed even when more accommodations were constructed. Debate on the consistency of this causal relationship is therefore quite common.

The causal chaining between different problem statements is therefore a setup that is always fragile and tricky to deal with. It is the object of debates, oppositions, confrontations, and its implementation is generally not simple. We must stress that the shifting of the problem that it brings about makes it possible to modify the terms of the debate and introduce two new components of the problem statement.

The first is the "guilty party", that is, the group which is to be condemned for having produced the problem. Linking problems to each other makes it possible to shift from a relatively vague problem to a problem which clearly identifies the guilty party. In the example of road accidents, highlighting the cause "drinking and driving" makes it possible to rule out many other guilty parties such as the road, the car, or the person who sells the alcohol, and concentrate on the driver who consumes alcohol (Gusfield, 1981). With regard to the housing problem, identifying the cause, "the markets inability to provide sufficient new housing", makes the market the guilty party, and not the homeless, the owners, or the social housing organisms which attribute accommodation. Designating the guilty party plays a key symbolic role both in understanding society and within political activity.

The second is the person "responsible" for the problem, meaning the group or institution that actors designate as being responsible for its resolution. Sometimes the guilty are the authorities who are asked for compensation and sometimes not. It is therefore necessary to clearly distinguish these two notions of guilty and responsible party. In the case of reduced working hours, the designation of the guilty party, the State, which enacted the law, is also the responsible party, and the one expected to repair the damages. However, in the case of housing, for example, it is not towards the guilty party, the market, to which solicitations turn, but towards the responsible parties who are the public authorities charged with compensating their weaknesses.

Designating who is responsible is therefore a major issue as it implies defining who will be responsible for solving the problem. The person accountable is not necessarily the guilty party or even, to take up the distinction proposed by Gusfield, the owner. By ownership, the author means the person who establishes the definition. Gusfield highlights the example of environmental associations which designate cars as guilty parties and the manufacturers as responsible for air pollution. Here we can see that for environmental stakeholders, the issue is to maintain the ownership of the problem all the while placing responsibility elsewhere.

Designating a responsible party is all the more interesting, given its additional particularity: it suggests that a solution is possible without necessarily specifying which one. Storms or tsunamis are natural phenomena. They lead to victims, those whose property or even lives are damaged; they are often designated as problems and have natural causes as well. However, no one can be held accountable, nor is there any solution to prevent the next tsunami. On the contrary, were the tsunami to be linked to the larger problem of climatic change which in turn was to be linked to the guilty party which is human activity, it would then be possible to designate public authority as the responsible party. Designating a cause and responsible party accords legitimacy to the institution thus identified and introduces it as the bearer of an awaited solution.

The fourth phase: the making of an apocalyptic future

A problem statement depends not only on the label attached to a situation, the identification of a Public of victims as well as a cause, but also on the perspective of its future consequences within the society which transforms it into an unacceptable problem. This perspective of an apocalyptic future was developed from the "narrative" concept advanced by authors such as Eymerie Roe (1994), Deborah Stone (1989), and Claudio Radaelli (2004).

Using a term from literature such as "narrative" is neither new in philosophy nor in social sciences. For instance, we find this term in Paul Ricœur's hermeneutical philosophy or in Paul Veyne's conception of history for whom history is "nothing but truthful narrative" (Ricoeur, 1976, 1984; Veyne, 1971). According to Ricœur and Veyne, a narrative is a global epistemological project which makes it possible to develop a philosophy of history (Veyne), and an epistemology of social sciences (Ricœur, 1984).

For Ricœur, a narrative is a particularly fertile concept that seeks to understand the problem of time and historicity in analysing the present and the immediate. Focusing on the phenomenology of the present, he proposes a break away from the paradox which makes phenomenology incapable of reflecting on time and on history through the use of narratives. As he himself argues, "temporality cannot be spoken for in the direct discourse of phenomenology but rather requires the mediation of the indirect discourse of narration. (...) Our working hypothesis therefore amounts to taking narrative as the guardian of time insofar as there can be no thought about time without narrated time" (Ricœur, 1984, p. 242). A narrative is therefore a specific discursive process which enables individuals to give meaning to their actions by situating them within a narrative, a narrative of past events, sorted, selected, and plotted, but also fictional narratives aimed at bringing the future back into the present.

A narrative must therefore be understood as a process involving the specific construction of the present based on the past or on the future. This concept has been used by authors working on problem agenda setting who, as we have seen, are particularly receptive to discursive approaches. This is the case of Joseph Gusfield, for instance, who focuses on scientific production and on how knowledge devices have contributed in shaping the dominant discourse on drinking-driving.

Gusfield argues that considering science as a form of art means "examining its style, its modes of persuasion, its fictional components – in short, its literary substance. That science is not literature is accepted. I treat it as if it were literature in order to bring out those aspects which are better understood through literary analysis" (Gusfield, 1981, p. 18). The author therefore takes an interest in how knowledge, which is uncertain and limited at the outset, emerges from this ambiguity by creating fiction and a dramaturgy, "a dramatic image of the drinking-driver as a person of evil and blame results" (Ibid., p. 53). According to Gusfield, dramaturgy is therefore a discursive strategy to construct meaningful knowledge.

Gusfield uses the "narrative" concept to show that the production of knowledge is far from scientific in terms of a science capable of producing valid and complete knowledge. "Science as a literary art" therefore produces articles which form narratives, "a story with a beginning and an end involving change" (Ibid., p. 87), which seek to persuade an audience.

Inspired notably by the studies carried out by Gusfield, Deborah Stone developed the concept of "causal stories" towards the end of the 1990s in order to grasp the problem agenda setting process. The author focused in particular on how actors did not stop at grasping the causal compre-hension models of phenomena but rather composed "stories" from misdemeanours and difficulties and used these stories to legitimise their call for governmental intervention. She therefore evoked the notion that actors use narrative story lines and symbolic devices to manipulate the construction of problems. Establishing a typology of causal stories, Stone insisted on the empirical dimensions of a narrative which make it possible for individuals to grasp the moral mechanisms in blaming those who bring about the suffering.

Since the 1990s, Roe and Radaelli's studies have largely contributed to reinforcing this concept in the public policy field. While for some authors a narrative is the form that social sciences, which do not wish to be caught up in positivism, should use, for others such as Roe and Radaelli, the narrative is first a discursive form that actors develop. According to Radaelli, it enables them to describe "*scenarios* not so much by telling what *should happen* as about what *will happen* according to their narrators if the events or positions are carried out as described" (Radaelli, 2004, p. 366). A narrative is therefore important as it enables the dramatisation of the future through the presentation of fictions which appear as the logical continuation of an organised past.

By proposing "temporal causal sequences" (Radaelli, 2004) as its fundamental characteristic, the narrative appears as a heuristic concept that explores how actors analyse the present by making of the past a story which has meaning and whose meaning determines an unaccept-able future. By depicting and dramatising a foreseeable future that is a generator of disorder, the narrative contributes in legitimising the need for public intervention, the first step in a different process summoned to ward off the apocalyptic future and restore order in the present.

The fifth phase: taking necessary immediate action

During the definitional process of problem agenda setting, identifying a responsible party and the future consequences of a complex situation contribute to the emergence of the last phase, that of requesting immediate action from the responsible party. The actors who define a problem by underscoring the disorder it generates within society strive to make this situation unacceptable.

Felstiner, Abel and Sarat (1980) evoke this as the "claiming" phase. As has been shown by J Baumgartner and Jones (2005), while the obligation to act is difficult to grasp, it is nevertheless easy to recognise empirically. Indeed, the two authors observed that the agenda setting process was accompanied by greater awareness among the actors concerning the pressing need for change, even though shortly before, prudence reigned.

Rather than consider this phenomenon as the result of an "awakened awareness", we would like to insist on the definitional activity carried out by actors which shows that the resolution of problems cannot wait. Indeed, the obligation to act is based on the manner in which the statement illustrates an apocalyptic future but also integrates another essential temporal dimension. Contrary to other phases which often refer to processes not anchored in time, this phase raises the question of immediacy. Indeed, the particularity of social problems is often their oldness and their longevity. Irrespective of whether they deal with accommodation, unemployment, or inequality, problems appear to transcend the ages and stand the test of time. However, this apparent atemporality contrasts with the ephemeral temporality of the agenda setting process. In other words, faced with the construction of a problem statement portraying an apocalyptic future, the question which arises, and to which the actors bearing it must respond, is why non-intervention is more intolerable today than yesterday.

Admittedly, some problems are more recent than others but the issue of their continued relevance remains unchanged. The environmental problem is undoubtedly more recent than that of inequality but despite this, it can only remain in the sphere of problems due to its compelling topicality. As Kingdon (1995) has convincingly argued, the world of problems is a world that is particularly agitated where problems on the agenda succeed each other with frightening speed. One problem replaces another depending on the latest events. The problem of the nuclear power station in Japan occupies all the news until that of the Arab spring replaces it or that of the tribulations of an elected official makes big headlines. It must be noted that problem agenda setting is undoubtedly linked to the world of media and the latter only survives because of its ability to report the latest events which change often enough to maintain the attention of individuals.

In this volatile process of problem agenda setting, the immediate temporality of the event is therefore a major element. In the first phase, we saw that the definitional process of labelling involves a taxonomic activity which makes it possible to shift a situation from its singularity and associate it to a more general problem. We would like to posit here that this is a two way process, meaning, while the labelling of a situation within a more general problem enables it to de-singularise itself, the situation brings topicality to the problem definition thereby facilitating the immediate obligation to act.

The current relevance of situations therefore constitutes an essential resource for problem owners but requires a complex and tricky process which involves associating immediate singular situations and more general public problems. This facilitates the media's agenda setting of these problems on one hand, as the media is often keen on generalising singular situations, and on the other, that of the owners who request these symbolic resources that the latest events bring them.

It is therefore this dialectic between singular events and general problems that constitutes the cornerstone of the need for action.

Propagation or suppression: controversy on the bias of a definitional strategy

To grasp the entire definitional process which is at the core of problem agenda setting, it is also necessary to focus on the strategies that actors use, as well as on their struggles to impose a problem statement. One of the principal debates which structures this question is the manner in which the statement propagation process is considered and the conditions of its inclusion in the government's agenda.

The first pluralist studies showed that the problem propagation process depended primarily on the result of struggles and on the power relations between groups of competing actors, with each group bearing its own definition of the problem defended (Bentley, 1908; Dewey, 1927; Dahl, 1965). Questioning these pluralist approaches, many studies have underlined the phenomenon of the trajectories of problem obstruction or suffocation. These authors argue that by focusing on definitional struggles between concurrent issues, the observer overshadows the earlier processes of sorting and selection which have already contributed in eliminating numerous problems. In other words, by observing only the problems which make it to the agenda, researchers grasp only the visible part of the definitional process which, in reality, is longer, more selective, and more complex.

Schattschneider (1975) is among the first authors to have high-lighted this phenomenon of obstruction. To achieve this, he first distinguished the direct conflict between several protagonists, which created a problem from the process and further enabled this problem to expand beyond the protagonists directly implicated. The author cited an example of a riot in Harlem which took place in 1943, started by a simple fight between a black soldier and a white policeman. This fight rapidly degenerated into a riot and threw the Harlem neigh-bourhood into disarray resulting in almost 400 injured persons and several millions of dollars in material damage. Its degeneration was not directly linked to these two men who had fought and who had in reality no direct relationship with the riot. It was primarily because the inhabitants associated this singular event, the fight, to the problem of racism, thereby making it lose its singularity and transforming it into a societal problem.

However, while Schattschneider highlights the importance of a defi-nitional activity, which makes it possible to redefine a singular situation into a public problem, and he insists on the interpretation, which enables generalisation and the expansion of conflict, it is primarily to further stress the existence of definitional strategies which seek, conversely, to obstruct this expansion. According to him, actors set up strategies in order to contain conflict. For example, notifying an individual that he has no chance to win a conflict is a method that dissuades him from trying. Modifying or limiting the subject under conflict by preventing all generalisation is also a method that prevents conflict.

He therefore underscores the "bias" which actors use to prevent the problem from spreading and concludes that only a few problems manage to avoid all bias and go through to the end. He therefore describes the definitional process as a major political task whose objective is to master the expansion of conflict.

In the 1960s, Bachrach and Baratz largely contributed to popularising the studies carried out by Schattschneider and in making the issue of mastering the contagion of problems an essential issue in understanding the emergence of problems (Bachrach and Morton, 1962, 1963). Written in 1962 and updated in 1963, their article on "non decision" was largely publicised among the political science community.

Bachrach and Baratz thus evoke all the constraints that limit the access of problems and insist particularly on invisible constraints such as values, ideas, rituals, or the procedures which favour certain problems over others, or certain groups over others. To designate all this, the two authors borrow the "bias" concept from Schattschneider as well as the process of the "mobilisation of bias". The "mobilisation of bias" is therefore a particularly restrictive process which takes place upstream. Restricting the field of possibilities or selecting acceptable forms are key issues that these authors propose to analyse.

Thanks to the agenda metaphor that they largely popularised but did not invent,[2] Cobb and Elder pursued the studies carried out by Bachrach and Baratz (Cobb and Elder, 1971) by focusing on the conditions which obstruct propagation as well as those that enable the resolution of a problem. They particularly insisted on the process of expanding a conflict based on the definition of the problem. In so doing, they created a second type of process which focused less on the forms of suppression than on the costly forms of mobilisation which make it possible to propagate and to publicise a problem.

The authors thus attached particular importance to the language used and its mastery, to the mobilisation of symbols, and to the generalisation of rhetoric. Associating a problem to a long tradition of conflicts for instance constitutes one of the strategies that individuals develop to expand conflict.

The process by which actors fabricate and impose a more or less expansive definition of a problem is therefore, according to them, one of the key factors to analyse. Thus, for example, the more ambiguous a problem, the greater will be its social implication; the longer it lasts or the less technical it appears, the larger will be its chances to expand itself. The struggle in problem definition is therefore an essential aspect to enable or hinder its contagion.

Between propagation and suppression: the discontinuous careers of problems

More recently, other authors have worked on reconciling these two visions by considering propagation as the result of the struggle between the actors who work on problem agenda setting and those that are opposed to it and set up numerous obstacles in their path. While propagation is based on the capacity of the acting spokespersons of a problem to interest other actors to join them in this particularly costly and difficult process (Olson, 1978), obstruction reveals the existence of opponents who fight to hinder the emergence of these problems. By no means linear, the "career" of a problem (Gusfield, 1981) presents itself as an oscillation that depends notably on the agreements and conflicts among actors.

In recent studies, Frank Baumgartner and Brian Jones (2005) have attempted to carry out a synthesis between the two models, with regard to how agenda setting is understood, by proposing the theory of punctuated equilibrium. On the one hand, it involves showing that over long periods, the dominant actors of a public policy sector ensure an equilibrated and stable situation by mastering and monopolising upstream problem definition processes. Thus according to the two authors, there are stable rules of the game which ensure the stability of configurations and dominations. All new action, entailing "frictions" therefore becomes too costly to implement. Moreover, the two authors take up the notion of the cognitive limits of individuals who prefer stable ideas to new ideas,[3] reinforcing the stability and the impossible outbreak of problems.

On the other hand, during often unexpected moments, a new problem arises on the public scene with new spokespersons who throw a system into crisis and provoke change. On the long calm river of incremental processes, Baumgartner and Jones evoke the frenetic shifts in the agenda which lead to specific and sudden attention to a given public policy sector.[4] While the incremental and stable process is structured around an orderly and continuous temporality, punctuations occur in a chaotic and unexpected manner. It is for this reason that the model loses its predictive character, all the while preserving its underlying potential.

The phenomenon of political attention therefore makes it possible to understand how the actors, incapable of dealing with everything in one go, direct their attention to the problems suddenly highlighted, thereby developing their still limited perception of reality. It is the emergence of new information, of a new interpretation or of a new definition which provokes the feelings of urgency and the necessary punctual mobilisation of actors. From this point of view, the two authors suggest that bounded rationality explains stability as well as change.

To some extent, problems therefore follow "careers" (Gusfield, 1981), which, far from being linear and marked by oscillations between success and failure, partly depend on the amount of support accompanying them. David Easton (1965) showed for example that taking a problem into account depended not only on transforming its definition, but also on the capacity of the actors bearing the problem to garner support. In a different register, Bruno Latour and Michel Callon worked on the importance of increasing interest and enrolment. They observed the processes through which new actors solicited by the spokespersons supported the problem (Latour, 2006; Callon, 1986). Their key argument is that problems consolidate themselves based on the success of enrolment or, on the contrary, end up forgotten due to lack of support (Latour, 1993). In this enrolment process, the redefinition of the problem is as important as the argumentation which supports it (Chateauraynaud, 2011).

2.3   Conclusion

In conclusion, we can say that the numerous studies on the agenda setting of public problems have made it possible to highlight the significance of the definitional and propagation processes driven by actors in order to impose a problem. In this comprehensive perspective of the agenda, the definitional process, which is also considered to be a meaningful process notably based on the cognitive skills of the actors, plays a central role.

It is first a transformation and translation process which makes it possible for actors to analyse a situation by naming a problem, identifying the victims and the guilty parties, designating the causes and those responsible or even by giving an account of the consequences. It is also a propagation and obstruction tool which makes it possible for actors to diffuse their own definition of a problem by multiplying interactions, arguments, and tests.

This definitional task is particularly an essential politicisation process which makes it possible for actors to point out social disorder thereby rendering public policy necessary. Making reality unacceptable, showing the fragmentation of the Public and transferring to the State the obligation to act thus contributes primarily to the policymaking necessary for their agenda setting.

Taking into account this definitional process around problems echoes Dewey's studies, as well as studies by contemporary French authors belonging to this prevalent school of thought of pragmatic sociology with Luc Boltanski, Bruno Latour, and Francis Chateauraynaud. These authors have taken a particular interest in the role of knowledge devices, of analysis, and even of the critical production that actors mobilise.

Rejecting the asymmetry between the sociologist as the one who knows and the actors, Boltanski (2009) proposes to shift away from critical sociology to sociology of critique, inspired by pragmatic philosophy and ethnomethodology. This approach attaches to the actors themselves, when they are in a given situation, the competence to produce and to use the knowledge on the social reality around them.

The sociology of critique therefore proposes to take an interest in the activity of critiques and of disputes, as well as in justification and agreement. As Boltanski argues "the sociology of critique undertook to describe the social world as the scene of a trial, in the course of which actors in a situation of uncertainty proceed to investigations, record their interpretations of what happens in reports, establish qualifications and submit to tests (...) the intention was to make a form of normativity emerge from the description. Work was initially directed towards clarifying the normative positions on which actors can base themselves, in order to criticise or to justify themselves in the face of critique" (Boltanski, 2009, p. 48).

Analysing the definitional process that actors use to critique society by making the reality unacceptable and the action of the State necessary therefore makes it possible to better grasp this agenda setting process. It gives account of how the actors politicise a problem by making it the symbol of a society in disorder.

3
Defining Solution: A Complex Bricolage to Solve Public Problems

While problems have given rise to numerous studies that have focused on the construction and definitional activities driven by actors, solutions have often been seen as neutral tools requiring no specific definitional activity. Moreover, literature on public policy has employed the term "definition" exclusively to tackle the problem agenda setting process. Authors have generally used the term "formulation" with regard to solutions (Jones, 1970). As a consequence, "to formulate" a solution primarily refers to finding a solution by resolving a problem, rather than defining it. While the concept of "formulation" presupposes a single, unique, and non-debatable meaning, that of definition presupposes varied interpretations. Finally, while "defining" a problem means acknowledging that problems have political implications, "formulating" solutions seems to be more neutral.

The difference between the problem when it is "defining" and the solution when it is "formulating" is undoubtedly linked to the fact that many public policy authors are less interested in grasping political phenomena, as in the case for problems. Rather, they seek to identify by themselves new solutions that are more scientific or more rigorous in problem resolution.

Nevertheless, "solutions" and "problems" share many common features, beginning with their autonomous and independent existence. Since the studies carried out by Simon and Lindblom, we know that they do not result from a simple rational treatment of problems but rather, from a complex cognitive bricolage which often has multiple paths (Simon, 1945; Lindblom, 1958). The studies carried out by March, Cohen, and Olsen have also shown that these solutions often exist well in advance of the problems and independently of their resolution (March, Cohen, and Olsen, 1972). Nonetheless, the significant progress in understanding how solutions are produced has however not challenged their comprehension, nor led to a genuine opening of the black box in which they are formulated.

In this second chapter, we would like to call into question this attempt to grasp solutions as neutral tools in order to show that this must be understood as a construct that depends on the definitional activities of actors. As genuine normative statements, solution proposals are rarely produced by coupling them to a problem found in a garbage can (Kingdon, 1995) but rather, are genuine definitional activities produced through "coupling" an already existent tool with the problem it is expected to resolve, the consequence that it is to produce, or even the public policy that it is to transform.

To understand the coupling process, we must first focus on how actors, incapable of rationally resolving the problems that they find exceedingly complex, deploy cognitive stratagems in order to find solutions which mobilise nonetheless, subjective rather than bounded rationality. This is the assumption from Simon and Lindblom's initial studies that is forgotten far too often, and that we would like to revisit here before expounding on it using a pragmatic approach that takes into account discursive practices.

Far from being a simple bricolage, the coupling process can be considered as both a genuine definitional activity that makes meaning, and as a genuine political activity of restoring order in the disorder brought about by problems.

3.1 Between stratagem and cognitive bricolage: the contribution of Simon and Lindblom

To understand policy definition processes, we must first address the manner in which actors produce knowledge in order to tackle exceedingly complex or even insoluble social issues. A traditional concern among many philosophers, and particularly pragmatic philosophers, the processes of knowledge production have also been of interest to the first authors who worked on the decision-making process such as Herbert Simon or Charles Lindblom. Herbert Simon was indeed among the first authors to highlight the existence of an insurmountable gap between the limited cognitive capacities of individuals and the complexity of the social issues that they had to tackle. However, while we often retain the concept of "bounded rationality" from these studies, we generally neglect the importance that Simon attached to the subjectivity of rationality and to the activities that individuals, conscious of their limits, deploy to resolve these insoluble problems. Referring to the "bricolage" and "stratagem" concepts, Lindblom pursued Simon's studies by taking an even greater interest in the strategies that individuals deployed to address insoluble problems.

Understanding human behaviour: from bounded to subjective rationality

While the concept developed by Simon on bounded rationality is well known, that on subjective rationality which he refers to primarily in his preliminary studies on decision-making remains widely unknown. Simon notably employed this concept in his book written in 1945 (Simon, 1945). The original intention of this book was relatively simple. As he explained in his introduction, his objective was to provide adapted concepts and language in order to describe an administrative organisation. He challenged the traditional opposition used by the sciences of administration to grasp decisions, and notably between facts and values, or the means and the end. He thus proposed to focus on the chainings between means and ends that actors implement practically, and which respond to their subjective rationality.

Focusing on the science of administration literature in the first half of the 20th century, Simon began this book by first drawing attention to the importance of distinguishing between facts and values on one hand and on the other, the means and the end. By this, he sought to define a "good" decision. Indeed, this literature showed that a "good" decision was based on the initial choice of a clear value, a choice considered to be political, as well as on its "logical" translation into facts and practical means; the translation was carried out by the administration.

However, Simon noted that a majority of the decisions that he observed empirically interweaved facts and values as well as means and ends. He also considered that it was simply impossible to clearly distinguish them by following a logical and rational method.

He cited the example of a municipal policy of sports. The author noted that each attempt to identify its goals was always entwined with facts and values, and could always be considered as a means to an end, rather than as an end. Objectives such as "use time wisely" or "prevent juvenile delinquency" could be considered interchangeably as an end or as a means. Simon therefore highlighted the existence of a chain associating the means to the end; each end could transform itself into a means, thereby losing itself in the vague concept of bliss (Simon, 1945).

According to Simon, the reality of practices has little to do with the manner in which scholars have considered the decision-making process.

Contrary to the authors who politically identify objectives by prioritising possible outcomes and choosing the best means to achieve them, Simon begins by showing to what extent it is impossible to imagine a distinct theoretical border between the means and the end. While prohibition is a means that was conceived to encourage temperance, temperance cannot be considered as a final outcome (temperance for what purpose?) but as a means to achieve other more important outcomes. In addition, prohibition cannot be considered as a means without values; it is linked to issues of freedom. Using a simple and logical demonstration, Simon highlights this impossible neutrality and reinforces his argument. Put differently, it is impossible to distinguish between facts/values and means/end in a decision-making process. Moreover, there can be no simple and possible relationship between facts/values and means/end.

Simon thus showed that it was impossible to distinguish between politics and administration. Political decisions are rarely simply political, and the administration is never neutral in relation to the decisions taken. For instance, they can deform or sabotage them. These borders therefore construct themselves rather pragmatically in decision-making.

Hence, Simon no longer distinguished the means from the end but rather privileged the idea of a chaining. This led to both means and ends drawing their strength and their meaning depending on their position within this chain within a statement. This is an essential notion that Simon does not develop further but one that we will take up later:

> The significance of the 'means–end' relationship now becomes clear. It is clear the 'means–end' does not correspond to the distinction between fact and value. What is the connection between the two sets of terms? Simply this: A means–end chain is a series of anticipations that connect a value with the situations realizing it, and these situations, in turn, with the behaviors that produce them. Any element in this chain may be either 'means' or 'end' depending on whether its connection with the value end of the chain, or its connection with the behavior end of the chain, is in question. (Simon, 1947, p. 62)

After assuming that there was no theoretical distinction between facts and values and means and end, Simon then proposed to show how the decisions taken by an individual could not be objectively rational. This is undoubtedly the most famous aspect of his work. Demonstrating the impossible "objective" rationality through reduction to absurdity, he suggests that rationality should be seen as subjective.

For a decision to be objectively rational, Simon argued that an individual must have clearly defined an objective and identified all possible alternatives. He must also have identified all the consequences of each alternative. Finally, he must be able to compare the consequences depending on his objective and choose the best one. In other words, Simon clearly defined the perfect and ideal rational model of decisions in order to better underscore its dysfunctions. He outlined various elements which disrupt this model.

First, he insisted that it was necessary to take into account temporality within this schema. For him, this implies clearly distinguishing between the time to make a decision and time within the decision. In other words, when an individual must make a decision, he can only imagine the consequences of each alternative; if these have not occurred, he cannot consider them as true but only as probable or possible. Moreover, empirically, time is never-ending. This means that an individual is constrained and does not generally have the time to consider "all" the alternatives, for instance. Finally, time often limits possible options as it situates a decision within its context. Put differently, decisions are generally made in advance, restricting the scope of possibilities. If you set up a shoe factory, you cannot decide to manufacture cars the following day. Past choices condition future choices by restricting the possible alternatives.

Simon also stressed the importance of the limits of knowledge within the decision making process. This begins by the incapacity to clearly define an objective, to distinguish the means from the end or to determine the consequences of a choice in advance. The latter must be elaborated by taking into account a number of significant uncertainties. How can one really know the consequences of an alternative? Admittedly, it is possible to use past experience, use the regularities for example, and consider that what held true for the past will also hold true for the future. However, these regularities are often rough estimates, depending on a singular context and do not ensure the future reproduction of past events. For Simon, this was the major and nonreducible difference between scientific discovery which establishes the verifiable laws by their reproducible capacity, and a decision-making problem which must be resolved in uncertainty without systematic reproduction.

According to Simon, it is therefore impossible, for all individuals, to attain a high level of rationality in decision-making. An individual can explore only a limited number of alternatives. He is often a victim of constraints or stimuli which his environment imposes on him; the information available to him is limited and his capacity to predict the consequences of his choices is poor, especially since there are often unintended consequences to his decisions.

This impossible objective rationality in no way means that the individual's choice is irrational or totally constrained but rather, that his choice depends on subjective rationality. This is our third proposal. In other words, despite the fact that an individual is constrained by the environment, that his own capacities are limited, that his knowledge is always fragmented, that he only has a vague intuition of regularities, that he possesses a simplified schema of what reality is, and that he can only consider a limited number of alternatives, he always has a choice between several possible alternatives and he makes this choice depending on the reasons that motivate him. As the author argues, should an individual take medicine that does not cure him, this in no way means that he has acted irrationally but simply that when he chose to take the medicine, he thought that this would cure him. In other words, an individual takes action depending on subjective rationality as well as on what he believes to be the best solution at the decision-making moment. This is what Herbert Simon calls a "satisficing" solution.

Faced by the complexity of the environment which surrounds him, an individual subsequently develops what we can call cognitive strategies of simplification. The simplicity of the human spirit is also an asset in grasping this complexity. It is in this way that Simon analysed different techniques that individuals use in practice. For example, he showed how an engineer develops planning techniques in order to grasp his object and reduce it to knowledge that he can then exploit. In other words, it is not because an individual is incapable of enumerating and calculating all move sequences in chess that he does not play chess. Indeed, the individual mixes intuition and subjective rationality to reduce the number of options until he reaches a number he can calculate, and then makes his choice.

Simon thus focused on the human process of knowledge production and particularly, the processes of simplification that are indispensable and inevitably subjective; individuals nonetheless implement these processes to resolve insoluble problems.

Incrementalism: a stratagem to surmount the impossible rational treatment of problems.

Based on Simon's assumptions in which social problems are too complex to be resolved through objective rationality, Charles Lindblom proposed to extend this reflection by focusing on the cognitive bricolages that individuals nonetheless use to resolve insoluble problems. While incrementalism remains the most popular of these bricolages, Lindblom classifies it within the larger perspective that involves observing the different stratagems that actors use. Here, we focus on the forms of knowledge production as bricolages.

The notion of cognitive bricolage appears for the first time in the book that he writes with Robert Dahl in 1953, "Politics, Economics and welfare" (Dahl and Lindblom, 1953). Following Simon's argument that none of the stages of the decision-making process can unfold in a perfect manner, these two Yale professors question the multiple forms of bricolage that actors mobilise within such a context.

The two authors show how individuals, when confronted by a world that is exceedingly complex, undertake to reduce and simplify the information at their disposal in order to reduce the quantity and render the content more manageable. They therefore analyse how actors reduce the number of variables at their disposal, draw up samples and construct common orders of magnitude in order to enable comparison. Reductionism is therefore seen less as a problem than as a necessary bias in the management of information.

The authors also focus on the second stage of the decision-making process, that of the identification and the choice of alternatives. Like Simon, they consider that individuals are faced with an overwhelming abundance of alternatives and they cannot study them all; they therefore highlight the cognitive bricolages that actors engage in.

First, and this is a significant development in their studies, they show that contrary to common belief, the choice of great values (liberty, equity, security, etc.) or great "isms" (capitalism, socialism, liberalism, etc.) do no reduce the number of alternatives chosen. In their opinion, there is no logical descendant link enabling one to choose an ideology in order to deduce the appropriate tool. To illustrate their position, they cite the example of inflation. Dahl and Lindblom note that States which claim different ideological methods use nonetheless the same tools when it comes to mastering inflation. In other words, the authors undermine the common belief that a public policy can be logically deduced from a value or an ideology.

In the same way, they emphasise that linking the means to the end, an aspect previously highlighted by Simon, cannot follow a deductive and rational link. The means do not stem from the end, and moreover, the means always have unexpected consequences which distance them from these ends.

Contrary to this notion, they attempt to show that actors reduce the scope of alternatives by generally favouring the solutions which are closest to those already in place. The actors therefore prefer groping, making trials and errors. These actors are faced with major uncertainty with regard to the consequences that their choices can generate. Therefore, they draw from incrementalism, a method that reduces uncertainty. This method draws its inspiration, as has been underscored by the authors themselves, from Popper's studies and his willingness to set up piece-meal social engineering (Popper, 1945). In a book written during the Second World War, Karl Popper, who decisively rebutted historical determinism and historicism, advocated for a trial/error approach as the only means through which knowledge and society could move forward.

Incrementalism is therefore a cognitive stratagem which results from acknowledging that the means do not arise from the end, or the values or the ideologies; it is a scientific method of problem solving through trial and error. The authors defend themselves in considering incrementalism as a political or ideological method which seeks to favour "small" rather than "large" changes. The distinction is not easily detectable at first glance. It lies within the rational and scientific trait of position. If the authors defend incrementalism, it is simply because it represents the only rational method for decision-making within a world of bounded rationality. In other words, their argumentation to legitimise their method is not political but rather scientific.

While incrementalism became famous especially as of 1958 when the article, "The Science of Muddling Through" (Lindblom, 1958), was written, it is in the book, *Strategy of Decision*, where the author gave it real coherence (Braybrooke and Lindblom, 1963) before expanding it using the stratagem notion (Lindblom, 1979).

He therefore attempted repeatedly to clarify his argument in order to respond to the multiple erroneous interpretations that his model had brought about. First he used the term "the science of muddling through" (Lindblom, 1958) to signify both the existence of a bricolage from which actors are unable to extract themselves, and the necessity within this bricolage to introduce a scientific method such as the trial and error method. In a conference that he gave in 1970, the author therefore highlighted to what extent the term "muddling through" had led to confusion, with many considering that he had chosen to replace rationality by resourcefulness even as, in his opinion, the absence of rationality was a matter of observation and not of intention. It is this incomprehension which led him to substitute the notion of "muddling through" by that of "disjointed incrementalism" (Lindblom, 1979).

Nevertheless, he noted that several years later, this change in terminology did not seem to sufficiently clear up the ambiguity. He therefore proposed to better dissociate what qualified as descriptive, and bring together the methods individuals used to resolve excessively complex problems, from what qualified as prescriptive – the method he recommended or sought to improve.

He therefore developed the "stratagem" concept first and then the "strategic analysis" concept (Lindblom, 1979) in order to underscore the different forms of cognitive bricolage. He identified seven forms and considered incrementalism only as one of them. In addition, the author identified the stratagem of the reversibility of decisions. Here, individuals make a choice whose particularity it is that they can turn back if they find the option unsuitable. They can voluntarily make a bad choice in order to study the unexpected outcomes; they can choose uncertain choices and endeavour to ameliorate their choices as they go along; they can divide problems into several manageable problems; they can make voluntary partisan choices.

Cognitive bricolage as a stratagem: Simon and Lindbom's contribution

When we consider them from a descriptive and comprehensive angle, Simon and Lindblom's studies enable us to shape our thinking with regard to three key points.

First, their studies make it possible to grasp the difficulties that individuals come across when they are confronted with social problems, difficulties generated by both the cognitive limits of the individuals, and by the consistently unexpected consequences of solutions. By making absolute rationality and the synoptic approach a myth, and its use a bricolage among others, the authors ensure that knowledge production within the decision-making process is a problem that actors must always resolve subjectively. Lindblom's final study specifically concerns this theme of knowledge production (Cohen and Lindblom, 1979).

The two authors developed this problem not only within the process of the definition of objectives, goals, values, problems, or solutions but also within the construction of the chains which associate them. By underscoring that the same tool can be mobilised within different ideological frameworks, they showed that a tool cannot be determined through logical deduction based on ideological frameworks.

Once again, this link is a problem that the actors must resolve. This idea that was particularly innovative at the time was however, unlike the previous one, not particularly exploited. Indeed, in contemporary studies, we frequently find a logical chain between these elements. In the studies carried out by Peter Hall or Paul Sabatier, for example, public policies are structured around a hierarchical system of levels ranging from the core of values to the more brittle core of tools (Hall, 1993; Sabatier and Jenkis-Smith, 1993). In these cases, a hierarchical system simply organises different elements joined together by a logical and stable link.

The third major development worth noting from these two authors is the notion that actors do not get disillusioned by their incapacity to find solutions when faced with exceedingly complex problems; rather, they deploy multiple stratagems to get around these difficulties and thereby act accordingly. Lindblom and Simon point out the activities of simplification, fragmentation, combination, and chaining as bricolages destined to resolve the problems associated to definitions and to links.

Nevertheless, while these three developments are fundamental in understanding the processes of public policymaking, the two authors neglect two particularly problematic questions.

The first: Why do actors feel the need to carry out almost illusory bricolages instead of simply grasping the solutions available to them, and admitting that it is simply a question of bricolage, which must simply be made more stringent? And why have all the efforts of camouflaging this bricolage made by the tenants of rational choices been more successful than Lindblom's "science of bricolage" project? Our two authors who were involved in this fight against rationality, and who strongly associated description and prescription, undoubtedly found it difficult to step back and reflect on the more general question of restoring order among these elements, as well as on the underlying issue of meaning.

This leads us to the second question that has remained in the shadows: what is the relationship between the world of knowledge, including limited and subjective knowledge, and that of collective action? Although both authors agree that decisions generally result from collective action and not from isolated individuals, this problem hardly finds its place in their reflection. While Simon effectively points out that the decision-making process can only be understood at the core of collective action, while he notably takes an interest in the phenomenon of loyalty within groups, he remains evasive with regard to the relationship between collective action and subjective rationality.

Lindblom is also very interested in the issue of collective action and tries to integrate it into his reflection on disjointed incrementalism. He therefore evokes the notion of mutual adjustment in order to analyse the outcomes of collective action on the development of incrementalism. In 1965, he devoted an entire book to mutual adjustment in order to underscore the importance of taking the plurality of actors into

account, as well as the exchanges involved in decision-making processes. These reflect the need for agreement among the large number
of participants and make reference to a process, that can be described
as the invisible hand of the market, to explain sharing and regulation.
However, quite curiously, this link remained elusive in the book he had
written two years earlier on incrementalism (Braybrooke and Lindblom,
1963, Lindblom, 1965).

3.2   From cognitive bricolage to language games

The studies carried out by Simon and Lindblom make it possible to grasp
the cognitive bricolage regulating the chaining between the different
components of a solution. However, they face difficulties in linking these
processes of knowledge production to the manner in which knowledge
thus fashioned circulates between the actors and serves as the basis of
their agreements and, more broadly, of their collective actions. In our
opinion, this difficulty can be explained by the distinction that they
make between the world of thought and the world of action or interaction. By dealing with these two aspects separately from the outset, they
can no longer reconcile them at the end of their argument. On one hand,
the mere construction of an individual's reasoning without questioning
his relationship to others, and grasping the negotiations between the
actors without questioning the manner in which this reasoning structures and impacts the very nature of the interactions on the other, leads
to an impasse. By separately studying the phenomenon of incrementalism and that of mutual adjustment, Lindblom is then unable to grasp
the connection between them.

To overcome this impasse, we propose to assemble the reflections from
the linguistic and pragmatic shift of philosophy and social sciences.
Indeed, this calls for blurring the boundary which separates the world of
thought from that of action by directly observing discourse "in action".
This simultaneously constitutes access to the knowledge produced, as
well as the essence of the exchange between the actors. Discursive practices such as definition, argumentation, conviction, and persuasion are
therefore characterised as much by their content as by the interactions
that they reveal.

In this chapter, we would like to expand on the key developments
of this linguistic shift and, in particular, present the seven facets of
discourse "in action" often neglected when analysing the processes of
public policymaking. These seven facets enable us to consider the definitional activity of problem solving as both the result of a patchwork

production of knowledge as well as a social interaction around which agreements and disagreements are built between actors.

Discourse, the overlooked aspect in policy change theories?

While the linguistic shift has largely permeated all social sciences and has influenced the majority of public policy change studies tackling the issue of problem agenda setting, it has had very little impact when tackling policy-making and decision-making processes. With the exception of studies which claim to follow the interpretative approach, few authors have questioned the role of discourse even while, like Aaron Wildavsky, they often want to "speak" truth to power (Wildavsky, 1987) and make their studies an argument in transforming practices.

Political discourse as such is not absent from these studies but it is often used as a counterpoint in relation to the practices that the researcher would like to highlight. As a consequence, discourse on "reform" or on "significant change" often serves as a contrast in order to better highlight the public policies which finally, do not really change. Discourse expressing the political will of the decision-maker is often used as the point of departure for a demonstration which seeks to prove the powerlessness of the decision-maker. Discourse is somewhat the expression of a "spectacle", to borrow the term used by Murray Edelman (Edelman, 1988), which masks the reality of the practices that unfold behind the scenes and which the researcher undertakes to reveal.

When we distance ourselves from the sub-discipline of public policy change studies, we naturally find researchers who are specialists in the analysis of political discourse. Their studies are primarily based on the semiotic analysis of available texts. This calls for studying a text or texts by seeking to understand, either qualitatively or quantitatively, its meaning, the links which structure it, the type of arguments mobilised, the representations voiced, etc. Here, textual analysis is the methodological key through which researchers read reality. To achieve this, they often rely on Saussure's studies which distinguish "internal linguistics" from "external linguistics" (De Saussure et al., 1986), as well as discourse from the manner in which it is produced and set out.

We will not go into the different streams which structure this field but it must be noted that these studies did not only fail to convince public policy analysts, but in addition, the latter also probably reinforced their conviction to decline this aspect of the studies undertaken by others. Subsequently, they defend the idea that their bias is fundamentally different in view of the fact that for them, reality is to be found in actors' actions and not in their discourse.

At this stage, we would like to turn away from both the semiologists and the public policy change researchers and defend the idea that they both share a similar epistemological conception of discourse and of practices which are based on a clear distinction between these two activities. On one hand, this distinction makes it possible for semiologists to analyse discourse without focusing on all the practices in which they are embedded and to which available texts do not give access. On the other hand, the distinction makes it possible for researchers to disregard the epistemological status of language even as they use methods such as interviews or the reading of written documents which are nothing more than discursive practices.

We therefore need to go back to how discourse is addressed by considering it not as an element that is separate from practice but rather as a fully-fledged practice. It would be wrong to consider that political discourse is limited to what Vivien Schmidt rightly calls the discourse of "political communication", meaning all the official discourses destined to a large public within a coordinative policy sphere (Schmidt and Radaelli, 2004). Not only can these discourses be understood exclusively through the analysis of the conventions that they are part of, but in addition, they only represent a very small part of all the discursive practices which prevail in the decision-making space.

Consequently, all the discursive practices present within the process that one seeks to study must be encompassed within "discourse". Each discursive practice is therefore singular because it expresses itself under particular circumstances, specific times and places, and between given audiences. From this perspective, the discursive activity becomes much richer and diversified than it originally was. Owing to the fact that it also has materiality as opposed to an idea, for example, it also becomes observable, definable and reconstitutable even if this gives rise to numerous methodological problems that would need to be addressed.

In this respect, we focus on discursive practices as they constitute the central activity that we find in decision-making processes. Making a public policy, passing a new law, or modifying technical devices are decisions which result from numerous discussions within administrations, political bodies, multiple groups, etc. Without further elaborating what constitutes a decision for the moment, our priority is to consider, alongside public policy analysts, that a decision is never a man, a place, a moment; rather, it is a complex process that is notably constituted of multiple discussions which structure all agreements and organise conflicts (Lindblom, 1979). This is the point that has been ignored.

To take these discursive practices into account, it is therefore necessary to first focus on what they specifically show in our field. To achieve this, we would like to develop the seven facets of discourse that we are particularly interested in.

Discourse as a transgressive and indispensable filter of reality

First and foremost, discourse must be understood as the primary means through which actors deal with reality. Consequently, it not only means taking up Dewey's argument that one cannot grasp reality without knowledge devices, but to add as well that these knowledge devices cannot be separated from the discursive activities within which they are embedded. To put it differently, language is the filter that we use to grasp and debate on the world around us, a filter that is both indispensable and transgressive.

To understand these two dimensions of discourse, we must first address the studies of the linguistic turn in greater detail. Indeed, it is at the heart of this turn that authors sought to dissociate themselves from a philosophy of conscience favouring the internal (ideas, representations), by elaborating a philosophy of language. This postulates that knowledge making is inseparable from other activities such as speaking and acting, as they use language as a common core to grasp reality.

Jürgen Habermas, a key philosopher within this turn, thus explains that language is an indispensable filter that we use to grasp reality. Moreover, this language that we use to reason cannot be distinguished from the one that we use to speak or to act: "our cognitive ability can no longer be analysed independently of our linguistic ability and our ability to act (...) For us, language and reality inextricably permeate one another. Experience is linguistically saturated such that no grasp of reality is possible that is not filtered through language. (...) the reality facing our propositions is not 'naked' but is itself already permeated by language" (Habermas, 1999, p. 181).

This language filter is of interest to us not only because it is indispensable but also because it is not neutral and transparent with regard to the object, the idea, or the fact that it seeks to state or describe. On the contrary, to take up Michel Foucault's reflection, discourse is an act of "violence that we do to things, or, at all events, as a practice we impose upon them" (Foucault, 1971, p. 55). In order to reinforce his demonstration, Foucault wonders: if discourse is neutral, why are certain subjects, certain words struck by prohibitions?[1]

Given that discourse is neither transparent nor neutral, it acts on what it describes. Consequently, it is no longer about getting caught up in a discussion on the validity of the description, absorbed by what Wittgenstein calls "sovereignty of meaning", but placing discourse at the same level as the practices it is to analyse. Discourse therefore becomes a supplementary practice whose precise role is to seek to encompass the other practices, to establish order, to smooth them over or erase them, and to give them meaning.

Postulating that language is an indispensable and transgressive filter of reality therefore means underscoring that we cannot access reality without language. It is this complex relationship between language and reality that leads to endless problems.

Michel Foucault has made extensive efforts to develop the complex relationship between discourse and reality. According to him, while discourse and reality are not equivalent, they are nevertheless mutually significant. While defining a "fool" depends on the society in which he finds himself, and on the moment when this society determines this definition, and furthermore is a constructed concept, this does not means that "fools" do not exist but simply that truths primarily express themselves within a given framework and period.

It is therefore important to understand to what extent one cannot do away with discourse to attain reality. Discourse is the indispensable filter that grasps reality without absorbing it completely. In physical sciences, we can compare this to the problem of quantum mechanics. In order to tackle the infinitely small, researchers construct specific devices. The problem invariably encountered involves the interference arising from the device in relation to the reality observed; this interference cannot be eliminated. What they observe is a complex in-between, between reality and nothingness.

Language games in the construction of meaning

The third characteristic of discourse expands on the first two by integrating the issue of meaning. Language is not only an accumulation of words which makes it possible to grasp reality, it is also the means used to give it meaning, and is necessary in constructing thought as well as communication.

To grasp the construction of meaning, we would like to borrow the concept of "language games" that has been used by Wittgenstein. This concept makes it possible for him to consider actions such as define, select, analyse, sort, conceptualise, translate, or problematise as discursive operations based on language, as well as the multiple associations that it makes possible. The author therefore considers that "the processes of naming the stones and of *repeating words* after someone might also be called language games (...) *I shall also call the whole, consisting of language and the actions into which it is woven, a 'language-game'"* (Wittgenstein, 1958, paragraph 7).

Refuting the obvious, Wittgenstein thus plunges into numerous reflections in order to grasp or at least encircle these multiple language games of which he can only identify the aspects. Subsequently, he prefers to give examples, all the while conscious that these examples can never completely cover the whole, but rather, that the definition of a whole is generally overwhelmed by examples.

> Here the term *'language-game'* is meant to bring into prominence the fact that the *speaking* of language is part of an activity, or of a form of life. Giving orders, and obeying them; Describing the appearance of an object, or giving its measurements; Constructing an object from a description (a drawing); Reporting an event; Speculating about an event; Forming and testing a hypothesis; Presenting the results of an experiment in tables and diagrams; Making up a story; and reading it; Play-acting; Singing catches; Guessing riddles; Making a joke; telling it; Solving a problem in practical arithmetic; Translating from one language into another; Asking, thanking, cursing, greeting, praying. (Wittgenstein, 1958, pp. 11–12)

Language games are, among other things, heuristic techniques to tackle reality. According to Wittgenstein, language games are not confined to word games but rather regroup other activities, for instance making an object based on a drawing; this occurs through language. What matters therefore is the diverse usability of language through these multiple games, rather than the view of language as a set of words. Language games are central activities which give meaning to words. In our opinion, they are central when addressing public policy. They structure, organise, prioritise, and make sense of a tool by transforming it into a problem solving tool within a larger public policy in which it is embedded.

Such a prospect actually makes it possible to go back to the developments advanced by Simon and Lindblom, offering them a new perspective. While these authors had also grasped the importance of the processes of simplification and the multiple bricolages that actors produce, they had tackled this only in terms of knowledge and not in terms of language and meaning. Nevertheless, integrating meaning makes it possible to understand the essential activity of restoring language order which often tends to do away with the traces of cognitive bricolage.

In other words, while actors struggle to understand a problem or resolve it, they must also grope around in an effort to restore order for their discourse to make sense. Contrary to what Lindblom had hoped for, this does not imply acknowledging bricolage in order to make it more rigorous, but rather understanding that erasing it is a supplementary bricolage that makes it possible to produce meaning.

From this perspective, the concept of language games makes it possible to reconcile this double cognitive and semantic dimension of discursive bricolage.

Discourse as action

The fourth characteristic of discursive practices is that they are actions in their own right. Discursive practices constitute actions which do not only exist for themselves, for their content, for the way in which they grasp the world, for their literal meaning, but also for what they achieve. Discursive practices therefore express the intention which shaped them and are therefore actions. They also have consequences, and this involves another form of action. The expression "consequence" is particularly significant here as the consequences of a discursive practice are often unintended.

The author who has taken the greatest interest in this aspect of language is Austin. Dissatisfied by traditional philosophical approaches and considering as well that ordinary language is the filter through which we access reality, Austin proposed to study ordinary language in order to implement what he called linguistic phenomenology. Here, language is not studied for itself but rather for the phenomena that it illustrates (Austin, 1962). Austin sought to emphasise that language is not only descriptive, responsible for describing reality, and confronted with determining whether a description is true or false, but that it is also performative, meaning that saying something makes it possible to do something.

To illustrate his argument, Austin cites examples of words which are not intended to describe, to be true or false, or to inform, but simply to perform. The first example which is probably the most well-known is "I now pronounce you husband and wife". When the mayor uses these words, nothing is described and these words are not true or false but they are performative. In the same way, Austin cites other performative utterances such as the "'I do' of the bride or groom pronounced on the wedding day", "I name this ship the 'Queen Elizabeth'" or "I give and bequeath my watch to my brother" as occurring in a will or "I bet you sixpence it will rain tomorrow". These utterances do not describe an action, they are not true or false, they inform no one, but they are performative. To speak about something is equivalent to performing an act with words.

Consequently, Austin brings an important nuance to his argument. Not only can the same act exist without words, such as the betting act, but circumstances are essential especially in order to transform a statement into an act. In other words, if an individual walking in the streets comes across two passers-by and tells them "I declare you husband and wife" or if he advances towards a boat at random and names it, these utterances do not transform themselves into acts. It is indispensable that these utterances take place in appropriate circumstances, that is, the individual must be empowered to carry them out according to a set of conditions defined elsewhere. Hence, to name a boat, one must be empowered to do it. To get married, one must not already be married. Betting, which is a more complex issue, presupposes, in order to be an act, that it has been accepted by the person with whom the bet is laid. The other also needs to take me seriously. The statement "I give you" presupposes that the words are accompanied by gestures.

Numerous performative utterances therefore exist and these can be contractual, for example betting, or explicit, for example "I do" or "war is declared". In any case, it is words that constitute acts. Even if an individual does not respect his bet, the very fact of having said the words, at the moment he says them, makes him act. Words are acts: saying is doing.

Austin therefore begins his reflection on the act of saying based on the most significant performative utterances. These he names explicit performative utterances since it is the utterances which generally begin with a striking expression such as "I bet", "I promise", "I bequeath". Less explicit words exist as well. For instance "go!" can be considered as a command, that is, as a speech act. Here as well, as is the case for a baptism or a marriage, the utterances only constitute an act from the moment they are pronounced under special circumstances and before specific persons.

We often wrongly assimilate the speech act with a real or imagined sincerity of utterances. We will come back to this as it is a classical situation in political sciences. An example is if one says "congratulations" without meaning it. Or when a judge says "having been found not guilty, you are hereby acquitted" even while he thinks an individual is guilty. Austin insists that in such cases, the speech act has been pronounced nonetheless and that words are, and remain, an act. Even if the judge is not sincere, the individual is acquitted. Similarly, the failure of an act does not mean that the act did not take place. If an individual says "I bet" without the intention of keeping his promise when he utters these words, or on the contrary, an individual declares "I give you" and the object to be given is ultimately unavailable, in either case, this takes nothing away from the fact that the utterance was an act in its own right.

Subsequently, Austin establishes a distinction within performative utterances between a locutionary act, an illocutionary act and a perlocutionary act. A locutionary act is simply an act of saying something (Austin, 1962). An illocutionary act is the performance of an act in saying something (Austin, ibid.). A perlocutionary act is what we bring about or achieve by saying something (Austin, ibid.). It is not easy to grasp this distinction, especially as Austin continues to make it even more complex.

In any event, there is a first distinction between intention, the intentional and the unintentional outcome. Acts have consequences that are not necessarily sought by the individual who produces them. This nuance implies that it is necessary to distinguish the intention of the subject who speaks from the outcomes, given that these are not necessarily intended.

An illocutionary act is an act characterised by intention and by the intentional effect. On the contrary, a perlocutionary act is characterised by the consequences of an act, be they intended or unintended. Accordingly, "he said to me 'shoot her'" is a locutionary act because the simple act of speaking constitutes an act. "He advised me to shoot her" expresses the intentionality of the speaker. On the contrary, "he persuaded me to shoot her" centres the utterances on the locutionary act.

The illocutionary act ("he advised me") is a speech act itself because the words of advice perform the act of advice. However, it does not necessarily bear consequences on the individual to whom it is addressed. "He persuaded me" also shows that action passed through words, through an exchange. It is not necessarily linked to the illocutionary act even if in this case, the probability is high. Hence, if we add "without intending to, he persuaded me to shoot her", it still refers to a perlocutionary act as it is the speech act which led to the act of shooting as an involuntary consequence.

The distinction between illocutionary and perlocutionary acts subsequently enabled Austin to reconsider his boundary between performative utterances where the key to understanding is success or failure, and constative utterances where the response is either true or false. Indeed, according to the author, constating or describing is an illocutionary act that is at the same level as the others. It designates an intention just as suggesting or convincing for instance.

With these reflections, Austin makes a significant contribution to how the role of speech is understood. He illustrates to what extent utterances are discursive practices which bind the speaker vis-à-vis the person who is addressed, and how they can have intended or unintended consequences. It is therefore an act provided that it is taken into account within its singular context. This does not imply taking the content of a speech and judging it in relation to the acts it gives rise to but rather, considering discourse as a fully-fledged act. Moreover, it involves taking into account all the underlying conventions which can give it meaning.

In light of Austin's reflections, we can go back to our discussion on how political discourse is confined to "official discourse" and is either analysed by semiologists based on its content, without taking into account the surrounding conventions, or rejected by public policy analysts due to its link with reality.

Official discourse is an act that falls within a set of conventions. It does not seek to express a speech that a researcher must analyse based on its veracity. On the contrary, it must be considered as a locutionary act in which the speaker is conscious that there can be consequences. Hence, when discourse refers to the "coherence" of the State, an example often quoted by researchers, it should not be assessed on the basis of its content and compared to the reality of practices; this would reveal a puzzling and incoherent bureaucracy. Rather, it should be grasped as an act in itself. It is not a question of determining whether the person responsible for this speech believes it or not but rather understanding that saying "the State is coherent" is an act which can have consequences, including the consequence of producing coherence. Should the head of State say "the State is incoherent", he could be heavily criticised for these words in which commentators could identify a possibly destructive intentionality.

To understand official discourse, it is necessary to understand the intentionality, which is not necessarily explicit, of the person producing the discourse as well as the conventions in which this was produced. This must then be separated from the consequences of the speech act which are not necessarily linked to the intentions. It is probable that the consequences of this discourse could be very hard to assess as they often have a general scope and a very large audience. Moreover, official discourses that have consequences which go beyond the respect of conventions within which they fall are rare.

More generally, Austin's reflections make it possible to avoid restricting the researcher's interest to official discourse and enable him to focus on all the discussions which take place in the midst of processes. Speech is an act and as such, must be considered as a set of acts destined to elucidate words. It must always be placed within its underlying context in order to understand it and distinguish it from its consequences which also constitute acts.

It is for this reason that we would like to address all discourse and discursive practices in view of the fact that we consider that an utterance is an act. Discourse is an act which presupposes an intention from the individual who pronounces it and can lead to consequences. In the event of discussions, the limited number of participants makes it possible to grasp the illocutionary and perlocutionary acts differently.

Thus, for instance, the intention to convince is an illocutionary act that we will devote considerable attention to hereafter. The intention to convince does not necessary lead to the success of the act but it is nonetheless an essential activity.

Discourse as an interaction

The fifth characteristic of discourse is that it is not only an action – it is also an interaction. Discourse allows interaction but is also forged within the interaction. A discursive practice is always located between at least two individuals and creates a relationship between the interlocutors. Regardless of the forms that they take – addressing a monologue on radio targeting a public, making a declaration before the National Assembly, taking part in a one on one discussion or taking part in a group discussion – discursive practices always link individuals to each other.

The majority of authors that we have quoted so far pay particular attention to how discourse generally constructs itself within interaction. As Wittgenstein points out, language games can only be understood within the actual and complex relationship in which they have taken place. This complex relationship is structured around the meaning that the speaker decides to give to his words and the meaning perceived by his listener (Wittgenstein, 1958). If two persons in direct interaction define the same words differently, we can easily assume that an external observer will also understand the word in a different way. Taking into account the interaction in which discourse is situated also implies considering the transition from a monologue to a discussion, and primarily understanding discussion as an attempt at constructing mutual understanding. By this, we do not seek to claim that discussion is where ambiguities dissolve, but rather, to understand that it is here that discourses are put to th and where they rarely come out unscathed.

Moreover, discussion is primarily a discursive interaction where exchange is forged and where discourse is put to the test. This exchange engages the concerned parties and can sometimes lead to an agreement, or on the contrary to conflict, but it rarely leaves indifferent the two parties confronted with the test. Discussion is therefore not a neutral space or solely unidirectional. It engages the interlocutors in an entanglement that is difficult to undo. It poses its own dynamic and can even produce, according to Habermas, its own rationality.

Nevertheless, taking interaction into account within discursive relationships calls for a deeper level of reflection. Undoubtedly, Mead was among the first to focus on these interactions (Mead, 1934). He argued that it was insufficient to restrict interaction to a confrontation of already existent thoughts; rather, it was necessary to situate the actual construction of thought within these interactions.

To illustrate his theory, the author cites a boxing match in which the feint of one boxer provokes the reaction of the other, forcing him to adapt his attack. This underscores that interaction is a phase that cannot be understood through observing each individual separately, but rather, through observing an interaction in which everyone adjusts to the other. Similar to the individual's gestures or the words of the speaker, the boxer's punch cannot be grasped independently of the scene of interaction where "mutual adjustment" is developed. The significant punch, gesture, or words lead to adjustment in the one to whom it is addressed. "The primitive situation is that of the social act which involves the interaction of different forms, which involves, therefore, the adjustment of the conduct of these different forms to each other, in carrying out the social process" (Mead, 1934, p. 133).

This is a significant point as it reinforces the assumption of the singularity of words. What we say depends on the listener to whom we address. The arguments and the words that we deploy cannot be understood as general words but rather as situated, oriented, and specific words. The text of a political discourse intended for a given "public" is not the same as the words that the actor uses during discussions.

Nevertheless, Mead proposes to go beyond acknowledging this game of mutual adjustment within discussions. He applies the concept to the individual himself and to how his thoughts are developed. The stimulus that our words rouse in others, leading to their adjustment, also affects us. "In the case of the [vocal gesture], the form (the organism) hears its own stimulus just as when this is used by other forms" (Mead, 1934, p. 65).

An individual therefore begins to formulate thoughts in discussions with himself but also with the others to whom he addresses his thoughts.

According to the author, using structured language to formulate our thoughts rather than our own language, without paying attention to the order of words for instance, can only be understood because language is primarily a mode of communication and adjustment. Hence, according to Mead, language is only one part of the cooperation process which enables individuals to adapt their responses to each other. It falls within the construction of meaning that can be understood in relation to the other. It forges thought in a discussion with self as with the other.

Mead also insists on the manner in which the "self" is developed within an interaction between self and the other, rather than within a Cartesian relationship with self. "The process out of which the *self* arises is a social process which implies interaction of individuals in the group, implies the preexistence of the *group*" (Mead, 1934, p. 164). The "self" is reflected within a pre-existing social situation on which it depends. The proposal I makes therefore also depends on how I anticipates the reaction of others; this reaction is integrated in others' attitude.

According to Mead, it is therefore impossible to isolate the thoughts of an individual from language which mediates thought as well as from the social context and the interactions in which it belongs. Consequently, we cannot define the relationship between the individual and the society as two distinct and separate entities and/or entities in opposition as is often done by sociologists; rather, we can define it as an inseparable whole. Based on concrete social interactions, Mead expands on the pragmatic principle of John Dewey, which states that we can neither distinguish thought from action nor the individual from society.

Discourse as a material and singular practice

The sixth characteristic of discourse is its singular materiality. First and foremost, discourse exists because it is formulated, written, or spoken. It is placed out there, somewhere, at a specific moment and within a specific location. Discourse is not assumed or theoretical but rather material given its empirical existence. When we evoke a discursive practice, it is therefore not simply "discourse" on discourse but rather the existence of a space–time where practices take place.

Speaking of discourse is therefore, first and foremost, evoking its existence within the social practices which take place. In the same way as language is the indispensable filter to access reality, discursive practices are exclusive locations where discourse resides. Considering discourse as a practice therefore has two consequences.

The first consequence of this assumption is that it is impossible, or at least uninteresting, to distinguish discourse from the practical context of its materialisation. It is therefore impossible to have an idea as an objective and immaterial concept on the one hand, and, on the other, discursive practices which can only partially show an idea transcending discourse. Discourse exists only in its materiality and has meaning only in its specific deployment.

According to Michel Foucault, this "materiality" which is a central characteristic of discourse is an occasion to reject the search of a thought transcending discourse or even the search for hidden meaning. In his opinion, one should not move "discourse towards its interior, towards the 'hidden nucleus' at the 'heart of signification' because behind the discourse 'there is nothing'".[2]

For Ludwig Wittgenstein, highlighting the significance of the materiality of language games implies recalling that what is important is neither the unambiguous character of the meaning behind words which a classical philosopher could seek to establish, nor the polysemous character of words that a linguist could clarify endlessly, but rather, the unambiguous meaning that polysemous words take at the specific moment they are used.[3]

Wittgenstein argues that it is not language but rather its uses that need to be examined; we have called these discursive practices. It is this practical character which forbids the analysis of discourse, separated from its context of use, where it takes on meaning. For instance, seeking to grasp the meaning of a text by analysing it out of its practical context of uses is irrelevant.

Although dissimilar in many aspects from the aforementioned authors, Pierre Bourdieu's approach on this issue is rather interesting; it also takes, as its point of departure, the error of linguistics in separating text from the context in which it is established. More generally, it focuses only on that which is possible to grasp materially, like transcribed words, and not on the daily linguistic unwritten exchanges between agents for instance. He therefore argues that a semiotic analysis interested in the internal analysis of a text should be rejected, and on the contrary, special consideration should be granted to the conditions of discourse making that are essentially social. Bourdieu therefore takes the example of "position-taking" in politics which can only be understood within the distinct context in which it belongs. From this perspective, the term "position-taking" is significant. The author focuses notably on politicians' practical sense to master the game and the rules of the game relative to the positions taken (Bourdieu, 2001).

This leads us to the second consequence triggered by this materiality, that of its empirical singularity. It is problematic to empirically reveal an idea – a transcendent, universal, and objective concept, which could only lead to distorted displays. It is much simpler for the researcher to seek an effective and singular practice.

As discourse is a practice situated within time and space, it must first be understood in its singularity. In other words, each exchange, each meeting takes place primarily within its own space-time. It takes a singular form not only because the context is singular but also because the exchanges are unique.

According to Michel Foucault, this singularity makes discourse reside in minor events such as notarial acts or parish registers, as well as in major events such as laws or wars. It is multiple and multi-faceted. It takes place at any moment and ends the desperate search of a cause and effect relationship or of a relationship to a universal core. Foucault defends the singularity of discourse against the universality of an idea or a thought. This means that thought does not only exist in a transcendental manner but also, that it cannot be separated from the discourse used to express it. Thought does not exist in the background of discourse but rather within discursive practices.

This singularity makes it possible to reject the concept of ideas that is rather convenient in policy studies. It has also made it possible to do away with the concept of discourse. Indeed, most public policy studies fall within this approach which seeks to highlight actors' practices by revealing what is behind their discourse. Where the actors claim coherence, researchers point out incoherence. Where the actors defend their willingness to resolve problems, researchers highlight that it is often the solutions which seek out problems. Where actors defend a notion, researchers show that they are outsiders with regard to notion defended. While the idea is a concept which enables objectivation and the decontextualisation of concrete scenes, discourse compels us to return to the concrete study of all discussions by constantly bringing back an idea to its materiality, that is, to its specific enlistment within discursive practices.

Discourse as the acknowledgement of the subject

The seventh characteristic of discourse is that it is not only the expression of knowledge, a means of action, or where interaction takes place, but it is also a space where the speaker who engages himself is acknowledged through the words he speaks. Through the similarities that they generate and the dissimilarities that they provoke, discursive practices participate in forging the identity of the speaker.

As previously stated, one of the major differences between an approach through ideas and an approach through discourse is based notably on the singularity and the materiality of its utterances. Admittedly, this singularity must be understood as the indissoluble link which unites the words spoken and the one who speaks them. The existing link between discourse and the subject who speaks is actually what makes impossible the objectivation of discourse. Objectivation here refers to a process that seeks to eliminate the subject. Ideas do not fly in space, they only exist when they are shaped concretely. For an idea to disappear, it would suffice that no one speaks about it anymore. It is rather like a word that disappears from the dictionary when its use diminishes.

Discourse engages the subject who utters it. It brings him to life, immortalises him. As we have previously seen, the individual produces discourse depending on his interlocutor, discourse in which he anticipates the possible reactions and puts them to the test.

The discussion in which an individual is involved is a discussion which engages him and engages his position in the complex game of social relationships in which he is nested. It not only involves personal interest but, to take up Mead's reflections, it involves the construction of self. From a social interaction point of view, the construction of I and Me entails highlighting similarities and differences.

We can evoke resemblance given that the subject seeks to identify his belongingness to a group with which he would like to be able to discuss and to identify with. Discussion is therefore based on a common set of signs and language meanings which make comprehension possible. The individual can reinforce the conditions for his integration through his discourse in advance. However, in parallel, the "I" associates itself to a "me" in which the individual has a tendency to distinguish himself from others. It is through this distinction that he forges a part of his identity and constructs what has been referred to as his interest.

This is a relatively classical aspect of sociology which consists in considering the individual within the construction of his social identity. The practices driven by individuals, in which we have hence integrated discursive practices, participate in identity construction. The political discourse of a politician must therefore also be understood as the manner in which an individual constructs his own identity within the political and social game to which he belongs. Referring to Mead, Murray Edelman argues that politicians construct their identity, what they are, through their discourse and their practices (Edelman, 1988). He notably revisits the manner in which the concept of leadership is developed through the multiple practices that individuals drive.

It is in this way that a leader constructs his identity by positioning himself and by acting (this integrates discourse). He participates in forging his image partly by responding to what is expected of him and partly by surprising through his specificity. He relies on attitudes and on a specific language. It is in claiming his capacity for action, his representativeness or his capacity to solve problems that he forges his identity. His competence in mobilising a universe beyond his control and on behalf of which he acts is an essential element which must be taken into account. Similarly, the expert participates in forging his identity by using his knowledge; by claiming that this knowledge is objective, he describes himself as "neutral" or "objective".

The researcher must therefore neither focus on whether what is said is true, nor on its objectivity nor representativeness; rather, he must understand how the manner in which an individual mobilises these concepts defines his position and his identity within the games in which he is involved. To borrow Pierre Bourdieu's expression, discursive practices are not only knowledge but acknowledgement as well (Bourdieu, 2001). The challenge is therefore to take both into consideration within the same analysis.

Consequently, we would like to draw from Michel Crozier's work which opens up an interesting path on this issue. Crozier focuses primarily on how individuals act within bureaucratic organisations (Crozier and Friedberg, 1977). Considering that individuals always possess an incompressible liberty of action, he develops the notion that their identity resides precisely at the heart of this liberty of action and that they express it by making their behaviour unpredictable.

Put differently, the more an individual develops a capacity to do what is unexpected of him, the more he is able to exist within the space around him. To achieve this, he must develop the conditions to render others dependent on him by developing specific knowledge, singular know-how or social relationships for which he holds a monopoly. It is this dependency which enables him to exist and find his place within the organisation in which he belongs. However, at the same time, he must avoid being a mere executor of an order, in which case he would disappear as an actor of the organisation. He must therefore develop some independence which translates into his capacity to refuse to satisfy the demands for which he is solicited.

Depending on others and independence from others therefore constitute a complex and contradictory whole which is perpetually unstable. According to Michel Crozier, actors constantly develop defensive strategies in order to preserve their independence of action and offensive ones to make others even more dependent on them. An example which illustrates this complexity is the difficulty faced by machine maintenance workers in a factory. They only exist within organisations if machines break down and they are called upon. Fixing machines is the act that makes it possible for them to construct some form of recognition through the dependency of the machine users. Consequently, they must be able to fix machines from time to time. But they must also be able to negotiate their intervention, a negotiation that must not be automatic. They therefore take their time, do not respond immediately to queries and negotiate their intervention. In order to preserve their identity, it is also necessary that the machines do not malfunction frequently. Crozier also cites the example of chess players who must respect the rules in order to play together but, in parallel, must have freedom within the rules of the game to avoid losing the game in advance.

Nevertheless, the author comes across two major difficulties in his approach. The first is that he seeks an explanation for the resistance to change within organisations based on these assumptions which show, on the contrary, the instability of behaviour. He thus constructs a model which considers that dependence and independence are excessively complex relationships that stabilise with time. Moreover, he argues that all attempts at change result in too much uncertainty for the actors. Liberty is no longer translated within the instability that it requires, but rather within the presumed capacity of instability. Between the unstable image of the actor's behaviour and the smooth and stable image of the organisation, it presents itself as a complexity that Crozier's explanation has not been able to adequately address. Moreover, Crozier does not focus on the specificity of the organisations which he analyses, and political scientists have been quick to criticise him for not differentiating political organisations from other organisations.

Crozier does not centre on discourse and the discussions that actors may engage in among themselves. While the interview is his key tool, he does not propose an epistemological status of language. Actors develop and deploy strategies while interacting; they get into power relations but at no moment is the role of discussions taken into account.

We would like to take into consideration this complex apprehension that Crozier develops in relation to actors and, in particular, in how they construct their identity between dependence and independence. However, we would like to consider that the actions and strategies that actors drive cannot be apprehended without taking into account the subjective meaning that they give to their actions, and the manner in which this meaning is constructed within discursive interactions.

Put differently, we would like to revert to the public policy-making process and consider discursive practices as strategies driven by actors to develop or oppose a public policy proposal, which it is at the heart of these strategies that they forge their identity. To achieve this, they engage in discussions in order to set up agreements, express disagreement, convince others, or persuade them.

In other words, within their discursive strategies, actors set out their intentions in which their identity is continuously elaborated. They select those they wish to convince and those against whom they wish to fight. They decide either to allow time for discussion or not. They assemble arguments to convince different actors.

Through the concept of discursive strategy, this therefore implies bringing closer language games and actors' games and observing the manner in which they are intertwined. Once again, it is undoubtedly about maintaining the distinction between intentionality and consequence. Consequently, if an individual uses a discursive strategy to meet a mayor and, once in his presence, develops arguments to convince him, this does not mean that he will succeed in convincing him. The consequences can even be the opposite of the desired effect. Nevertheless, by having chosen the mayor as the person to convince, by having been received by him and by having used certain arguments, the actor contributes in shaping his identity as well as the mayor's.

The three principles of the rarefaction of discourse

With these seven characteristics, discursive practices become a key practice that enables an observer to follow public policymaking. They offer him the opportunity to identify the actual knowledge devices, the actions and the strategies that actors drive, the interactions they organise, the identities, and the forms of acknowledgement that they shape. They are no longer taken as content whose validity must be verified but rather as essential social practices which reveal intentionality and generate often unintended consequences, making agreement possible and structuring conflict.

Our intention here is not to claim that all social activity must be observed through discursive practices – a debate that would be too broad to consider – but rather, we claim that all activities that seek to give form and life to a public policy proposal are essentially discursive practices.

However, to sum up this initial overview on discursive activities, we need to tackle a major problem that the study of discursive practices generates. We have seen that one of the major interests of discourse is its materiality which enables the researcher to search for it. "Who said what, when, to whom and where?" is a question that a researcher can start by asking when he wants to grasp the manner in which a proposal takes shape.

Nevertheless, this materiality has a setback – its specificity. Indeed, if all discursive practices are specific, if all events are singular, what remains of the sociologist, the historian, or the political scientist? How can one avoid being overwhelmed by the infinite multiplicity of discourse?

It is here that we would like to resort to the concept of statements. By statement, we mean discourse whose particularity is that it is repeated within numerous discursive interactions in varied terms. This is a particularly fragile core of our argument. On one hand, we have avoided considering a concept such as that of ideas which, in our opinion, is objective and disembodied. We have sought to make singularity and the association discourse/subject/situation central to our analysis. On the other hand, we have sought a way to circumvent the excessively diverse situations available.

To circumvent this problem, we would like to begin by borrowing from Michel Foucault the assumption that beyond the plurality of discourses, their rarefaction operates. His idea is simple: it is not only the observer who finds himself confronted with infinity but the actors as well. To address this infinity, the latter set out discursive strategies of rarefaction within discourse.

According to the author, there are many processes involved in reducing the puzzling infinite freedom of discourse, the dangers and mastering the hazards; he names these the principles of rarefaction. He therefore argues that: "In every society the production of discourse is at once controlled, selected, organised and redistributed according to a certain number of procedures, whose role is to avert its powers and its dangers, to cope with chance events, to evade its ponderous, awesome materiality" (Foucault, 1971, p. 10).

Michel Foucault therefore identifies three principles of rarefaction in discourse: the limitation of power, averting hazards and the rarefaction of subjects. According to him, discourse "is not simply that which translates struggles or systems of domination, but is the thing for which and by which there is struggle, discourse is the power which is to be seized" (Foucault, 1971, p. 12). Prohibitions as well as the distinction between reason and folly or even the opposition between what is true and what is false are, for Foucault, principles of the rarefaction of discourse and of the limitation of its dangers. Consequently, this "desire for truth" at the heart of discourse is a system of distinction and exclusion which is based on a set of practices (teaching and pedagogy) and institutions (the book-system, libraries, laboratories, etc.). Foucault therefore differentiates between truth which has distinguished itself from power in the sense that having power no longer makes it possible to tell the truth: "since the time *of the* Greeks, true discourse no longer responds to desire or to that which exercises power in the will to truth, in the will to speak out in true discourse, what, then, is at work, if not desire and power?" (Foucault, 1971, p. 19).

Consequently, the rarefaction of discourse exists through all the procedures set up to distinguish between truths and falsehoods, but this rarefaction does not prevent the exercise of power which shifts within the very will to seek truth.

The second principle involves putting order within a space that is highly uncertain. To limit the untenable problems that result from the chaos caused by uncertain events, by the discontinuity of phenomena, by the incoherence within specific discourses, there exists a set of procedures internal to discourse and these endeavour to master it. According to Foucault, simply commenting on a text to understand it presupposes that the text is neutral. By limiting hazards and stating what the text does not actually state, a commentary violates the initial text by giving it meaning, coherence, and unity. Consequently, the will to distinguish coherence and continuity, for instance, from the specificity and the variety of each text, makes it possible to rarefy the multiplicity of discourses, to reduce them to a more simple expression, thereby averting hazards. How can one evoke Foucault if each text is specific? How can one comment on Foucault if each commentary repeats the same thing as the initial text? It is also the author's hope of unity which enables the researcher to seek the coherence of a text. Alongside or with the commentary, the author is therefore an element of the rarefaction of discourse.[4]

Foucault also focuses on what he calls discipline. This he defines by "groups of objects, methods, their corpus of propositions considered to be true, the interplay of rules and definitions, of techniques and tools" (Foucault, 1971, p. 32). Here, the primary challenge is not to identify the meaning but rather, the conditions of formulating new proposals. Discipline therefore makes it possible to produce new discourse at the same time as it ensures restriction. This restriction is notably the existence of conditions of access associated with the delimitation of objects and the rules of validity in each discipline. Foucault calls this "discursive police".

Finally, the third principle of the rarefaction of discourse involves the rarefaction of speaking subjects. While some discourses are open to all speaking subjects, others are limited, mastered. Rituals therefore exist which, for example, "define the qualifications for speaking subjects" (Foucault, 1971, p. 38).

The processes of the rarefaction of discourse do not therefore prevent the existence of new discourse but they reduce their possibility by setting up a significant number of conditions. It is this rarefaction that participates in creating an order of discourse, an order that makes words oscillate between singularity and repetition. It is this order of discourse which, to reduce the singularity and the infinity of words, encourages the existence of a discourse on ordering (Deleuze, 1986; Veyne, 2008).

While we do not seek to reproduce Michel Foucault's processes of the rarefaction of discourse in the strictest sense, we would like to focus on the very idea of rarefaction. Specifically, we would like to analyse the discourse that emerges following this rarefaction process.

Policy statement: a rarefied, stabilised and institutionalised definition

Taking into account discourse "in action" is a particularly interesting means to analyse the manner in which knowledge on a particular issue gets constructed, crafted, stabilised, and institutionalised. In our first chapter, we have shown to what extent knowledge issues are central in analysing the definitional processes of a problem, thereby transforming a given situation into an unacceptable public problem. We would like to suggest here that this process is quite similar with regard to public policy.

For this, we will first adopt the heuristic concept of statements. A statement is primarily a definitional institutionalised discourse. Consequently, it relies not only on the naming of its principal object but also on the definitional activity of linking the object named to a set of proposals which gives it meaning. It also relies on the stabilisation process which enables it to resist the test of time. A statement must also be understood as discourse "in action", meaning discourse made by actors with intentions.

Applied to a social issue, a policy problem statement presents itself as a discursive whole which comprises the naming and defining of a problem as well as the identification of its cause, of the public concerned and of the responsible party. Consequently, a problem statement is essentially a set of proposals chained to each other through equivalent links as well as of association, dissociation, inclusion, or causality which contribute in defining the problem and giving it meaning. A problem statement is also a discourse "in action" which expresses the intention of its bearer.

This seeks to denounce a situation, to make it "unacceptable" in order to better call for immediate action, and to appeal to the sense of responsibility of the person expected to act. A policy problem statement is a somewhat political weapon of its stakeholders who want not only to describe the disorder of our society but also to shape it.

Applied to a proposal, a policy solution statement once again presents itself as a discursive whole comprising the naming and defining of a solution. More specifically, it involves the identification of the consequences, of the problems that it must resolve, of the public policies that it must change and the authority figures that it must legitimise. Problem solving must also be understood as discourse "in action" which seeks to make the solution proposed "acceptable" or even desirable. Problem solving is the political weapon that makes it possible to propose to its bearers the restoration of order within society.

These two statements are therefore at once similar and different. They are similar as they are both structured on the basis of language games and on the intentionality of actors where each constitutes a major political weapon. However, they are different because on one hand, they reveal dissimilar intentions, between denouncing and proposing, and, on the other, they both rely on distinct forms of politicisation, one referring to order and the other to disorder.

However, beyond their similarities and differences, these two statements are often embedded within each other, and this sometimes makes their distinction difficult. In a problem statement, there is often another aspect concerning solutions, notably through the existence of strong criticism of the public policies in place. In policy solution statements, problems are also quite present and notably as regards their ability to be resolved. Within a form of antinomian dialectics, the problem and the solution feed off each other just like the order and disorder they bear.

While numerous studies on problems have made it possible to better grasp the role of definitional activities within agenda setting processes, a similar challenge exists regarding policy change statements. This has largely been neglected from the discursive angle even though in our opinion, it plays a major role in the setting up of a repertoire of acceptable solutions.

3.3   The five couplings in defining solutions

Enhanced by the contributions of the linguistic and pragmatist approach, the concept of bricolage developed by Lindblom can be considered as a language game that actors use in their interactions. Defining a solution therefore refers to crafting a proposal by associating to it other elements which give it meaning and make it possible for it to propagate itself within the interactions that actors have among themselves. To grasp this definitional process, we would like to re-examine the principal associations that actors frequently practice. Labelling a proposal, associating consequences to it, attributing to it values, problems to resolve and public policies to reform, constitute the major definitional stages which contribute to giving meaning to a proposal by transforming it into a "solution". Each stage must be considered here to be independent from the others and not indispensable. Consequently, there is no temporal link between these stages. They are numbered only for heuristic purposes.

The first stage: labelling solutions and owner titles

The labelling of a solution is relatively similar to the labelling of problems. Labelling is first attributing a name to a solution through a definitional process of association. This attribution is the first of the language games identified by Wittgenstein (Wittgenstein, 1958).

Labelling is primarily carried out on public policy tools, meaning, on public authorities' means of action. This can involve the development of legislation, rules, grants, equipment, tax, and so on. Consequently, it can refer to VAT, to a new rule on renting, a new high speed train (TGV) line, a new airport, a speed limitation, a military intervention, etc.

As Wittgenstein has shown for the concept of games, it is often exceedingly difficult to define a concept whose objective is to regroup highly dissimilar objects which only have in common a "family resemblance" (Wittgenstein, 1958). Undoubtedly, this point in common is based less on its content than on its producer, public power. From this perspective, recent studies on tools have made it possible to enrich the list and the perception of these forms of actions (Lascoumes and Simard, 2011).

Rather than embarking on a debate on the nature or the form of these public policy tools, we would like to focus on how actors decide to label such tools proposals. We identify two different situations. The first which is probably the most frequent is where the name is already glued to the proposal. Many of the proposals that actors formulate actually have nothing new and are often drawn from the already existent repertoire of proposals and, at times, have even been frequently tested. Increasing VAT, reducing speed limitations, reducing State expenditure, setting up a new railway line, or modifying the retirement age are proposals that have been formulated many times. By drawing from this repertoire of available responses, actors simply recycle solutions that have been repeatedly used.

While labelling is often considered to be unquestionable, there might exist a second situation where the name of the tool is subject to debate. It is precisely at such moments that we can better grasp the issues that come to the fore in the labelling activity. This debate takes place each time an actor accompanies his proposal with a new name. Debate can then take various forms and reveals that the already established labels are often accompanied by stable statements and an identified owner. Put differently, the creation of a new label presents itself as the means through which to construct a new statement or define a new owner.

In France for example, tax such as the VAT has become with time a fiscal tool perceived widely as "unfair". It has therefore been interpreted, making it difficult for a government to propose it without dealing with its unfairness. In the early 2000s, the French government of the time decided to propose an increase in VAT by working on a new label. It was no longer about increasing the VAT but rather, implementing a "social VAT". Through this new label, its authors attempted to absolve themselves from the dominant interpretation and create a new one. They therefore sought to alter the meaning in order to legitimise their proposal.

Undoubtedly, in addition to not being neutral, the labelling process also prompted reactions and attacks that sought to challenge it. Subsequently, the opposition called this proposal the "antisocial VAT" in order to better underscore its similarly unjust character. This labelling battle is thus a definitional struggle to impose meaning and to interpret the measures proposed.

In the United States, it is frequent to label laws with a new name in an attempt to impose meaning to the measures generated. For instance, in education, George W. Bush defended the law labelled "No Child LeftBehind", while Barack Obama launched an education programme which he named "Race to the Top". Labelling essentially exists to make it possible for actors to impose, or at least to seek to impose, the meaning that they desire to confer to a proposal. They do not therefore hesitate to explain a text in order to couple its meaning with the label and maintain mastery. Barack Obama therefore explains, after restating the name of the programme, the meaning that he would like it to have:

> I think the single most important thing we've done is to launch an initiative called Race to the Top. We said – we said to states, if you are committed to outstanding teaching, to successful schools, to higher standards, to better assessments, if you're committed to excellence for all children, you will be eligible for a grant to help you attain that

goal. And so far the results have been promising, and they have been powerful.[5]

However, the label does not only reveal the statement which gives it meaning; it is also inseparable from the owner who claims right of use. As opposed to problems where ownership titles are often complex and generally distinct from the designation of the responsible parties, the solution is often linked to a public collective actor who is both the owner and the responsible party.

While the ownership of certain tools can therefore not be challenged, others remain open to appropriation or to co-ownership. Measures such as the limitation of speed or the construction of a nuclear power plant, regardless of who requests it, can only be decided by the State. On the contrary, as the multitude of cross financing proves, there are numerous tools which can lead to multiple collective actions of actors. In the first case, choosing the label undoubtedly implies choosing the owner. In the second case, it opens debate on a generally restricted list of actors.

In any event, the solution is always owned by a collective actor responsible at least for its implementation. This corresponds more closely to the concept of "responsible party" that we referred to in the case of problems. This collective actor does not solely belong to national or local government; he can also be linked to an internal division of labour within each public organisation.

Beyond semantic differences, what distinguishes a house from a shelter in France is first the ministry which owns the label. The label "housing" is inseparable from the Ministry of Housing while that of "shelter" or of "emergency shelter" belongs exclusively to the Ministry of Social Affairs. The label here shows the right of ownership. This is apparent when we observe the heated debate which opposed these two ministries in the mid-1990s when the Ministry of Housing proposed to set up "emergency housing". Considering that "emergency housing" is simply "shelter", the Ministry of Social Affairs opposed this new and hybrid proposal which it considered to be set up by a Ministry lacking competence with regard to shelter. For the Housing Ministry, "emergency housing" was not "shelter". Beyond this semantic debate and definitional struggles, at stake was the ownership of the new policy.

In the United States, the commission of inquiry concerning the events of September 11 has shown that each administration has specific devices to fight terrorism and that they are the exclusive owners of these devices. For the FBI, the fight against terrorism involves collecting information on all suspicious foreigners arriving in the United States. For the CIA, this is organised through the protection of embassies. According to the Federal Aviation Administration (FAA), the fight is organised through the protection against the embarkation of explosive devices. Each administration therefore has a solution that it labels "anti-terrorist" of which it is the sole owner. Reports therefore show that organising a terrorist attack in a foreign country by hijacking an aeroplane and using it as a weapon corresponds to some sort of collective impasse.[6]

The issues of ownership are not exclusive to labelling. They are also present in other phases, making ownership a major issue in solution statements.

The second stage: identifying the consequences and the Public of beneficiaries

Whereas problems have causes, solutions primarily have consequences. The difference between the two is not only semantic it is also fundamentally temporal. While the causes of a problem can be found by exploring the past, the consequences involve determining the future; while the causes illustrate a public of guilty parties, the consequences show a public of beneficiaries; while the causes describe an unacceptable past, the consequences construct a desirable fiction.

To give meaning to a tool, actors therefore associate it to social fiction by outlining a transformed world and linking it causally to the implementation of the proposed measure. In other words, for the actors, it implies illustrating a world that is different from the present one and, in parallel, highlighting the existence of a causal link between this world and the tool proposed.

Working on consequences is essential as it is first the means through which the issue of the Public and of the society is introduced into debate on proposals. As with the causes of the problem, the consequences of a proposal make it possible to conceive a new public or a new structuring of the public based on the identification of new beneficiaries. Actors are therefore attached to showing that a proposal has unintended consequences on a specific public, the public of beneficiaries. Should the proposal be implemented, these beneficiaries would experience a change in their situation. Highlighting consequences therefore makes it possible to create a fiction in which the situation of the public of beneficiaries, and in turn, of the Public is transformed.

In his anti-gun agenda, for instance, Barack Obama underscores the importance of the link which exists between his gun control proposal and the consequences of such control, not only on citizens but especially on children. Consequently, children are here distinguished from the general Public and constitute an identifiable sub-group that can benefit more than the other groups from the consequences of such a measure. It is this process of associating a proposal and a public which makes it possible to develop a fiction, a fiction of a world without children hurt or killed by guns, and to legitimise the proposal by giving it a specific meaning.

In social policy, structuring the public of beneficiaries is a practice that exists in most countries. When the French Ministry of Housing proposed specific financial aid in the mid-1970s to help a specific category of individuals pay their rent, it partitioned the public by identifying a group of potential beneficiaries and demonstrated how this group would experience a change in its position socially. Through the consequences, it thus defined a fiction that the proposal made possible.

In these different cases, determining the consequences and the public of beneficiaries significantly contributes to giving meaning to a proposal by embedding it within the social space, thereby transforming it into a "desirable" proposal. However, this linking gives rise to innumerable problems. It must be noted that while actors attempt to show that their proposal makes it possible to shape a desirable world based on the consequences of the choices proposed, they find themselves confronted not only with the possible contestation of this link but, in addition, with the "unintended" consequences which we highlighted, meaning those that are neither wanted nor desired by the actors.

While uncertainty is valid for all the associations that we have described, the one generated by the possible consequences is undoubtedly the most significant. From this point of view, the famous "black box" described by David Easton (1965b) applies particularly within this phase of the process which links the tool to social transformation.

The notion that the consequences of a public policy are rarely restricted to those desired is not new. This notion resulted essentially from the experimentation of actors and it has largely contributed to developing specific knowledge on public policy. Notably, it was largely covered in debate during the prohibition era in the United States, which led to the surprising consequence of increased criminality, but it is valid for many other actions as well. It was also present in Keynes' critique of political economy in the 1920s (Skidelsky, 2003). More fundamentally, it underscores governing limitations as well as the impossible absolute mastery of tools whose consequences generally include undesirable elements.

The issue of consequences is therefore central and generally constitutes one of the most engaged-in debate topics, especially as it provides a footing for those who defend measures that can shape a world they desire, for opponents who find there uncertainties to invest in, for experts who can contest a measure without engaging political speech.

The third stage: coupling with a problem to resolve

Linking a proposal to a problem it is to resolve is also a major step in the definitional process. While problems do not need solutions to exist, a proposal can only become a "solution" from the moment it has a problem to resolve. Actors who are the spokespersons of a proposal therefore work towards establishing this link between the solution and existing problems. It is this linking that Kingdon names "coupling" and considers as a key moment in the change process of public policy (Kingdon, 1995).

The coupling phenomenon was identified by Cohen, March, and Olsen on the basis of empirical evidence that showed that, within change processes, solutions not only have autonomous trajectories but, quite often, they precede problems as well (Cohen, March, and Olsen, 1972). Observing such a gap made it possible to show that a solution does not only result from objectively treating a problem but that rather, it must be considered as a subjective bricolage of coupling. Far from knowing how to resolve insoluble problems, actors couple existent solutions to problems independent of them. To achieve this, they have a repertoire of solutions and a series of problems which successively pass through the agenda and draw their attention.

Nevertheless, while Kingdon addresses the definitional stakes of a problem, underscoring, for example, the role of a definitional activity which makes it possible to transform a situation into a problem, he does not deal with those that concern solutions. In his opinion, the repertoire of available solutions is primarily the result of a selective activity of a public policy community which determines what is possible as well as the acceptable solutions.

Consequently, the most interesting part of the pragmatist approach using the definitional process is to also address the definition of solutions. A proposal first becomes a solution when it is coupled with the problem, even if it succeeds it, and when it functions and makes sense. Coupling is therefore a form of language game which contributes to this meaning.

The issue ignored by Kingdon on the meaning of solutions nevertheless opens up the avenue to fundamental compatibility issues of coupling. For coupling to be possible, it must first make sense, that is, it must be prone to subjective rationalisation, even *a posteriori*. Nobody can couple a proposal on the speed limitation of cars with the problem of academic failure or housing shortage, given that this makes no sense. Meaning is a selective process necessary in producing coupling, and it plays a role, including via anticipation.

However, on the contrary, meaning can sometimes take surprising paths. For instance, at the heart of the riots in the suburbs in 2005, the French president Jacques Chirac, during a televised mission intended to show his capacity to respond to a crisis, proposed to reduce the age of apprenticeship from 16 to 14 years. The coupling between these two was not clearly understood and became highly contested. This new coupling proposed by Chirac was largely criticised. Nevertheless, this example shows that actors sometimes propose surprising couplings which defy logic and even imagination. Following Foucault's example on the Borges' Chinese encyclopaedia, we need to observe how new discursive associations between heterogeneous elements can create new ways of thinking (Foucault, 1966).

Coupling is not a rational process as the solution results from the objective treatment of the problem. Neither is it an irrational process in which it would suffice to randomly pick problems and solutions from a garbage can as has been suggested by Cohen, March, and Olsen. It is a key phenomenon, albeit selective, which makes sense, that is, it can be rationalised, both for those who establish the coupling as well as for others to whom they present the proposal.

The fourth phase: integration to a public policy that needs to be changed

A different way to define a solution is to associate it to "public policy", that is, to a larger whole that needs to be changed or completed. The relationship here is not causal but rather inclusive as it involves embedding an element within a larger whole that it is expected to transform. Consequently, the actors who propose this coupling must carry out a taxonomic activity to define the inclusions as well as a normative activity to define the expected change.

In our introduction, we evoked the difficulties that different authors come across when defining the "public policy" concept considered to be rather vague. While among these definitions we find the concept's governing character, which is never restricted to a single action but to the significance of its owner as well (generally public authorities), it remains difficult to draft a shared definition. It is surprising to note to what extent researchers have taken this definitional debate around public policy seriously, all the while paying little attention to the definitional debates that actors drive. We would like to consider "public policy" as a concept that actors mobilise to produce coherence and restore order in a chaotic world of actions and public tools. This does not therefore imply debating on the validity of described coherence but rather focusing on their discourse "in action" which ensures coherence within a specific strategy. Integrating a proposal within a larger whole therefore makes it possible to give it meaning by making it the lever of change.

Defining a public policy thus amounts to developing order from which it is possible to situate, and therefore give meaning to, a proposal that an actor seeks to legitimise. Linking compels actors to produce or reproduce an assumed coherent order in public policy in order to better illustrate the tool's limitations or shortcomings.

The association between a proposal and a public policy refers therefore to a double task: that of putting into order the public policy that it needs to define for the occasion and restoring order to integrate within it the proposal in question. It is at the heart of this ordering that policy change is mainly situated. The tool's strength is in making it possible to change a public policy much larger than itself. It is at this particular moment that the tool, vehicle for change, takes on meaning. It is also during this association that debates and controversies are organised.

Let's take an example highlighting a definitional struggle around association. In the case of noise control, a case on which we worked (Zittoun, 2009), actors came into confrontation with each other in relation to the proposal on speed reduction in Paris. They sought to determine whether this involved transforming a transport or an environmental policy. For some, speed reduction in Paris was part of a broader policy that sought to reconsider mobility within the city. For others, it was a tool that made it possible to complement the fight against noise and pollution within the capital city.

In each case, the instrument is attached to a distinct policy domain which gives it a specific meaning. In the first case, the group is known as the transport policy and it forms a whole that is *a priori* coherent and the tool contributes to this. The policy instrument therefore reveals the transport policy, giving it a reality and a materiality. In the second case, the group is known as the "noise control policy". Now and then, actors change the name. They speak of the "noise pollution policy" integrating atmospheric pollution by this new name, and assigning noise the name of "noise pollution" (Zittoun, 2007). Each time, the policy domain and the instrument make sense together. The policy domain feeds off the instrument to prove that it exists and the instrument feeds off the policy domain in order to find a place.

It would be difficult for a researcher to identify the policy domain in which this instrument is embedded. Moreover, it is evident that policy domains have ambiguous and unstable boundaries and the link between the policy instrument and the domain is fragile. It is therefore less about responding to this controversial question but, rather, observing how conflicts are structured, discursive practices set up, coherence established, and categories shaped.

Undoubtedly, the investment in definitional conflict is not purely semantic. It does not suffice for actors to determine a "good" definition or to develop an average definition which would make speed reduction a tool for both transport policies and noise pollution control. It is also a battle about ownership titles. As with labelling, public policies are primarily sets that belong to a specific collective actor, and thus relate to the division of tasks within public institutions. Transport policies are therefore the property of the transport division and of the deputy mayor of transport while noise pollution control is that of the environment division and of the deputy mayor of environment.

This definitional conflict is therefore inseparable from the ownership conflict which accompanies it and is reflected in the concrete problems of procedure. While speed reduction belongs to transport policies, it must be implemented within the mobility policy and debated within the participatory processes set up in this domain. If it belongs to noise pollution control, it can be implemented more rapidly within the pollution control policy represented by the division on environment and the deputy mayor concerned.

While it is also an essential battle of boundaries and ownership, it is important to understand that the discursive practices that they use do not solely constitute the veil which masks the "real" conflicts of interest. Quite the contrary, discursive practices are indispensable weapons which actors must use to do battle. There can be no "bare hands" battle in this type of combat. Moreover, these battles, far from being neutral, have consequences on the tools themselves. Consequently, linking them to the transport policy modifies the procedure and the scope through which the tools must pass to impose themselves.

Attention should therefore be paid to public policymaking as it reveals the actor's ability to produce coherency from scattered and incoherent public policies. Moreover, it expresses the fundamental organisation of the authorities who contribute in its constitution.

The fifth stage: the association to a referential framework and values to guide it

A solution can also be defined by positioning it within an ideological system or within a particular framework. To say that a proposal is Keynesian or neoliberal, liberal or conservative, is to attribute meaning to it by situating it with regard to a larger framework that it participates either in composing or decomposing.

The issue of values, ideas, and paradigms is particularly present in public policy studies. We come across it rather early in the studies carried out by Charles Lindblom or Aaron Wildavsky who use it in order to put at a distance the theories of rational choice which ignore them (Lindblom, 1968; Wildavsky, 1969). A public policy always relies, in their opinion, on values and on a certain ideology. In more recent studies, authors such as Peter Hall or Paul Sabatier have integrated the issue of values and ideological paradigms within their own model of understanding public policy changes.

On the basis of his studies on economic policymaking in Britain, Peter Hall considers that there are three levels of change, changes to the setting of existing tools, adoption of new tools and changes in policy goals (Hall, 1993). Each level corresponds to a hierarchical order which refers to a different level of change. Goal alteration is a radical change characterised by a paradigm shift. Given its significance, it is the least common and requires exceptional conditions. The other levels involve changes that are easier and more frequent. To put it differently, if a paradigm shift is rare and incremental change frequent, the idea that a radical change in meaning could intervene begins to arouse interest. According to Paul Sabatier for example, the system of belief is a key element of identity and a fundamental guarantee of the stability of a public policy (Sabatier, Jenkins-Smith, 1993). Giandomenico Majone uses the image of successive layers, which start from a core element, to peripheral layers with the notion that ideologies and paradigms constitute the stable core element, and the peripheral layers, more volatile tools (Majone, 1989). Here we undoubtedly find Thomas Kuhn's influence on these different authors as well as his theory of scientific revolutions in which the dominant paradigm constitutes the stable structure of a theory (Kuhn, 1962).

Nevertheless, these theories inspired by Kuhn attempt to reconcile the importance of ideologies and the empirical discovery of Dahl and Lindblom which shows that actors within very different ideological systems can use the same tools to fight inflation (Dahl and Lindblom, 1953). In other words, these authors highlight the absence of a logical or inclusive link between values and public policy tools. The paradigm concept, or that of a core composed of successive cores, poses a problem insofar as it presumes a certain coherence and a certain sequence even as empirical observation shows a reality that is more flexible and more malleable.

To overcome the deadlocks formed each time an author attempts to produce his own substantial categories, we would like to focus on how actors themselves develop links between tools and values, ideologies, or frameworks in order to give meaning to the actions they propose. Here, we posit that the link between a tool and the reference to a larger ideological system is not a logical link which imposes itself simply by reference to the tools, but rather is an association developed between two distinct heterogeneous elements where actors must prove their veracity and robustness.

The referential framework concept is an issue of interest to us, not as a representation of the world as has been defined by Jobert and Muller (1987), but as a concept which makes it possible to demonstrate the ideological or value references used by the actors to give sense to their proposal. Indeed, there exist a certain number of concepts and values which saturate the political space and to which actors like to refer. We can haphazardly cite certain fundamental value references such as equality, laicity, liberty, solidarity, or certain general concepts such as progress, modernity, growth, sustainable development, etc. What is of interest to us here is the use of any concept considered as a self-justifying reference which is sufficient in itself. Yves Barel has outlined a rather interesting profile in *La société du vide* (Barel, 1984) by evoking the importance of self-referencing in society.

As reference makes sense by itself, it is interesting for actors to associate it to a policy tool and to give it meaning through this language game. Once again, as with the association with public policies, when actors establish such a link between a policy tool and a referential framework, not only do they give meaning to the tool but they help describe the meaning of the framework itself.

Let's take an example once again to illustrate this. The tramway project in Paris is linked to the "sustainable development" framework. Although drawn up late, this link describes not only the meaning of the tramway, which has become a means through which to counteract vehicles, but also that of sustainable development, which has taken a concrete form. The researcher must therefore understand the challenges posed by such a link for all those who contribute in shaping it.

Defined as the mobilisation of a reference that is external to the proposal's scope within a statement, the "referential framework" concept makes it possible to understand the manner in which actors construct meaning. They grope around in their search for "good" associations which would legitimise their proposal and enable them to share it.

To better explain our understanding of a referential framework, we can also revert to its mathematical use. A framework is based on both the choice of an origin, the famous reference which forms the point from which all objects are redefined, as well as on a set of aligned axes which make it possible to give the details of an object within the referential framework in question. This is therefore a fundamental element in redefining the object by taking a point of reference and constructing links which make it possible to translate the definition of an object in its terms of reference.

Here, reference is a concept that is neither hollow nor saturated. It is not hollow given that there are many statements that accompany it, and these sometimes constitute evidence. "Sustainable development" has sufficient statements on the need for long-term interest and on the importance of taking into account economic, social, and environmental issues. However, when actors start building motorways within the "sustainable development" framework, they are confronted with evidence on the fight against road development, which is also associated with sustainable development. References are however not saturated. Actors continuously work towards redefining them in order to enable their integration. To put it differently, each time an object is translated within a new framework, this comes at a cost for both the object and the framework itself.

3.4   From coupling to restoring political order

The coupling activity constitutes a fundamental step in the development of a statement. It makes it possible for the actor bearing it to associate a proposal to different elements which contribute in defining it and giving it meaning. Linking the policy tool to a label, to consequences, to a problem, to a public policy, or to a framework, contributes to creating a "solution". From this perspective, the "coupling" concept initially developed by Kingdon (1995) makes it possible, above all, to understand the process through which actors associate previously distinct and heterogeneous elements within their discourse, such as a problem and a proposal, and to therefore better grasp the phenomenon that solutions often emerge before problems.

However, while the "coupling" concept makes it possible to better understand that a policy-making process does not fall empirically within problem solving, it is insufficient to explain the reasons why certain couplings are never proposed, starting with absurd coupling, or why others are ephemeral and do not withstand the criticism they come across. Moreover, it does not make it possible to grasp the importance of the process of rationalisation, which is often carried out *a posteriori* and which transforms a proposal into a real "solution".

In order to understand the processes at work in policymaking, it is therefore necessary to focus on what we have called the "assembling" phase, a phase that consists of realigning the different coupled elements for them to form a whole – a coherent "whole" – that makes sense. While "coupling" illustrates the disorganised association of a solution to a problem, "assembling" reflects restoring order and schedule within statements which makes it possible for a solution to be perceived as the result of problem resolution, and policy tools as factors of transformation of public policy. Assembling is all the more important as it makes it possible to erase the traces of a cognitive bricolage. Moreover it also depicts the political will of a capable collective actor, should he choose this proposal, to act on the world and restore order.

The coupling concept issues

The coupling concept makes it possible to exclude the idea that a solution is the result of the rational resolution of a problem. However, it is unable to comprehend that the association between a problem and a solution is not a free association, without constraints, and it is not simply explained through chance. Noting that not all couplings are possible, Kingdon rejects the notion of chance and analyses the conditions which contribute in making coupling possible.

In his book *Agendas, Alternatives and Public Policies*, Kingdon therefore demonstrates that coupling is a complex process which takes shape on the basis of three selection processes. The first one exists within each stream. The problems stream essentially involves selecting problems which attract decision-makers' attention. The policy stream is also a process which selects a limited number of solutions. The second selection process falls within the coupling process itself; although a solution has been selected, it cannot be coupled with each and every problem on the agenda. The third process is the political stream which also sorts out the couples.

Nevertheless, by allocating only one paragraph to the selection process of each stream in his conclusion, the author remains very evasive on the procedures of selection, and notably on that of coupling itself, only evoking as an explanation the risks of coupling in relation to another coupling.[7]

This response remains quite unsatisfactory as it fails to explain, for instance, why some couplings seem to be possible while others do not. It does not enable us to attain a fundamental understanding of what makes couples emerge, develop, and hold out while others do not exist or resist with time. Moreover, it does not enable us to understand why order and schedule is generally restored among the couples which resist, that is, the tool is presented as the result of the resolution of the problem. Finally, it does not make it possible to grasp why solutions, which develop independently from problems, need problems in order to impose themselves.

While the coupling concept has the merit of highlighting the cognitive bricolage, which enables reconciling a problem, a solution, a framework, or a public policy, it does not make it possible to take into account the significance of the process that erases the traces of this bricolage. Nor does it enable the restoring of order and schedule within the statement to ensure that ultimately the solution is well presented as the result of the resolution of problems, as an element which makes it possible to change the public policy to which it belongs, as an expression of values, or of a reference.

Discursive practices to assemble a solution and a problem

Restoring order within a statement must first be understood as one of the key elements which make it possible for an actor to make a statement hold up and pass from a simple coupling to what we can call "assembling". This assembling must not be taken as the second distinct phase of statement making. It must be understood through the anticipation of actors' conscious of having to justify their proposal by presenting an ordered statement. This anticipation contributes to selecting conceivable couplings. The anticipation of this assembling process thus functions as a selection system for possible couplings.

To grasp the assembling process at work, special attention should be paid to how actors develop a series of discursive strategies which enable them to transform an "unacceptable" problem into a "treatable" problem and an "acceptable" solution into a "ready to be embedded" solution.

Transforming an "unacceptable" problem into a "treatable" problem is a process that can be described as substitution or translation (Latour, 2006). To understand its origins, there is a need to address the language games that actors practice as from the moment the cause is identified. For the actor, stating that a problem has a cause is not only about establishing a link between two phenomena, the first preceding the second and provoking its existence, but it is also about substituting one phenomenon with another. Stating that a problem has a cause is therefore stating that the resolution of a problem comes down to treating its cause. From this perspective, establishing a cause makes it possible to substitute an "unacceptable" problem with a treatable cause, the problem and the cause are often two equivalent phenomena.

To understand this process, let us look at some examples. Evoking the "unemployment problem" makes it possible to become aware of the existence of an unacceptable problem. Attributing to the unemployment problem a cause such as the rigidity of the Labour Code does not only amount to creating a link between two distinct phenomena, unemployment, on one hand, and the Labour Code, on the other. It also amounts to substituting a problem (unemployment) with another problem (the rigidity of the Labour Code). This is a genuine shift of the problem which, through this language game, is no longer the same as before. This shift makes it possible to make unemployment a treatable problem. Admittedly, making the insufficient productivity of companies another cause of unemployment amounts to identifying a different problem and lays the groundwork for a distinct treatment.

As regards the housing policy in France, the actors have significantly contributed to making the insufficient number of houses constructed each year the cause of the problem. This association between two phenomena makes it possible to substitute a largely undefined and untreated problem with a treatable problem – the insufficient amount of housing constructed. While the actors do not know how to resolve the housing problem in general, they can always tackle its cause which, on the contrary, is treatable.

Similarly, actors can transform a proposal by coupling it with consequences. This coupling process is therefore based on highlighting a causal link between two phenomena: the consequences and the proposition that generates them. It is also based on the substitution that it makes possible. The measure proposed is thus replaced by a mastered fiction. By linking a solution to its consequences, actors thus transform an "acceptable" proposal into a new proposal that is better placed to couple with a problem.

In the case of employment, the proposal "facilitate dismissals" or "reduce minimum wage" comes with its desired consequence – an increase in the number of new jobs created. In the case of housing that we evoked previously, actors couple the proposal "develop construction aid" to its expected consequence – an increase in the number of houses constructed.

Having transformed the problem into a cause and the proposal into a consequence, the actors may proceed to an assembling operation which enables them not only to couple them to each other but also to firmly restore order and schedule. While coupling a problem to the initial proposal is neither logical nor rational, coupling the cause of the problem with the consequence of the proposal takes a different form. Indeed, the consequence of the solution is often a mastered fiction in which the cause of the problem has disappeared.

Let us go back to the housing policy. In order to link investment aid to the housing problem, its spokespersons highlight both the proposal's intended consequences, the construction of more new housing, and the cause of the housing problem, the insufficient number of new housing constructed each year. It is the coupling of the cause with the consequence that thus serves as a means of assembling the problem and the proposal. Similarly, while the link between the proposal on facilitating dismissals and the unemployment problem makes no meaning and can even be considered as antinomial, passing by the causes and the consequences makes the assembling feasible.

Cause and consequence participate in the translation process which transforms the problem and the proposal into two "ready to be embedded" phenomena. On the one hand, we find problems that are often vague, insoluble and general and, on the other, proposals that are sometimes inarticulate on their own. The actor's activities therefore depend on simplification and translation processes which make assembling possible. While vagueness makes it possible to weaken criticism – vagueness that is often present in problem construction – assembling obliges an exit from this vagueness and to increase the possible scope of contestations and challenges. It is for this reason that this activity is rather delicate.

Assembling is therefore based on language games which make shifting and translation possible. It makes it possible to restore meaning to a simple coupling by constructing a feasible path which leads the problem towards its solution. It also makes it possible to rationalise *a posteriori*, transforming the proposal into a solution, a result of problem resolution.

The imperative of restoring order: issues in politicising solutions

Highlighting the assembling process makes it possible to understand the manner in which actors, unsatisfied with the couplings that they establish between the problem and the solution, can restore meaning to the problem/solution couple and even make it rational. Restoring order must nevertheless be understood not only as a traditional game which makes it possible to restore meaning to a proposal but also, as a specific political process which contributes in making the solution a legitimate public policy proposal.

Restoring order within a statement primarily makes it possible for actors to develop a communicable political discourse. The actors who propose to couple a solution with a problem are aware that they must, sooner or later, publicly justify their proposal by using arguments which prove that their solution is not absurd for resolving the problem they associate with it. No actor can claim to propose a solution in relation to a problem, simply because he had a solution at hand and took a problem present on the agenda at that moment. Within the political sphere, actors therefore need to make sense and must be able to state what they can defend, justify, and communicate (Edelman, 1988).

Restoring meaning also makes it possible to develop a response not only to a problem but also to the disorder generated by the latter. While the politicisation of the problem passes through highlighting a society in disorder, assembling a proposal to a problem contributes in transforming it into a political tool that restores order.

This politicisation process begins first by linking the proposal to the intended consequences and, in more precise terms, to the mastered fiction that it portrays of an ordered and stable world. This process is then prolonged by the reconciliation between the solution and the cause of the problem. Through this reconciliation, a link is thus established between the disordered world of problems and the organised fiction of solutions. Subsequently, it is this reconciliation that makes the proposal a tool for restoring order within a society in disorder. Here we find the antinomial dialectics of order and disorder that we previously evoked in our introduction and which remain an essential element in politics. Solutions need problems to exist as order needs disorder and vice versa. These contradictory concepts feed off each other in order to make sense and form a self-referenced system. Restoring order finally makes it possible to display the political will of the actors. While societal problems are complex and insoluble, actors' ability to propose tools capable of illustrating a different world is also an occasion to highlight that, through their will, these actors can act on society.

Illustrating through fiction that a solution can produce a reality that is different from the present reality first underscores that actors have a capacity to act on what is real. Developing a statement, which shows that a solution makes it possible to change a public policy in place, also underscores that this change is the result of actors' activities. To put it

differently, while problem statements illustrate a world of the unacceptable and project a tale of the inaction of public authorities, solution
statements extol, on the contrary, the capacity of man to act on the
world and to shape society. Restoring order within statements therefore stands for a genuine theory of public policy change where political interventionism occupies its rightful place. Even if the actors are
muddling through in order to produce solutions, they take into account
the capacity of these solutions to solve the problem and become the
symbol of their capacity to act.

3.5   Conclusion

Simon and Lindblom have highlighted the absence of objectively
rational links between problems, objectives, solutions, tools, values,
causes, consequences, and ideologies. By this, the authors have shown
that assembling them involves public policy and cannot be considered
as a simple deductive activity, which starts from a central point or a core
element, such as values or objectives. However, while this link cannot
be considered as evidence, this does not mean that it does not exist.
On the contrary, Lindblom has shown that this link corresponds to an
empirical reality and can therefore be seen as the result of a complex
cognitive bricolage driven by actors in order to find solutions to insoluble problems. By suggesting that empirically, solutions often emerge
before problems, the studies carried out by Cohen, March, Olsen, and
Kingdon have reinforced this idea of bricolage which is essentially a
coupling process.

Taking language games into account makes it possible to broaden this
perspective by focusing not only on the coupling of scattered elements
but also on restoring order so that the elements can make sense. The
issue is no longer restricted to knowing whether the problem or the
solution came first, or to what public policy such an action should be
associated; it also involves restoring order among all these elements.

It must be noted that monitoring the restoration of order has two
major advantages. First, it makes it possible to understand what we could
call the career of a proposal, in reference to the better known "career of
a problem" (Gusfield, 1981). Given that coupling is not a neutral operation, this often calls for redefinition which makes it possible to "glue"
the coupling. Moreover, restoring order makes it possible to grasp the
political dimension which is at the very heart of fabrication. By developing a proposal, actors show to what extent means exist to solve societal problems and govern societies.

4
Propagating Solution: Argumentative Strategies to Cement Coalitions

Analysing language games in discourses "in action" makes it possible to understand how actors use discursive strategies to define policy solutions by assembling an instrument, problems, public policies, and/or values. Solution statements therefore take shape and meaning through the definitional activities we have previously described.

However, shaping statements does not suffice to understand what we can call, in reference to Gusfield's studies on problems, the career of solutions (Gusfield, 1981). While solutions are usually supported by a relatively large coalition of actors when they are imposed, the transition from a solution supported by a few to a solution supported by a coalition must not be considered a natural or obvious phenomenon. Simply developing a statement proposal, regardless of how solid it is, does not mean that the proposal will be implemented. Nor is it enough for the individual who advocates the policy proposal to belong to an organisation or network, as all the members of this network may not be in agreement and may not back the proposal.

In this chapter, we would therefore like to highlight the propagation of solutions. We consider this to be an issue that actors who want to promote a solution must address, rather than as a natural or evident process. This involves analysing how a few actors bearing a solution manage to persuade others to join them in defending a similar solution, thereby forming a coalition.

We assume that a solution statement is the link which makes it possible for actors to come together with regard to a policy proposal. Simultaneously, the constructed coalition cements together all the scattered elements of a statement through a gluing process. On the one hand, the statement is reinforced and stabilised as it spreads and gets support from an increasing number of actors. On the other hand, the coalition continues to take shape as the statement constitutes a common discourse shared by the actors.

To highlight the propagation process, we would first like to understand how actors develop genuine argumentative strategies to reinforce their statements and make them more feasible. In a context where a solution is primarily the result of discursive bricolage, arguments play a fundamental role in making a statement more convincing and easier to share. Nevertheless, far from being a one-way process, argumentation takes place most often within a platform of discussion where not only the arguments and the statement itself are challenged, but the identity of the protagonists as well.

Once persuasion has been identified as the means through which actors propagate their statements, we must focus on how all these disparate interactions participate in the same action at the meso level – stabilising a statement and building a coalition around it. To this end, we would like to highlight two phenomena: the need to convince and mutual adjustment. These two phenomena both contribute to unifying the solution statement and cementing the coalition.

4.1   Arguing to persuade

In the previous chapter, we showed that the definitional activity makes it possible to construct meaning by transforming a policy tool into a public solution. It must be understood not only as the restoring of order of a cognitive bricolage but also as a means through which sharing a policy proposal is made possible. This means considering the production of meaning not for itself but for what it enables – persuading actors of the validity and the pertinence of a proposal. To put it differently, the only interest of language games here is their capacity to support actors' games.

We would therefore like to focus on the persuasion process, understood here as the means through which a proposal is propagated. This activity is all the more interesting because it is not limited to stating proposals and to making couplings which give it meaning, but rather is developed from an argument which supports the solution statement in order to confirm as well as contribute to its solidity. This necessitates focusing on the concrete use of argumentation in order to better grasp its role within the process, which enables an actor to claim ownership of a proposal.

Argumentation is a discursive practice that is interesting for two reasons. First, it makes it possible to consider the significance of the consolidation activity of cognitive bricolage with regard to the individual who argues. Second, it takes into account the cognitive skills of the individual receiving the arguments who does not adopt a new point of view merely because of a simple assertion. More generally, focusing on argumentation helps us to better understand the significance of the knowledge and meaning test during interaction; this corresponds to a pragmatic view of knowledge that is always built in social action.

Argumentation as a social activity of thinking beings

Aristotle's *Rhetoric* proposed focusing on the use of speech as the ability given to man to influence other men. He saw speech as a social action always situated within a real communication process that sought to persuade. Nevertheless, his successors have progressively transformed rhetoric into a study of the figures of style and artefacts which seek to persuade or take advantage (Amossy, 2006). As with the study of political discourse, which is considered to be veiled or deceitful, rhetoric has participated in separating the form from the substance as well as discourse from the social activity in which it takes place.

This "restricted" rhetoric has thus largely contributed to studies in the figures of style used within political discourse. However, it has significantly impoverished, even belittled, studies on argumentation. According to Paul Ricoeur, the history of rhetoric is an ironic tale of *"peau de chagrin"*.[1] Ricoeur argues that while Aristotle developed rhetoric based on three fields – a theory of argumentation, a theory of style and a theory of the composition of discourse – rhetoric has been progressively reduced to the study of style, becoming an "erratic and futile discipline" (Ricoeur, 1976).

To consolidate our idea that argumentation is a specific social activity, we would like to evoke the studies of Chaïm Perelman, a philosopher who has largely contributed to renewing rhetoric. As from the 1950s, he proposed to abandon "restricted" rhetoric and revert to the fundamentals of Aristotelian rhetoric. Moreover, he argued that argumentation is an activity deployed in a communication setting. However, his studies would not have any impact on linguistics before the 1970s (Perelman et al., 1958).

We focus on Perelman's studies primarily because they re-establish argument as a practical philosophy, that is, as an essential social activity within society. Perelman proposes to re-establish ancient rhetoric in a new way and recommends that the study of figures of style out of context, "like flowers dried within a herbarium", should be abandoned. The author argues that focus should be on the dynamic of the persuasive context within which arguments occur. He thus focuses on discourse "in action", discourse situated within a singular interaction between a specific speaker and his particular audience.

According to him, by studying analytical reasoning alongside dialectic reasoning, Aristotle is the father of the theory of argumentation. Analytical reasoning is a demonstrative and impersonal reasoning based on an assumed and non-debatable premise. Using a series of inferences, it leads to a logical conclusion. Put differently, conclusions are not concerned with the truthfulness or the falsity of premises but rather with the formal rigour of reasoning. On the contrary, for Aristotle, dialectic reasoning is based on premises considered to be true or at least likely and it draws its strength, not from binding inferences, but rather from the convincing characteristics of arguments.

To better understand Perelman's assumptions, we need to elaborate on the opposition between truth and likelihood which forms the basis of his theory. Perelman criticises Cartesian philosophy which rejects "likelihood" for the benefit of "truth" that reason must produce. On the contrary, he considers that the field of likelihood and the plausible, which is that of argumentation as well, concerns reason more than the field of truth and demonstration.

First, he establishes a clear difference between what he calls demonstration, which according to him is applicable only within the field of mathematics, and argumentation, which prevails within other domains. Formal logic involves demonstrations which result in absolute truths. Consequently, this domain is particularly limited and relegates to plausible all that does not fall within mathematics. In other words, Perelman suggests that all discourse other than mathematics falls within the plausible domain and not that of truth.

However, for the author, it is precisely when one leaves the domain of demonstration and evidence that he actually invokes reason. Demonstration and evidence do not require proof, an audience, or a subject. They reject the other's existence and, therefore, his mind and logical reasoning. For Perelman on the contrary, all argumentation seeks to gain the adherence of minds and assumes that an intellectual contact exists (Perelman et al., 1950). In other words, it is the individual's reasoning which is set within the argumentation process, both for he who argues and for he who listens to the argument.

This is the fundamental point of his reflection – that argumentation is not a disembodied demonstration but a rhetoric which integrates the existence of the other. As a consequence, this new rhetoric that he proposes is based on how argumentation is shaped both by the speaker and by the audience he addresses. While "ancient" rhetoric involved the audience only when it was necessary to call on the art of persuasion with regard to beliefs and sentiments, the new rhetoric integrates the audience within a process which calls for reason (Reboul, 1991).

By focusing on argumentation and not merely on arguments, Perelman thus argues that to understand arguments, one must take into account the speaker as well as the audience that he seeks to convince, his readiness to listen, and the effectiveness of his argument on the audience. He focuses on argumentation as a social and discursive concrete activity which equally shapes the speaker and the audience. In his opinion, any rhetorical theory is an audience theory which will "study discursive techniques able to *provoke* or *increase adhesion* in the minds of those to whom propositions are presented for agreement" (Meyer, 2004, p. 21).

Argumentation to persuade and convince

Argumentation must therefore be understood to mean a specific activity that an actor uses during discussion in order to gain adherence to the idea he lauds, meaning, in our case, to the validity and relevance of his statement. To fully grasp this process, we would now like to distinguish persuasion and conviction activities based on Perelman's thesis. Indeed, the author suggests that activities should be differentiated depending on the nature of the audience rather than on reason, as conviction traditionally refers to reason and persuasion to manipulation.

One of the most successful assumptions developed by Perelman considers that arguers develop their arguments by taking into consideration their target audience. It is not only about assuming that the audience influences the speaker by its reactions and its objections, its agreements and its disagreements; rather, it is about bearing in mind that an argument is already developed by integrating the specificity of the audience as imagined by the speaker. Consequently, the speaker is not alone in shaping arguments – his audience does as well – or at least what he conceives as his audience. Thus, an argument is a strategy designed bearing in the mind the individual that it is to influence

With this hypothesis, the author distinguishes conviction when a speaker addresses a universal audience from persuasion when he addresses a specific audience. This distinction seems particularly relevant within the framework of our study as it makes it possible to distinguish between two very important activities within the political sphere: the first is the activity that Vivien Schmidt calls communicational discourse

(Schmidt, 1999), whose specificity is not only the non-negligible size of the audience but also the absence of real reactivity. The second is the activity which seeks to persuade a specific individual by sharing the validity of a statement or even its ownership through arguments which target him specifically.

All too often, when the term discourse is evoked, it refers to the notion of a powerful orator who speaks within specific instances and targets a universal audience. Consequently, as discourse seeks to convince, it has often been analysed depending on its soothing content and on all that it leaves unsaid. The study of discourse as well as all discursive forms has thus been characterised as unnecessary acts.

We would like to take into account persuasion, which is defined as a specific process essential to the propagation of a statement. We would also like to reinstate conviction, particularly with regard to its significance in persuasion. The persuasion process associates a speaker supporting a proposal he intends to share to a listener who accepts to listen to what the speaker would like to say. Admittedly, as Perelman has also argued, an audience of a single listener transforms discourse into dialogue. It is therefore the listener who asks questions and objects. Consequently, persuasion is primarily an interactive – and not a one-way – discussion which flows from the speaker towards the listener.

Nevertheless, while persuasion falls within the category of discussions, it is, in our opinion, a specific discussion marked by the differentiation of positions. Multiple forms of discussion exist. During negotiation, for example, individuals can have equivalent positions – which does not mean that these positions are balanced – since the two parties are committed and interested. On the contrary, during persuasion, individuals do not hold equivalent positions. We can distinguish the individual who is motivated by his intention to persuade and elaborates an argumentative strategy to this end, and the one who listens to him but is not necessarily interested and could decide not to commit himself any further. To persuade, an actor cannot restrict himself to developing the conditions of an argument with an individual as is the case with negotiations; he must also interest his listener and encourage his enrolment.

Analysing the singular process of persuasion therefore implies taking an interest in both the arguments which contribute in making the statement likely as well as the specific process of involvement which motivates an actor to join a discussion. When we can make this heuristic distinction between making likely and being involved, it is possible to come back to the distinction that Perelman proposes between persuading and convincing.

The arguments that contribute to making a statement likely often claim universality. Admittedly, they are used within a specific discussion but they are also intended to be recyclable within discourses that target a universal audience. Arguments which contribute to the specific involvement of an individual do not necessarily emerge from "silent" discussions. To put it differently, at the heart of persuasion lies the claim of enabling future conviction. Persuasion, the activity which seeks to encourage adhesion, unfolds from argumentative practices of feasibility and involvement.

Persuading to change public policy, the 1960s intuition

Persuasion must be understood as a discursive process that makes it possible for a stakeholder advocate of a statement to share it with another stakeholder. It is a discursive practice, meaning it is a concrete interaction which takes place based on the intentionality of the one who organises it, targeting a given individual in order to make him adopt a position that he does not hold. The importance of a face-to-face encounter as a space which enables discursive exchange and the use of arguments is thus a fundamental issue here.

Focusing on persuasion therefore implies empirically observing the manner in which stakeholders act in order to persuade others to adopt a statement they are advocating. This means taking into account who they encounter, the type of arguments exchanged, and the content of the discussions in which they participate. It also implies analysing whether this attempted sharing is satisfactory or not. Observing such a practice therefore means considering that it does not involve evidence but rather construction, and that success or failure cannot be understood without analysing the contingent activities which make it possible. Consequently, what we propose here is to put these argumentative activities at the core of empirical observations by focusing on the intention of the spokesperson who targets a listener, on the content of the discussions, and on the effect of these discussions on the listener as well as on the bearer of the proposal. We therefore posit that focusing on the observation of these discursive practices paves the way for a better understanding of the process of disseminating discourse and of its transformation into a statement.

Few authors have addressed persuasion in detail. Nevertheless, a few significant political science studies carried out in the 1960s focused on this issue. In particular, these studies opposed the ruling elitism and their taken-for-granted hegemony. Three authors seem to have paved the way, which unfortunately has not been followed up. For instance,

Richard Neustadt focused on the foreign policy of the United States and subsequently carried out a significant empirical study on the activities of the President of the United States (Neustadt, 1960). He came to the conclusion that the president's core activity was persuasion. In his opinion, the president spends his time persuading other stakeholders to implement public policies. Despite his position that confers upon him authority, he spends his time arguing and using his charm to persuade others to share his proposal. Neustadt showed, for example, how the president persuaded a senator, through arguments – rather than through force, threats, or authority – the extent to which a project was in his interest and was his responsibility. Without further elaborating on the conceptualisation of his theory, Neustadt illustrates that persuasion is a difficult activity and that being president is by no means sufficient in enabling the sharing of a point of view.

Neustadt's studies make it possible to underscore that, what holds for the president of the United States also holds for other actors who engage in a proposal. This is because generally, stakeholders involved in the development of public policies spend a considerable amount of time persuading other actors. The researcher must thus take this activity seriously.

Robert Dahl is another exception to the rule. With his influential study, *Who Governs?*, he sweeps aside different ways in which to tackle the issue and outlines a particularly successful avenue between influence and persuasion (Dahl, 1965). In his book, he tackles the issue of governments by challenging the theories which simply consider that power is a matter of position. He proposes to take up the issue of power by considering that he who has power is he who concretely influences public policy. We will focus on the second section of this significant book. Here, after showing the plurality of the elite, Dahl analyses the division of influence between the different groups of elites on one hand and between these elite groups and other citizens on the other. To specifically analyse this influence, he proposes to study two public policies in particular: the urban renovation policy and the education policy in New Haven (Connecticut, USA).

With regard to urban policy, Dahl specifically analyses influence using two operations. To simplify the excessively long list of participants in decision-making processes, the first operation that he proposes simply consists in identifying the stakeholders behind the origin of ideas. He shows that in 57 initiatives, half result from two people – the mayor and development administrator – and the rest from 23 other people. By initiative, Dahl does not only mean origin, as it is often difficult to determine the exact origin of an idea, but also how the idea is initiated and developed within multiple decision-making circuits in the city. He notably insists on the phase which makes possible the transition of an idea into a project. This presupposes that critical resources such as money, time, energy, attention, skill and political support are dispensed (Dahl, 1965).

The second operation on which Dahl insists is that of negotiation or how the bearers of a project construct around them a "bizarre" coalition. For this, they negotiate with other leaders, heads of service with regard to "winning support and gaining the necessary adhesion" (Dahl, 1965, p. 127). This phase is all the more interesting as it is not a question of negotiation in the sense where two parties attempt to merge their interest by drafting a compromise. It is rather for the bearer of the project to persuade his listeners that the project is indeed tailored to their aspirations or, at least, does not oppose them.[2] It is the leader bearing the project who influences others. This is based on his capacity to persuade "sub-leaders" of the significance of the project, as well as on his capacity to interiorise the expectations of the "sub-leaders" whose ability to cause trouble or obstruct seems large. In other words, for a project to be adopted, its bearer must persuade certain leaders but also know how to adapt it to the expectations and to the real or imagined limits (when they are expressed during discussion) of the organised stakeholders.[3]

Similarly, Dahl underscores the manner in which citizens influence the project, given that the mayor, keen to receive the support of his voters, anticipates what he conceives as his fellow citizens' wishes. By insisting on citizens' indirect influence, he shows that the political system is not a simple oligarchy but a genuine "polyarchy"; it is on this occasion that he coins this term which he progressively develops (Dahl, 1971).

The third author who deserves particular attention is Edward Banfield (1961). In a book entitled *Political influence*, he analyses the way influence works within the city of Chicago. By mobilising several empirical terrains, he challenges the mythic image of the elite who monopolise power and act concurrently to dominate the world. Banfield analyses the specific processes of influence implemented by actors with fragmented power who are often in disagreement. He thus begins by defining influence as the capacity to make others act, think, or feel as one intends. This is equally true for a mayor who convinces his voters to approve his project and for a businessman who persuades a mayor to take an action. Consequently, and this is Banfield's key hypothesis, public policy always takes place within a system of influence that seeks to convince the "right" persons. From this standpoint, analysing influence consists of analysing the forms of government of a society.

This hypothesis leads him to focus on analysing the influences at work between stakeholders. As a consequence, it means considering "who has influence with whom and with regard to what?" Banfield's idea here is to underscore that influence is a process that is inevitably specific and that one person can have influence on another with regard to a given subject but not to another. It also implies analysing how influence works. Banfield also identifies several forms of influence: influence by obligation or authority, by gratification, by logic, by transforming representations, etc. Finally, he focuses on the terms upon which influence is expended.

Banfield's empirical and theoretical study is all the more significant as the author shows that while all coordination is complex given the autonomy of stakeholders and the formal fragmentation of power, it is inevitable for new action to emerge. As a consequence, influence must be understood as the means that these dependent stakeholders use in order to cooperate around an action. Influencing is therefore not only about persuading but also deceiving, recompensing, punishing, or inducing. Consequently, the power to influence can be analysed based notably on the ability of actors to block, or on the contrary, to propagate new actions. Banfield goes as far as characterising a political system depending on whether its system of influence makes possible the emergence of all proposals (radicalism), impedes them (conservatism) or takes other more complex forms.

Analysis as an argumentative persuasion strategy

Among the argumentative strategies used to persuade interlocutors of the validity of a statement, analysis plays a key role. We have already addressed this issue in the previous chapter and underscored to what extent it contributes to policy statement making. We would like to revert here to its role within discussions as well as its persuasive function.

The analytical activity is all the more interesting as it is the method that has been used most often by researchers to describe and analyse a public policy and, sometimes, to "objectively" prescribe policy change. It therefore enables us to step back from a policy analysis by considering it as an objective activity carried out by the researcher, and as a discursive strategy which stakeholders drive in order to persuade others.

The idea that analysis is an argumentative strategy follows the works of several authors who were the precursors and who we will address here before taking our reflection further. Charles Lindblom is probably the pioneer of this approach. As from the 1970s, he has made an attempt to understand how public policies are produced by focusing on the role of analytical strategies. In a short book on the policymaking process and, in particular, in the first edition of this book, Lindblom abandons his traditional defence of the incremental model, a model that is both descriptive and prescriptive, and evokes the importance of different analytical strategies that analysts use during the policy-making process (Lindblom, 1968). In this book, Lindblom no longer speaks like an analyst but rather as an observer of analysts. He thus describes their ingenuity in developing numerous analytical techniques destined to reduce the complexity of the problems to be tackled and to reduce the number of alternatives that they need to choose. Lindblom takes up the different simplification processes he had identified earlier to underscore the diversity of the methods that individuals use to carry out their analyses.

This change in perspective modifies Lindblom's relationship to his methods as well. For instance, while he had shown that ideologies have no direct link to public policy in his early works, he underscores that, on the contrary, they participate in an analytical process that enables simplification. He therefore argues that the issue is not in knowing whether ideologies are true or false but rather understanding that policy-makers believe in them and that they help them to choose, which would otherwise be impossible. More broadly, Lindblom considers that all the methods he identifies to solve problems are nothing more than analytical strategies that stakeholders use to help them choose one: settling for a "satisfactory" choice; the trial and error approach (a sequence of choices, feedback, and renewed choices); the error method (voluntarily make small errors to avoid making a big one); the law of series (considering that public policies respond to laws in order to deduce the right solution); the bottleneck method; and incrementalism. Nevertheless, what we find particularly interesting in Lindblom's study is that he goes beyond conceiving these analytical methods as cognitive strategies to enable individuals to deal with their choice. He also sees them as discursive strategies that stakeholders use to make conflict or cooperation possible. Lindblom suggests that the plays of power are primarily actors' games that mobilise analyses.[4]

Considering that decision making is a complex process requiring significant cooperation, Lindblom suggests that analysis is one of the methods that actors use to cooperate. The analysis suggested by one actor to another marks his quest for cooperation, but it also makes cooperation possible given that it offers the other a possible channel through which to resolve problems. According to Lindblom, it is only when persuasion fails that authorities intervene to establish coercive cooperation. While Lindblom was one of the rare authors to initiate this idea, little attention was paid to it and it curiously disappeared with each new edition of his book. The book which was nevertheless relatively successful was edited thrice and has been widely used as a manual rather than as a genuine research study.

The 1990s argumentative stream in public policy

It was not until the 1990s that the first wave of studies placed argumentation at the heart of public policy. In this emerging stream, two books stand out in particular and deserve special attention (Durnova and Zittoun, 2013). The first, Giandomenico Majone's book, *Evidence, Argument and Persuasion in the Policy Process* (Majone, 1989) and the second, Frank Fischer and John Forester's collective work, *The Argumentative Turn in Policy Analysis and Planning* (Fischer and Forester, 1993). While these two books belong to different registers, they are similar in that they conceive argumentation as fundamental to public policy analysis. Majone's book focuses on analysing public policy as an intellectual construct based on arguments. He insists in particular on the importance of understanding and of persuasion in the processes which contribute to the emergence of a proposal. Majone is probably one of the first authors to underscore the importance of argumentation. He thus lays another building block in this field even though, on numerous points, he confines himself by remaining relatively vague on the significance of argumentation and conviction in renewing how these processes are understood.

According to Majone, discussion and argumentation is at the core of public policy processes.[5] By reducing public policy processes to issues of power, influence, and negotiations, too many studies exclude debate and arguments from understanding the process, even while they are a study through which actors make judgements and public policy choices. Indeed, it is at the heart of discussions that stakeholders adjust their vision of reality and modify their position. As a consequence, Majone argues that, within a system that governs by discussion, public policy analysis has less to do with formal techniques of problem resolution than with processes of argumentation. He therefore considers that the analyst's specific task is to produce evidence and arguments that can be used in the course of public policy processes.

Persuasion must not therefore be understood as a manipulative process where an individual sells his arguments and ideas, but rather as a discursive exchange in the course of which actors learn and mutually adjust their own vision in order to make it more compatible. Many judgements therefore emerge during discussion, rather than from isolated thoughts. Considering that values and facts are always linked, Majone insists in particular on the power of arguments which present "facts". He thus shows how the image of a public policy analyst who claims to be capable of distinguishing values and facts and who positions himself as the one who, once the object determined subjectively by others, is capable of objectively defining the best way of achieving it, is misleading.

One cannot rigorously demonstrate the conclusions of a public policy analysis and the alternative options that it implies. This is because it is always necessary to artificially limit the problem, eliminate all uncertainty, and lead others to believe that one possesses all the relevant information. Subsequently, analytical activities belong to argumentation. Majone does not suggest that proposed analyses are false or unnecessary but rather, that they are arguments which illustrate the likelihood of a proposal. He proposes that first, discovery should be distinguished from justification. In his opinion, how a proposal is discovered is not always linked to how it is justified. This holds for both sciences and politics. In the sciences, a discovery can be made by accident but can only be presented to a scientific community via the presentation of a body of evidence which sometimes is discovered *a posteriori*. In politics, an actor's motivation in defending an idea is not always linked to the arguments he uses to justify his choice. It is therefore important to understand that actors are aware that while it is insufficient to make a choice for a decision to become legitimate, they must also legitimise their choice by using a set of justifications. Once an actor has made a choice, he must inevitably justify his choice, explain it, and persuade. However, while choices precede arguments, it is generally rare that at the moment when they make their choice, actors have not anticipated the justification phase and that this has had no influence on the choice taken. In any case, these post-decision-making arguments often correspond to a rationalisation process. Majone thus evokes the study carried out by the American defence secretary, Robert McNamara, to convince senators of the relevance of his choices during the cold war, by using cost-benefit analyses. Analysing defence policies is therefore a particularly efficient persuasion argument.

Considering analyses and rationalisation as arguments that support a solution, Majone therefore revisits the distinction generally made between policy analysis and policy advocacy. Taking up Aaron Wildavsky's idea (1987), he shows that analysts are nothing more than craftsmen who use cognitive bricolage to formulate their proposal and the arguments which support it. He shows that analysts simply compile data from collected samples using approximate methods. He argues that to transform the collected raw data into useable "information", these analysts use know-how that enables them to reduce the amount of data, group it and transform it into simple and useable elements. Using averages, indicators, and parameters, these types of processes fall within reduction processes. Finally, information is transformed into indisputable and true facts which no longer require evidence.

Majone then identifies different arguments that he considers significant. First, there are feasibility arguments. These are arguments that highlight constraints and impossibilities, be they physical, technical, legal, economic, financial, social, political, implementation related, etc. These arguments reduce the possible alternatives. From this perspective, persuasion concerns both public policies and the societal background in which they operate.

Majone focuses on public policy tools in particular. He highlights that there are always multiple possible tools which make choice difficult. This choice makes it possible for numerous economists and public policy analysts to develop specific knowledge aimed at helping decision-makers. While many authors consider that this choice can solely be based on the technical character of an instrument, Majone shows that, on the contrary, such a choice cannot overlook the fact that instruments are never ideologically neutral. Choosing between an expense or tax deduction, between a control measure or an incentive, is more ideological than technical. Moreover, their social impact is not identical, and especially with regard to redistribution between social groups. Finally, tools cannot be clearly distinguished from objectives. While objectives are often vague, tools can acquire meaning beyond their instrumental value.

Majone therefore argues that the performance of a tool depends less on its intrinsic properties than on the political and administrative context in which it operates. Often tools are considered within ideal situations, whereas concrete problems only emerge within specific situations and actions take shape only within specific contexts. No concrete problem can be resolved using a theoretical solution. According to him, choosing a tool is not a technical exercise that one can entrust to an expert but rather an exercise that integrates all the dimensions of public policy, that is, political, moral, and cultural dimensions. It is for this reason that Majone argues that no technical argument can suffice in demonstrating the superiority of one tool over another. Technical arguments only play a minor role when it comes to selecting one tool over another.

Majone thus suggests conceiving a dialectical relationship between public policy and what is said of it; this he calls a "public meta-policy", meaning ideas, concepts, and proposals put forward by all kinds of actors. A public policy is not an object that assembles an up-to-date list of decisions, stakeholders, and institutions simply waiting to be discovered. It is primarily an intellectual construct and an analytical category. Our understanding of public policies cannot be separated from the ideas, theories, and criteria through which we analyse and evaluate them.

While he lays the base for a new approach, Majone remains relatively sketchy on how this approach makes it possible to evaluate public policy processes. The author suggests constructing a new model to understand change. This model should distance itself from technocratic models which describe change as the result of the changing preferences of actors based on an objective change. It should distance itself as well from "political" models which understand change depending on the reconfiguration of dominant interests. He thus suggests that a change generally originates from change involving beliefs and values.

Despite strongly criticising models which inevitably forget context and reveal the singularity of institutional situations and arrangements, Majone also proposed a model which made it possible to understand change based on a very broad metaphor between the core element and the peripheral layers. The core of public policy is relatively stable and evolves slowly while the periphery is ever-changing and unstable. In this model, the innovation and production of proposals belongs to the community of public policy experts while the activity of selection belongs to the political arena. He thus suggests that the interactions between a public policy community and a political arena make it possible to understand the dialectical relationship between public policy and public meta-policy.

But how can one distinguish an object from what is said of it (public policy and "meta")? How can one identify a central core and distinguish it from the periphery without referring to objective knowledge on public policy even though it involves a constructivist perspective (public policy analysis is a construct) which rejects the notion of objective knowledge?

Indeed, Majone highlights, like Lindblom and Wildavsky before him, that public policy analysis does not involve sciences in terms of rational demonstration or technique (theories of rational choice included) but rather of discourse and, in particular, of argumentative processes which seek to show a proposal's credibility. He thus suggests that argumentation should be the assumed centre of an analyst's activity. However, by focusing on the analyst's role, he does not take into account Lindblom's proposal that also considers analysis as ordinary knowledge which all participants shape. He therefore finds himself faced with the content analysis paradox he also continues to produce albeit differently, although he had shown its limited and rather relative character.

Borrowing from Majone's work, the collective study published in 1993 and edited by Fischer and Forester also marks a significant shift from traditional public policy studies. The authors take up the idea that all analyses, including those that claim to be "neutral", "technical", or "rational" are nothing more than normative or ideological arguments. They thus encourage researchers to adopt critical positions that unveil the normativity behind the "objectivity" claim, as well as a committed approach which pushes them to develop communication methods that contribute to new methods of analysing public policy. The book assembles twelve authors who, each in their own way, attempt to prolong Majone's first reflections. In its introduction, Fischer and Forester concur with Majone that public policy is composed of language and that argument plays a central role at each step of the public policy process. They explore the notion that public policy analysis must be considered as a practical argumentative process (Fischer and Forester, 1993).

Their primary interest is in understanding what analysts do with public policy, language, the representations they use which impede their work, and the forms of description and characterisation that they use. Their arguments interest the authors less for their veracity or falsifiability than for their partiality and normativity, or the manner in which they select an analytical framework and the role they play (descriptive, predictive, evaluative, symbolic, etc.) In particular, arguments place analysis and the analyst within a deliberative and argumentative approach and make him give up all claims concerning the production of rational knowledge produced from scratch, for the sake of coherence and internal logic. The authors thus distance themselves from a rational analytical posture which encloses debate on the veracity of analyses and move towards a critical approach which highlights the normativity of analytical developments in order to open them to criticism. This therefore involves illustrating the conditions under which analysis is carried out and the stakes involved in problem construction. It is also about highlighting the underlying multiple biases in order to open up debate.

Fischer and Forester suggest that analysts must constantly pay attention to the two aspects of arguments – their content, meaning their internal logic, and their efficiency, meaning their ability to convince. In some way, they dismiss those who, like the scholars of rational choice, are only interested in the logic of argumentation and qualify as irrational all those who remain unconvinced. They also dismiss those who attribute importance only to efficiency, without paying attention to content. In their opinion, the strength of argumentative analysis is in associating internal coherence to external conviction.

The argumentative turn primarily depends on the manner in which analysts create the problem on which they seek to reflect. This structures and limits the alternatives which are then available for analysis. One must also bear in mind the manner in which these arguments are produced not only in terms of content but also in terms of where they will be deployed, the public targeted, and the terms under which they are formulated. The book seeks to encourage a practical turn in public policy analysis by broadly underscoring the perpetually contingent and contextual character of analytical practices as well as their normative and political character. It highlights the entangled use of arguments with regard to public policy and the exercise of power.

Most importantly, the argumentative turn is a critical view concerning the analysis of public policy content. It is somewhat the unveiling of the flaws of rational analysis to show its character that is both constructed and political. By showing the political and relative character of each analysis, the authors contributing to this volume suggest that public policy should no longer be the means to underscore the irrationality of politics but on the contrary, should put politics back in the centre.[6] Furthermore, the argumentative turn presents two main advantages in our opinion. First, it points out that each policy analysis is no more than a discursive construction which forms the basis of argumentation in legitimising a choice. To put it differently, when analysis is placed within its context of creation and fabrication (who, what, when, for whom), it becomes an argumentative practice that makes it possible to legitimise a proposal. Secondly, this turn highlights the normative aspect of all knowledge on policy studies.

The uses of persuasion: promoting and criticising

While the aforementioned authors have been able to highlight the significance of argumentative practices in analysing public policy, it remains clear that their primary concern in seeking to fight rational choice by developing an alternative applied theory of analysis through argumentation and deliberation has not made it possible to take reflection on policy process further. They have therefore encountered difficulty in overcoming the "science of muddling through" paradox that we highlighted in the previous chapter, revealing the tension between a descriptive and a prescriptive point of view. First of all, they describe the activities of analysts who produce analysis which is nothing more than normative, and powerful arguments used to persuade, rejecting the idea that an analyst can have a neutral effect. Second, they prescribe a new role for the analyst who can become a "facilitator". A facilitator helps reveal the normative framework of any analysis and facilitates debate, discussion, and argumentation struggles in order to reach an agreement. This second possibility supposes first that it is possible for him to reveal the normative aspect of argument without using a normative point of view; second, that this analyst can participate in actors' games without taking into account the power struggles that arguments, his own included, involve.

If, consistent with the argumentative turn, it is possible for a researcher to highlight the significance of argumentation in the policy process, then we can consider that all stakeholders involved in policymaking, including "facilitators", develop knowledge that is always normative, and the statement is always intentional. Moreover, we can consider that stakeholders, the "facilitator" included, are all involved in power stakes and power games. It is therefore particularly complex to group together descriptive approaches, including post-empirical approaches which take into account the values and norms present in arguments, and prescriptive approaches, which must be based on strong assumptions with regard to the power struggles of both participants and the researcher, in order to exist. This complexity is present in Habermas' studies which present two types of action which refer to two conceptions of power: strategic action which supposes that power resides within actors' dominant positions and the communicative action which supposes that power resides within arguments.

Although we will address this issue in the next chapter, we would like to take up our highly descriptive position on the policy process by focusing on discursive practices and, more specifically, on persuasive action as a central social activity that policymakers use to propagate or eliminate a policy proposal through critical argumentative discourse. Following Boltanski's idea to shift from critical sociology to the sociology of critique (Boltanski, 2009), we argue that it is necessary to shift from critical policy studies to the study of policy critique based on a post-empirical perspective of the policy process. Our main assumption here is that at each stage of the policy process, all new policy proposals provoke much argumentation and critical discussion within the conflict arena of policymakers, even if a lot of these discussions are generally discrete discussions inside a black box. This can be explained by the fact that no policy proposal can be adopted without sufficient policymakers to sponsor it. As the literature on decision and policy processes shows, no decision is the result of a single man, making his decision alone in his office, even if he is the president of the United States. He needs to find a number of policymakers, experts, bureaucrats, and interest groups who can sponsor his policy proposal. Second, this can be explained by the fact that no policy proposal can be propagated without intense persuasion by proposal bearers, who target other policymakers. Even in the internet era, it is somewhat complicated for a policy proposal to circulate from one policymaker to another without actual meetings and discussions. The third reason is that the policymakers' world is a real arena where many individuals are in competition. Within the State, we can empirically note that there is conflict between each minister and ministry, between the different departments within the same ministry, between different offices within each department, and between agents within each office.

For these reasons, propagating a new policy proposal is a complex activity that is quite interesting to observe empirically. This reveals the manner in which different stakeholders reach agreement or not. To grasp these different discursive activities within the policy-making process, we would first like to heuristically distinguish two types of activities which take place at the very heart of the policy process and which correspond to the different uses of argumentation.

"Promotion" is the first type of activity. This activity is based on policymakers' will to propagate their new public policy proposal and share its relevance with their interlocutors. To achieve this, actors establish arguments which predominantly support and prove the link they have established through their statements between the proposal and the problem it must resolve, the public policy it must change, the values it must promote and the future it must design. Promotion also applies to public policies already in place. Here, it is notably about emphasising that public policy does not require modification and protects stabilised statements from all unions emerging from new proposals.

We also find "criticism" which, on the contrary, is an activity that consists of pointing out a proposal's lack of credibility. As opposed to promotion, this activity highlights the brittleness of the links which connect the different elements of a statement. This therefore involves proving that a proposal does not respond to an identified problem and does not produce the anticipated changes or give rise to unexpected consequences which pose even more serious problems. This activity is also present when it involves showing that an existing public policy is problematic.

Naturally, policymakers do not confine themselves to a single type of argument and can alternate arguments to better persuade their interlocutor. Their intentions thus become central given that persuasion is primarily a voluntary act on the part of actors. We can use a diagram to represent two figures or two roles that policymakers play by intertwining these strategies. The first figure is that of the "promoter" or "activist" seeking to propagate an idea. He does this by alternating arguments promoting a new proposal and those criticising the public policies in place. The second figure is that of the "guardian" which on the contrary, seeks to prevent any attempt at change by promoting the public policy in place and criticising emerging proposals.

This typology is summarised in the table below:

Table 4.1   Typology of argumentative strategies

	Promote	Criticise
New proposal	Promoter	Guardian
A public policy in place	Guardian	Promoter

To clearly understand these different activities, let us take an empirical example from the housing policy in France. In 1991, housing stakeholders began developing a policy proposal that sought to relaunch the housing policy in France by increasing the number of new homes in order to solve the "housing crisis". This proposal was part of an intense "promotion" activity in which some policymakers defending this idea tried to persuade others that this was a "good" solution. The Construction Director of the Housing Ministry thus explained: "When I was in charge, I actively militated to obtain some measures to exit the crisis."[7] In highlighting the militant character of the activity, this high-ranking administrative official points out the importance of the persuasion he used to gain adhesion. First, he tried to persuade the Minister of Equipment, Housing, Transport and the Environment at the time – Paul Quilès – to become the spokesperson of this policy proposal. After convincing him, they both tried to convince the Prime Minister and even the President of the Republic that their proposal was "pertinent".

Each step was long and difficult. Paul Quilès met each stakeholder and used arguments criticising the policies in place and claiming that they were insufficient to meet the challenges. He promoted a policy proposal capable of responding to the crisis facing the housing industry.

These promotion and criticism operations primarily sought to have these measures taken seriously by the stakeholders who were at the same time highly solicited by others. In other words, the issue was not primarily structured around the "for" and the "against" but rather between the "promoters" who sought to attract attention and the uninterested actors. To be militant therefore implied raising both awareness and interest. As the proposal spread and became "serious", the promoters were confronted by other policymakers who presented themselves as the guardians of the economic policy in place. They promoted the existing economic public policy, criticising the new policy proposal.

To counter this new proposal, two Finance Inspectors from the Ministry of Economy wrote a brief to François Mitterrand, then-president of the French Republic. The objective of this synthetic brief was two-fold: it promoted the existing policy and criticised the new proposal in order to persuade the president against adhering to it.

The following arguments were presented in the brief:

A re-launch of domestic demand is not the right response to the economic situation (...). A choice must be made between two possible strategies which cannot coexist:

- Maintain an economic policy of competitiveness which we have defended over the last ten years. This will contribute to higher growth in the medium-term by gaining market share over our competitors while mastering our domestic demand in such a way that it keeps in line with that of our partners.
- The policy that M. Quilès recommends concerning a re-launch of domestic demand through an increase in the budget deficit, notably for the benefit of construction firms. This will lead to a discrepancy in terms of our domestic demand compared to that of our principal partners and to the long-term weakening of our economy. (Zittoun, 2000)

In this excerpt, we can first underscore the significance of argumentation in the relationship between policymakers. For the two Finance Inspectors, this implies using arguments to persuade the President of the Republic not to adopt Quilès' proposal. To put it differently, without prejudging their effectiveness, the stakeholders embark on argumentation with the intention to inflect or rather, to prevent inflecting the President. To achieve this, they promote the "actual economic policy", which they labelled "competitive", and coupled it with a tool destined to "master our domestic demand" to consequences – "gaining market share over our competitors" – and to a fiction illustrating an "enchanted" future where "there are market gains". They also criticise the policy proposal by associating it to its consequences "an increase in the budget deficit" and "a discrepancy in terms of our domestic demand compared to that of our principal partners", the "real" beneficiaries who are not the economy but rather construction firms; they also highlight an apocalyptic fiction: "the long-term weakening of our economy".

Faced with such arguments, Paul Quilès' activism thus consists of responding to this criticism by developing new arguments to reinforce the previous ones. Quilès succeeded in persuading the President primarily because he fought for the proposal and knew how to use arguments against those of the guardians. While this is insufficient to inflect a position, it is a necessary condition.

Observing the different argumentative strategies

Persuasion is based on a specific argumentative practice which seeks to legitimise the discourse proposed. While an argument is specific and depends on both the speaker and the audience targeted, it is possible to identify the typology of the arguments that stakeholders use. The key point here is that while stakeholders are masters of their argumentative strategy and that this strategy varies depending on their audience, the type and the number of arguments used remains limited. They thus draw from a repertoire of available arguments which they then adapt in their own way, eventually transforming them. Sometimes, albeit rarely, stakeholders develop completely new arguments but these are often weaker and need some degree of legitimisation to consolidate.

Once again, we will rely on Perelman's studies and his famous treatise on argumentation. The latter identifies four types of argument. The first type of argument is the "quasi-logical" argument. As Perelman restricts truth to mathematical demonstration, he points out that what is likely can be constructed using quasi-logical arguments. In other words, these arguments appear logical; they use the logical approach but always have weaknesses which prevent them from becoming "logical". Consequently, with regard to reduction to the absurd which is very frequent in mathematics for instance, Perelman suggests argumentation through ridicule. The ridiculous makes it possible to underscore the contradictions and the incompatibilities of adverse reasoning. In the example citing the brief from the Ministry of Economy, pointing out that adopting the revival of housing leads to a reverse effect of the economic policy that has been in place for the last ten years, falls within this ridiculous argumentation. Within the quasi-logical category, there are also tauto-logical, transitivity, dilemma and, division arguments. Moreover, there is the definition which gives words or concepts meaning by defining an equivalence. It is therefore clear that "quasi-logical" arguments consti-tute a fundamental base in the construction of discourses and their insti-tutionalisation into statements.

The second type is what the author names "arguments based on reality". These are arguments that rely on the association between two events that exist or are likely to exist rather than on logic and its implica-tions. The causal links that make it possible to link two successive events is a good example of this process. Linking poverty and school failure associates two situations perceived as true in order to make one the cause of the other. Perelman also highlights what he calls the pragmatic argument which makes it possible to describe a situation depending on its favourable or unfavourable consequences, transferring somewhat the value given to one onto the other. Judging that a law is "good" because it has positive outcomes is typical of this transfer process.

The third major type of argument is not founded on reality but rather, founds reality. It is the use of examples, models or illustrations. It is also an activity that involves comparisons, analogies, and metaphors. In the debate over recent years on firearm prohibition in the United States, the significance of "dramatic cases" is clear in the argumentation driven by President Obama and his administration.

Finally, the fourth major type of argument is what Perelman names dissociation. Distinguishing, separating, dissociating, or dividing notions are processes which contribute to other types of argumenta-tion. Hierarchies such as man is superior to animals, as well as spaces – joint or specific – through which this hierarchy can be expressed are essential. According to Perelman, dissociation is often used as an argu-mentation technique. For instance, the dissociation appearance/reality makes it possible to dissociate within reality what is the "genuine" reality from that which is only an illusion. Indeed, the author argues that all dissociation which separates two notions constitutes an argu-ment. Consequently, it is the case of the couple means/end, individual/ universal, multiplicity/uniqueness, subjective/objective, theory/prac-tice, language/thought, character/mind, etc. It is the production of lines of opposition which give a speech its comprehensibility.

This is not a question of strictly taking up this division or even evalu-ating its strength but rather, highlighting the existence of a possible diversity of argumentative strategies which offer stakeholders an impor-tant field of possibilities. In public policy, using arguments is particularly common in persuasion processes. Stakeholders generally do not simply make their proposals heard or quote a stabilised statement; they take the time to use diverse and varied arguments to make their interlocutor adhere to their proposal. For example, it involves proving the solidity of the link between a proposal and the solution of a public problem by providing a series of complementary arguments to establish this link. These arguments can be of different types and can circulate depending on their stakeholders' interest in them.

While we have defined statements as institutionalised discourses intended to be imposed without argument, they are often severely put to the test when they are present within the processes of promotion, guardianship or destruction. The argumentative process should therefore be seen not only as a process seeking adhesion but also participating in the institutionalisation of discourses by transforming them into evidence.

4.2   Discussion as a test of persuasion strategies

In the previous section, we distinguished conviction based on the existence of a public audience that is large, impersonal and voiceless, from persuasion which assumes that the speaker targets a specific audience among whom he can inflect positions. We have also heuristically considered until now that the argumentative practice is independent of the reactions of the listener and of its impact on him. We would like to consider here that while real encounter is inevitable in persuasion, unlike in conviction, this cannot be contemplated as a simple monologue but, first and foremost, as an exchange or a discussion. Hence the listener does not simply listen to the discourse and the arguments of his speaker but asks questions, elaborates objections, raises doubts and critiques, and opposes arguments. Discussion therefore appears primarily as a test of the statement under construction and of the arguments supporting it.

Persuasion is consequently a specific type of discussion. On one hand is the speaker who uses discourse and an argumentative strategy. On the other is the listener who tests and through this shapes his own opinion of the discourse. Whether he adopts this discourse or not at the end of the discussion, this discussion will have contributed in testing the solidity of the statement and the arguments supporting it. While the results of discussion cannot be foreseen, we argue that discussion is an interaction whose outcome affects the listener, the speaker, and the statement itself.

Our argument on testing by discussion has already been developed within a different context by authors such as Boltanski and Thévenot (Boltanski and Thévenot, 1991). In their book, *De la justification*, these authors take a particular interest in how actors reach agreement through discussion. Actors focus on specific activities which are "public situations of dispute where action is confronted to criticism" (Boltanski, 2009). This therefore involves understanding how actors manage their disputes and emerge having reached agreement often during "reality tests". They state that,

> Justifiable acts are our focus: we shall draw out all the possible consequences from the fact that people need to justify their actions. In other words, people do not ordinarily seek to invent false pretexts after the fact so as to cover up some secret motive, the way one comes up with an alibi; rather, they seek to carry out their actions in such a way that these can withstand the test of justification. (Boltanski and Thévenot, 1991, p. 54)

This is how these two authors observe how agreements are reached within particular situations and how, during these discussions towards agreement, testing is carried out.

Boltanski identifies three types of tests (Boltanski, 2009). The first is the test of truth, meaning a test that involves confirmation. The second is the reality test which tests the compatibility of the approaches and the questions of the two interlocutors. Finally, the third is the existential test which is more directed towards offences. It is the reality test that has attracted the attention of most authors. In particular, it has made it possible to understand how actors seeking agreement must agree "on the relative importance of the beings that turn out to be implicated in the situation, whether the issue is, for example, the relative usefulness of two machines or two investments, the relative merits of two students, the competence of two business executives, or the tokens of respect that two local dignitaries owe one another" (Boltanski, 2009, p. 58).

Discussion as the testing of solutions

While we are interested in this notion of "testing" and would like to incorporate it within the public policy field, it is clear that we are not quite in the situation that Boltanski suggested. Be it promotion, guardianship, or demolition, the activities used within the public policy field do not necessarily fall within the context of dispute and, consequently, the imperative of justification.

In the different uses of persuasion that we have described, the stakeholders we analysed concentrated on increasing interest among indifferent actors and persuading undecided actors. Whether stakeholders discuss with opponents or not is of little importance. Rather, it is a question of understanding that a "dispute" situation is hardly general. We can even suggest that while negotiation and/or conflict are procedures that we come across when stakeholders defend opposing views, persuasion applies first and foremost in frequent situations where they are undecided, uncertain, or indifferent.

Consequently, in many situations that we encountered, the stakeholders with stable positions were not the only ones in opposition. The same was true for many undecided stakeholders who, through their indecision, occupied a central place in the promotion or the guardianship activities of the positioned stakeholders. In these activities, discussions and tests are fundamental in understanding the dynamics underlying policymaking.

Let us take the example of the reform concerning the housing policy in France in 1977. This reform was analysed in particular by Pierre Bourdieu who showed rather accurately to what extent stakeholders were clearly divided within a position-taking space. In this space could be seen the homothety between the positions taken and the social positions occupied by individuals (Bourdieu and Christin, 1990). There was therefore, on the one hand, a coalition of young bureaucrats from affluent backgrounds who bore a reform proposal that the author qualified as "liberal", and, on the other hand, a combination of older bureaucrats from less affluent backgrounds, politicians, and interest groups – guardians of the system in place. This relatively narrow vision sought to propose a genuine explanation of the stance taken based on position. However, it did not make it possible to understand how the reform was ultimately formalised even as one of its bearers, Raymond Barre, became Prime Minister.

This configuration offers a relatively timeless vision of the position of stakeholders. In other words, the process which makes it possible for a stakeholder to take a position that is often based on numerous discussions is overlooked. These positions unfold over time and it is interesting to follow the trajectories of proposals in the making. On the one hand are stakeholders transformed into "promoters", and others who position themselves first as "guardians" before becoming "promoters", convinced that reform is underway. They therefore turn their attention to the still undecided stakeholders who range from high-ranking officials to the President of the Republic, in order to persuade them to gravitate towards one position or another. Committed stakeholders do not attempt to persuade each other but rather race towards promotion.

The 1977 reform cannot be understood without grasping the progressive mutations of the proposal which, over the course of persuasion, constituted itself and was initially undesired by both camps. Moreover, it was not a simple result of negotiation between the two parties; it was the result of the twisting of a proposal tested through discussions and argumentations. In order to persuade the prime minister at the time, the stakeholders highlighted all the flaws and dangers raised by the first reform proposed. Certainly – and we shall return to this point – while they also attempted to create a power relationship, this relationship cannot be dissociated from stakeholders' demolition through argumentation.

Discussion as the testing of the relationship between a problem and a solution

Actors not only test solutions themselves but, more so, the relationships they establish based on the solution. This is the case of the relationship between the solution and its consequences or between a problem and a solution, for instance. As we stated in the previous chapter, the relationship between a solution and the problem it resolves falls within a limited causality where choice remains subjective and constructed. One must therefore focus on understanding how such a relationship is constructed, as well as how it is subjected to many tests within discussions around the proposal.

A proposal's legitimacy develops depending in particular on its resistance to argumentation during political struggles and technical disputes. On this issue, we argue that the relationship between a problem and solution is one of the most discussed relationships not only during visible and audible electoral debates but, more broadly, in more silent and discrete processes which are used within multiples spaces where public policies are discussed.

Such an assumption has consequences for one of the questions we evoked previously and which has continued to persist since the emergence of the garbage can model. It is worth repeating that Cohen, March, and Olsen empirically highlighted the existence of solutions which precede problems. In view of this, they concluded that reconciling these two elements was not rational and could therefore only be coincidental. Coincidence is nevertheless a simplistic solution that is hardly convincing. Kingdon, who takes up this model, expresses his doubts with regard to such a hypothesis by insisting on the role of "policy entrepreneurs".

How is it that solutions are associated to a problem by coincidence and at the same time, we rarely come across absurd or impossible associations? If solutions were associated to a problem coincidentally, we would witness surprising associations rather frequently. Within the public space for instance, nobody proposes that to solve the housing crisis, we must construct roads or improve health care. On the contrary, if associations were some kind of logical evidence, we would be rather surprised by certain associations which would transform unlikely problem/solution couples into legitimate couples, and particularly through solutions that precede problems. In other words, nobody proposes the construction of roads to counter the housing crisis. However, on the contrary, solutions frequently occur before problems, putting an end to all researcher attempts to construct a relationship *a posteriori*.

To some extent, a reasonable limit, or a rejection of the absurd exists and this means that a coincidence cannot suffice in understanding assembling processes. It is these limits that testing develops by defining the frontier of what is legitimate. These frontiers are thus not objective and we easily see that they can shift, transform, or are modified depending on contexts and on testing.

Testing arguments and statements must therefore be understood as a process where listeners test problem/solution unions and arguments in order to forge their own opinion. It is this activity that makes it possible to understand why the association of a problem to a solution, if it does not fall within a causal relationship, cannot be a coincidental or simple opportunity. Rather it has to go through an "obstacle course" to stabilise at the very least. Knowing whether the problem or the solution came first is of little importance; we must understand how actors end up considering a statement, which they deem together as being credible, before adopting it. Discussions must therefore be considered as both stabilisation and selection processes, as well as processes that eliminate projects which do not attract support. Obviously, as Gusfield has shown, there are proposals which actors do not take into account as their vision is rather biased.

Let us look at an example of this amazing process of testing problem/solution couples. One of the most famous and most significant in terms of empirical information is Graham Allison's study on the Cuban missile crisis (Allison and Zelikow, 1999). The author studied the manner in which the main leaders of the White House chose the naval blockade as a solution to counter the problem of the installation of missiles in Cuba. In this crisis situation, which could have ended up in a world war, Allison relied on the validity of several models of understanding in view of his empirical observations. Notably, he used Herbert Simon's and James March's model of organisational behaviour on one hand and, on the other hand, he used Neudstadt's model of political negotiation in a different part of the book.

In relation to the first model, Allison highlights that the naval blockade choice falls within a complex process which takes into account the bounded rationality of individuals and the constraints and organisational conflicts within which they evolve. As regards the second, he insists on the negotiation, which takes place between all political stakeholders, to reach a solution. The "blockade" solution thus finds an explanation in the cognitive bricolages that individuals carry out, the routines and the procedures, and the conflicts between semi-independent organisations. It is also explained by the persuasion and negotiation driven by the President in particular.

We have focused on discussion as testing in order to associate persuasion and negotiation practices to cognitive bricolage that has been dealt with separately in Allison's book. Validating a bricolage through assembling a ready-to-use solution and an emerging problem is at the heart of debate among stakeholders. Separating the thought processes of discursive practices from persuasion and discussion makes it impossible to understand the evolution which operates at the very heart of solutions and the manner in which stakeholders are able to identify a solution representing a compromise. The notion of testing is a reminder that no one actor or organisation can propose a solution without this proposal coming under testing through a complex game of argumentation, discussion, and negotiation. Through anticipation, the actors therefore limit the solutions whose coupling seems untenable. Certain solutions are rejected precisely because of their insufficient solidity. Assembling a diplomatic solution and the missile problem does not resist the criticism levelled against it by the leaders of the military staff, for example.

Obviously, this does not imply that the couplings with the "best" arguments are necessary but rather that critical twists which result in eliminating the weakest solutions are important. In other words, the capacity of statements to resist criticism and pass the testing that stakeholders put them through is a necessary but insufficient condition in imposing the implementation of a new solution. This therefore means abandoning the notion that stakeholders adhere to a proposal simply by seeing it and that the development of a statement and an argumentation is indispensable. Adhesion is a complex process necessary in the diffusion of a new solution and presupposes, at the very least, that the stakeholders consider the solution a "good" solution.

Discussion as testing the solution's owner

It must be noted that while these studies have highlighted the significance of analysis in argumentation, they have often neglected the second fundamental aspect of persuasion: promoting interest and testing the identities that all processes of this type involve. Discussions are not only spaces where solutions are tested, they also involve individuals who, by submitting to these tests, produce their identity.

It is important to understand that persuasion is difficult and costly for stakeholders. First, it engages and tests he who attempts it as well as the solutions and the arguments he uses. It also engages the individual who discusses the arguments and decides either to adopt the statement or not. Conscious of this commitment, stakeholders who wish to persuade must thus make use of their identity and take this issue into account when persuading, by promoting interest among their listeners.

Let us first begin by addressing the issue of the identity of the individual who engages in persuasion in order to promote a solution. This assumes that all stakeholders who test a solution and arguments also test themselves. Such an assumption can first be understood as the corollary of the interest we have paid to "discourse in action" rather than to ideas or discourses. The discourse pronounced concretely within a social interaction is what actually makes it possible to recall the inextricable nature of discourse and of the context in which it is stated. Solutions do not sail unaided; they are always accompanied by their promoter who states them and defends them.

Nevertheless, this inextricable nature does not suffice for understanding this relationship. To address it, we could first focus on a social practice that is rather common and which involves disqualifying the bearer of the solution in order to better destroy the solution itself. Considering that destroying the bearer amounts to destroying the proposal means that we maintain the view that there exists a strong link between the identity of the bearer and the tool's legitimacy. Disqualification as a practice has been notably analysed by authors interested in disputes, controversies, and public debates (Boltanski and Thévenot, 1991).

While demolition highlights the existence of a link for the proposal's opponents, observing promotion processes more directly makes it possible to underscore to what extent stakeholders often prefer defending a proposal whose ownership is not challenged. Through his empirical study on the Cuban missile crisis, Allison was among the first authors to highlight the link between a policy proposal and its bearer. While the Chief of Staff of the Air Force proposed an air strike as the solution to the problem, the Chief of Infantry proposed invasion – that of the Marine naval blockade, and the diplomat proposed a diplomatic solution.

While each actor defends his solution with his arguments when faced with a problem that must be collectively addressed, it is not simply an issue of "interest". Indeed, reflecting on the basis of one's interests leads to a sort of tautological reasoning: do they defend an air strike because it is in their best interests or is it in their best interests because they defend an air strike? In our view, it is preferable to speak of legitimacy and ownership. In order to be a legitimate actor during discussions, stakeholders favour proposals in which they have incontestable knowledge. If a diplomat were to defend an air strike or the army chief a diplomatic strategy, he would probably be told "you do not know what you are talking about".

This link between identity and the legitimacy of a solution is also visible when analysing how actors sometimes struggle to take possession of a solution. They do not only defend a proposal but also work towards integrating the solution within a zone where naming the owner is not up for debate. The individual's identity is therefore forged to a certain extent by the role he plays within the institution to which he belongs. The division of labour which organisations submit to thus participates in offering each stakeholder a role and an identity that he then must preserve or modify.

Obviously, we do not presume that roles constitute a key factor in understanding the processes of public policy but they contribute to it nevertheless. As Merton points out, a role is not only shaped by the individual who occupies it, but by the expectations and the outcomes of the social environment as well, and by all the roles within which it exists (Merton, 1965). While each individual occupies several roles in parallel at different moments, and while around the role exists what Merton calls "a smoke curtain", roles nonetheless bear resources, territories and conflicts. As a consequence, within bureaucratic systems, allocating roles makes it possible to organise the social space and establish individuals' actions as they structure conflict.

Association to a role and to an organisation is therefore an element of identity. It exists in many different ways. We find it for instance in the definition of the territory of problems. When municipality actors display a noise map of the city of Paris, this map stops at the capital city's borders not because noise ends there but because they have no legitimacy to cross the border at the risk of generating conflict by provoking the interest of new stakeholders (Zittoun, 2007). Interest and exclusion are thus an integral part of what is stated and of who states it.

Nevertheless, identity is not restricted to an assigned role. On the contrary, the transgression of roles can constitute an integral part of the enunciator's task to shape his identity. The proposal statement is therefore the very expression of a specific intention and of a particular identity. Moreover, it is often in the gap between a delay and the result that an individual's identity develops. Here we see the hypothesis developed by Michel Crozier which postulates that the liberty of individuals is expressed in their capacity to not do what is expected of them (Crozier, 1977). This is especially true given that each statement is a proposal of new action which participates in redefining frontiers and roles.

Connect, invade or avoid: battles within co-ownership

Making a solution statement is the first step for a stakeholder to become a policy proposal co-owner but, generally, it is far from sufficient. The existing or proposed solutions are often subject to battles and conflicts which reveal how difficult it is for a stakeholder to establish himself as the co-owner. It must be said that many measures do not only lack an obvious owner, rather they are also often situated at the crossroads between two or more owners. For example, because all solutions that require the mobilisation of budgetary resources reside at the crossroads of two ministries, the ministry which bears the measure must share its ownership with the ministry that handles the budget. Every solution which involves law must contend with the ministry that handles justice, etc. The appropriation of a measure thus often undergoes ownership battles whose objective is to become the sole "master on board". This form of ownership problems can also appear within a ministry, between two or more administrative departments, within one department, or within two or more administrative offices.

Every organisation and bureaucratic administration is organised based on the division of labour translated through the division of departments. However, because these divisions are rarely enough to determine who owns a policy proposal, ownership battles around a measure are rather common. Without claiming to be exhaustive, we would like to evoke three ownership strategies which we consider to be particularly frequent and significant, and which allow us to better grasp this appropriation process which is central in policymaking.

The first is the connection strategy. Stakeholders fight to develop a link between a measure under debate and a public policy which they incontestably own. It must be said that public policies often have an identified zone assimilated to the bureaucratic division of labour. The Ministry of Housing has therefore mastered housing policies; the Ministry of Transport, transport policies, etc. As a consequence, showing through argumentation that a solution proposal is linked to a public policy owned by a stakeholder corresponds to putting an "available" measure into a space within which ownership rights are undisputed.

In our studies, we analysed, for instance, the controversy on the reduction of speed limits in Paris (Zittoun, 2013a; 2013b). Two actors defended this solution: the deputy mayor in charge of the environment and the deputy in charge of transport. While both belong to the same Green political party, not only did they not combine forces to impose this solution proposal, but they also confronted each other in order to determine whether the measure was under the transport or the noise policy.

As we have seen, the link which connects a solution to a public policy is particularly weak. There undoubtedly exist arguments to show that this measure can be included in either of the two public policies. Nevertheless, the ownership issue makes it possible to understand why these two links cannot be combined. Each existing public policy established has a recognised owner. The deputy mayor for the environment does not dispute the fact that the transport policy is under the ownership of the deputy for transport and vice-versa. However, a new policy proposal has no evident owner. The fight for appropriation begins by an argumentative struggle to persuade the other stakeholders, starting with the mayor, that the new measure in question is part of "his" existing public policy. Here we can clearly see how the ownership issue is shaped. Each deputy mayor, when questioned on the issue of ownership, used the same argumentative strategy: not only did he claim ownership and disqualify his opponent who fought for "trivia", but he also underscored the incompatibility between the proposal and the policy belonging to the other mayor. Indeed, for the transport deputy mayor, the speed-reduction measure fell under the transport policy and would subsequently be factored into the deliberative process of the urban mobility plan, which was to last for a year. For the deputy mayor of the environment, the policy proposal was part of the noise policy and had to be integrated within the plan for combating noise that he was to present the following month. By transforming this appropriation issue into two incompatible choices, the two deputy mayors made consensus around a double appropriation impossible. Moreover, choosing between these two possibilities became a show of strength.

The stakeholders thus focused on two competing associations: the first associated speed-reduction to the traffic policy and the second to the noise policy. Beyond their capacity to defend the legitimacy of their connection, it was also their identity as leaders of a sector and of a public policy that was at stake. For example, the deputy for transport highlighted how he could lose his legitimacy by constructing urban mobility plans in which the speed-reduction measure was not included. Intertwining actor's game and language games within a statement which links both the proposal and the identity of its spokesperson, this connection process is nothing more than an appropriation game that consists of distancing certain stakeholders from the debate.

In addition to connection, we can identify other strategies such as those that concern invasion. We have already addressed the conflict that opposed the Ministry of Housing which owns the housing policy, and the Ministry of Social Affairs which owns the emergency shelter policy. When the Minister of Housing proposed a measure that he named "emergency housing", he invented a new concept that enabled him to gain access like a Trojan Horse to enemy territory without being challenged.

Lastly, the avoidance strategy is a fundamental strategy. For an actor, this implies being able to absolve self from ownership problems by developing a strategy that enables an actor to bypass the ownership of those whom s/he fears. In our studies on housing policy, we showed for instance how the Ministry of Housing increasingly confronted the Ministry of Budget, which fought to prevent all supplementary expenses. Faced with an increasingly strong adversary, the Ministry of Housing set up an avoidance strategy; it progressively favoured measures entitling tax benefits rather than budgetary opportunities. Consequently, instead of proposing an increase in the subsidy of financial aid when constructing a house, the Ministry of Housing favoured an equivalent reduction in VAT. While from an accountant's point of view the results are the same, from a "co-owner" point of view, the process is different. To spend more, one must fight with the budget department of the Ministry of finance, while to obtain a reduction in revenue, it is the tax department of the same Ministry who must be confronted. It is clear that actors seem to find avoidance easier, as there was an increase in tax deduction measures in the 2000s.

Searching for a new co-owner, interessement within discussion

During discussion, a solution's promoter therefore tests himself as he tests the solution and the arguments that he uses. However, he is not alone; the listener who discusses with the promoter also finds himself confronted with identity issues.

To grasp these identity issues, it is first necessary to situate the listener with respect to the promoter's intentions. The promoter can seek to simply present to his interlocutor the validity of his proposal or even the legitimacy of his identity. In this case, we can question the reasons which motivate the promoter to spend his/her time and energy. We can therefore suppose that the action of persuasion is not free; it requires identifying what the promoter hopes for when he gets involved in this action.

However, the most interesting case of persuasion is visible through the stimulation of individuals' interest and appropriation. As owning a proposal involves associating the owner's identity to a measure's legitimacy, a stakeholder cannot take ownership of the solution proposed by the promoter in a neutral manner. Indeed, simply consenting is not sufficient; there must be an interest in co-owning it.

We therefore propose to empirically study discussion as an activity of stimulating interest, meaning an activity in which the promoter attempts to interest his interlocutor in the solution. To empirically grasp this process, we must first revert to the concept of interest that is rather complex to use. It must be said that researchers often use this concept to objectify their behaviour by defining the "interest" in acting on behalf of the actor. Consequently, as we have stated previously, this is tautological; "interest" becomes both the justification of behaviour *a posteriori* and its motor *a priori*.

David Easton highlighted the ambiguity of such a concept in political sciences, underscoring to what extent the term is ambiguous as it interweaves subjective interest, that is the one the actor gives himself and objective interest, that is, the one given him by the observer. As Easton stresses, it is considered that groups act according to their interest (Easton, 1965b).

While we are primarily interested in the "subjective interest" that the actor gives to himself, the objectification of this interest by promoters rather than by the researcher, interests us just as much. Indeed, we would like to use the "interessement" concept to point out the persuasive activity that a promoter drives in order to show his interlocutor that it would be in his best self-"interests" to also become an owner of the solution, not only because the solution is "good" but also because it is compatible with his identity.

To better grasp the "interessement" concept, we can use Michel Callon's definition of the subject: "Interessement is the group of actions by which an entity (here the three researchers) attempts to impose and stabilise the identity of the other actors it defines through its problematisation. (...) The properties and identity of B (whether it is a matter of scallops, scientific colleagues, or fishermen) are consolidated and/or redefined during the process of interessement" (Callon, 1986, p. 186). The promoter primarily acts depending on what he imagines to be his interlocutor's interest. Interessement therefore refers to the promoter's objective interest. Discussion is where this interest is tested in the way the actor himself perceives his interest. This means that while interessement does not necessarily entail appropriation – it can contribute to it.

The mutation of solutions as the cost of appropriation

Just as persuasion does not necessarily turn into discussion, discussion does not necessarily lead to appropriation. As interessement does not always result in appropriation, we need to focus on this phase in a specific manner, as well as on the conditions that make it possible. While the success of appropriation is often determined empirically, it often leads to the mutation of underlying solutions and arguments. This process is somewhat similar to tagging which makes it possible for a new owner to identify with a proposal.

The solution's mutation must be understood via pragmatic testing itself. As we have seen, promoters are quick to adjust their arguments and solutions to their interlocutor. Interessement is thus already translated by a possible twisting of the solution and arguments to make them compatible with the interest imagined by the promoter. Discussion as testing is also translated by the possible modification of a solution and of its arguments. An argument that is swept away too quickly during discussion can disappear from circulation. Another argument "tested" for the occasion can, on the contrary, show its effectiveness. Stakeholders thus test the connections and interpretations they have established. This process can also lead the promoter to permanently abandon an argument, place a new one in his repertoire of available arguments, or even modify the solution.

On the contrary, interlocutors can not only make it difficult for the arguments and solutions proposed to succeed through critical argument but can also state the compatibility conditions of appropriation. In other words, they can condition their appropriation to the actual mutation of the solution. As a consequence, testing makes it possible for interessement to blend with appropriation.

The example of tramway line tracks studied by Benoit Demongeot effectively illustrates the process of statement mutation. Demongeot shows how in Marseille or Grenoble promoting actors' interest with regard to the tramway solution is translated by a series of mutations of the layout as well as of the device. Over the course of persuasion, we therefore observe both increasing curves in the tramway line as well as an increase in the attributes of the object itself (Demongeot, 2011).

Obviously, these curves have a limit. This means that the track, while it has never been straight – as it follows both physical constraints and political agreements, is nevertheless not an endless coil. Within mutations, "reasonable" character, "facts", or "objects" are part of the testing processes.

Although unsystematic – and we will come back to this point later – the mutation of a solution during discussion is essential. In particular, it makes it possible to grasp the key moments when persuasion is efficient, when actors define the conditions of their agreement, and when a solution proposal takes shape. From this perspective, the mutation of solutions is somewhat presented as the cost that interlocutors request to begin appropriation.

4.3   From persuasion to diffusion, building discursive coalitions

So far, we have focused on the personal relationship between individuals in order to better underscore the significance of concrete discursive exchange in propagating solutions. This has made it possible to emphasise that the transmission of a solution from one actor to another is a complex and costly process and that we would be wrong to overlook its analysis and comprehension. We would now like to step back and analyse this phenomenon on a slightly larger scale. In particular, we would like to focus on how this interpersonal phenomenon can be associated to that, more meso, of building coalitions. Our first question therefore concerns determining how persuasion processes which operate in a scattered, singular and disorganised manner, combine to enable the aggregation of actors around the same policy proposal statement.

Theories that have focused on the aggregation of actors have insisted on the prior existence of a network linking individuals among themselves. Each time, networks have been both the cause and the consequence of the aggregation of actors. Paradoxically, these theories have been unable to link actors' configuration to public policy. They are thus unable to explain the variation of coalitions depending on the projects, or the mutation of projects depending on aggregation. Our assumption here is that while the existence of frequent relations between actors can largely facilitate coalition building, a fact widely demonstrated by these authors,[8] it is insufficient in understanding how a shared solution is developed. By considering that agreement on solution statements forges the link between actors, we propose, on the contrary, to cement actors' coalition building and the development of solution proposal statements. A statement under construction is not only what actors propagate, but is also an object which mutates depending on aggregations and becomes the cement of a discursive coalition. The institutionalisation of common discourse and the relationships between individuals thus forms one process which results in a discursive coalition.

Following propagation to reconcile solution statements and discursive coalition

In order to associate actors' configurations to their proposals, we define a discursive coalition as all actors who share a joint solution and focus on the process by which a policy change statement and discursive coalitions are jointly developed and institutionalised. We therefore assume that it is the institutionalisation of a joint solution, what we have named the construction of a policy change statement, which unites actors and constitutes the cement of the coalition. This implies that the successive mutations of a solution illustrate coalition building.

This assumption makes it possible for the empirical situation to express and illustrate by itself the varying contours of actors' associations in a contingent manner. Moreover it makes it possible to associate an interpersonal action of persuasion through discussion to the building of a discursive coalition through the propagation of these discussions and convictions. The propagation of a solution therefore functions like a microbe which cannot propagate itself without contact between two individuals but which, with each propagation, boosts the number of its bearers and increases the contagion phenomenon. To put it differently, although a solution can arise from a very limited number of initial bearers, its propagation, which gives solidity to the discursive coalition, increases the number of potential defenders and therefore the possibility of propagation. The propagation process therefore becomes increasingly powerful as new actors are assembled. It is important to note that the more widespread a solution, the more it stabilises and becomes solid and can therefore easily convince. The intersubjective making of likelihood is therefore a self-sustaining phenomenon which reinforces itself with time, if it works.

It is this propagation and institutionalisation experience that we focus on. We need to apprehend it empirically and see it grow or on the contrary, stagnate, or even retreat. To achieve this, we need to increase both the number of discussions to be observed as well as the study duration. Undoubtedly, changing the scale poses major epistemological and methodological problems as it tends to make these moments of interaction invisible. Only the selective memory of actors, of which we know the methodological limits, or continuous empirical observation – largely impracticable over long periods – can make it possible to distinguish the two. However, it is by reflecting on the nesting and compatibility of an instantaneous process and of a process spread over time that comprehension can be achieved. In other words, changing the observation scale should by no means be a pretext for the researcher to exonerate himself from the reality he observes, as is far too often the case. We thus observe that persuasion takes place within concrete spaces and, when it succeeds, is part of a larger movement of discursive coalition.

To make these two types of observation compatible, we will use the statement concept both as the form on which actors agree and as an object which propagates and diffuses itself. Shifting from discourse on the solution to stable solution statements makes it possible to understand the interpersonal movement, the collective movement and the structural link between content and a gathering.

The conviction imperative to develop a joint public statement

The manner in which we have chosen to define a discursive coalition makes it possible to place the solution which cements it at the centre of its fabrication. However, it does not resolve all the problems posed by nesting at the micro level where persuasion takes place, nor at the meso level where discursive coalitions and statements are formed. We need to reflect, in particular, on how actors pass from persuasion (where a statement and specific arguments are developed) to a coalition regrouped around a joint public statement. We would first like to suggest that actors are subject to a conviction imperative; in a sense, they know that they must present their statement to a large public to convince it (convince in Perelman's meaning of the word) towards the end of the policy process. This imperative pushes them to consider joint public statements within persuasion and propagation during the earlier steps.

Before addressing the anticipation process, we must first evoke the phenomenon that we have named "conviction imperative" in more precise terms. Policy-making processes generally pass through a publicising phase and cover a public space in one way or another. A tramway relies on consultation before a municipal council, which checks its cost and its route. A housing recovery plan passes, at one moment or another, through the Council of Ministers and the National Assembly.

Notwithstanding these institutional phases, projects are often presented for debate by the stakeholders themselves via press conferences and other disclosure processes. During this phase, stakeholders must publicly expose a statement on their policy proposal and present arguments to justify it. Consequently, they are subject to what we call the conviction imperative, meaning they must seek to convince a universal audience that the tool they propose makes sense and should be implemented.

Conviction therefore concerns a statement and a repertoire of arguments that actors make public. While a statement and arguments can vary from one stakeholder to another, there always exists a common core, nonetheless, which displaces conviction from its orality and inscribes it in a codified text. This codification constitutes the common and visible core of the statement. This is a fundamental element that makes it possible for a proposal to travel from the decision-making field to that of implementation, meaning from actors in charge of the decision to those who must implement the measure. In other words, this codified formulation is the condition which makes it possible for a measure to break away from dependence on its enunciators and defenders and join another group. The codification of public policy has often been neglected because it does not make it possible to understand the often multiple interpretations that actors make of it, or the implementation of a measure which often had its own logic. Indeed, this codified formulation is the manner in which stakeholders define a sort of culmination within their action. It is on codification that stakeholders collectively base their agreement.

The installation of a tramway is codified by the project's text and by the map of its route submitted to the vote of elected representatives of the municipal council. It then leaves the realm of certain stakeholders and joins another scene where, within the framework of the text and the map, the conditions of construction are discussed. The discussion on its implementation can be found in particular in the Finance Law. Speed reduction in Paris exists first within a text before being put on a road sign.

By no means do we claim that this codification always exists. A technician could place a speed-limit sign in the absence of a text voted within the municipality or signed by the police commissioner. It is possible as well for a driver to destroy the sign which would suddenly lead to the disappearance of the limitation requirement which cannot exist in the absence of the sign. It is also possible that the sign will not lead to any adjustment in the driver's behaviour, making it unnecessary. Finally, it is possible for the police commissioner to decide, or not to decide, whether to delegate two police officers next to the sign to penalise those exceeding the limit regardless of the fact that no codification has taken place.

Let us put aside for the moment all these multiple forms of public policy and focus only on the cases in which codification exists. Here, we will focus on the support material on which a statement is engraved before its implementation. Although this undoubtedly involves multiple interpretations, it is possible for actors to interpret personal care for instance in numerous ways and to project its evolution in different ways as well as the problems it can resolve. But regardless of these multiple interpretations, actors have to agree on a reference text: legislation, a decree, a law, etc.

It is thus based on these material codifications that actors reach an agreement at a given moment, fight, come together, or oppose each other. These codifications say nothing of the reality of what action becomes but rather focus on how actors end up reaching an agreement over a statement. It is this codification that we focus on here because it constitutes what actors must agree on at a minimum. The tramway is a concept but, when associated to a tram layout, it begins to have a debatable materiality before its fabrication. Stakeholders can more or less agree on the stakes of the tramway, on its prowess, and on its virtues (Demongeot, 2011). They can forge distinct associations. For some, the tramway is the best means to upgrade the city while for others it is an efficient transport system. In many cases, we note that the bearers of these interpretations ultimately come together to defend a single joint public statement to the extent that they become one indivisible coalition. In such a case, it is interesting to analyse how the aggregation of a new mayor to the defence of the tramway and the curving of the route become inseparable. The layout thus symbolises both the flexibility of the public statement but also its limitations, as no route is strictly zigzag.

From this point of view, although this depends on subjects, the notion of vagueness is neither satisfactory nor sufficient. Vagueness or multiple possible interpretations always exist but this is hardly the issue. In most cases, there exist projects on which stakeholders must reach agreement, and these constitute the smallest common denominator of the coalition.

Mutual adjustment to shape a joint public statement

The process of building a coalition and making a joint public statement can therefore be envisaged as the result of the progressive assembling of a coalition's stakeholders. As the coalition grows, a joint solution emerges and is institutionalised and transformed into a joint statement.

One only has to think of this process to understand the fragility of assembling stakeholders as well as of the mutation of solutions.

While a statement mutates each time a stakeholder joins, or small groups of stakeholders join, the coalition there is no evidence that this mutation will be accepted by all stakeholders. Each mutation facilitates assembling but weakens the pre-existing equilibrium. It is rather like the wooden game where each one adds an element to the structure with the objective of enlarging it and giving it weight, but this could collapse each time a new element is added.

To understand this process, we have borrowed the concept of the "mutual adjustment" of actors and of a joint statement from Charles Lindblom, who is undoubtedly one of the actors who has had the strongest intuition for this type of phenomenon. While his mutual adjustment concept in his first studies was in reference to the "invisible hand" theory that he had borrowed from economics, in his later works he focused on persuasion and mutual adjustment based on actual contacts. He used the term negotiation to underscore that it covers too many distinct possibilities and evoked the notion of mutual persuasion between policymakers.

According to him, this term makes it possible to underscore that A seeks to persuade B or that A and B seek to mutually persuade each other. In either case, Lindblom insists on the importance of understanding this phenomenon not only based on its results, which could simply be considered as manipulation, but also with regard to how he who attempts to convince must adapt himself to the situation and modify his words and his attitudes (Lindblom, 1990).

Lindblom first questions the coordination process. He poses a rather simple question: How do actors coordinate themselves without a coordinator? This is an issue that he borrows from economics which analyses the invisible hand linking Brazilian agriculture to the American coffee drinker and for which he develops the mutual adjustment concept. He thus underscores that this is coordination between individuals that does not respond to established rules. This does not imply limiting the use of concepts to simple coordination between political leaders and their decisions. Lindblom first highlights the interdependence of leaders and decision-makers. In particular, he stresses that coordination must be understood as a process, and not as a result, driven by individuals with multiple and varied values in order to reach agreement on a decision.

To put it differently, while the decision-making concept was until then primarily considered as an individual process, either depending on bounded rationality or not, Lindblom made decision the result of a collective process. Admittedly, he is not the first; he referred in particular to the studies carried out by Truman (1951) and Bentley (1908) who highlighted the influence of interest groups in the decision-making process. However, the process he studied was more subtle and complex as it did not consider that an agreement between individuals resulted from a compromise between a few groups but, rather, highlighted the existence of multiple adjustments which made it possible to make the divergent interests of interdependent individuals compatible.

Consequently, Lindblom showed that among 15 individuals participating in a process, the combinations which made mutual adjustment possible were multiple. In particular, he distinguished discussion with a view to cooperation and mutual adjustment. In the first case, individuals seek to develop common objectives through discussion. In the second, actors are primarily individuals who act depending on their own objectives, their own definition of public interest, and conceive their interrelation as a nexus of conflicting relationships. This is what Lindblom called partisan mutual adjustment which assumes a series of individual adjustments among stakeholders who pursue their own objectives in order to make collective decisions.

Lindblom identified two major possible forms of adjustment among stakeholders. The first was adjustment through adaptation. X makes a decision and Y somewhat adapts to it. The second was adjustment through reciprocal manipulation. X and Y interact. Their interaction can be a negotiation, a trade-off, a partisan discussion or compensation. It is not necessarily symmetrical and balanced but primarily an exchange.

After defining the different forms of mutual adjustment between two actors, Lindblom showed that this process existed on a large scale within government and was combined with a form of hierarchical coordination. He therefore suggested that numerous autonomous stakeholders exist in government: political leaders, ministries, interest groups, Members of Parliament, and ministers. It is undoubtedly the partisan mutual adjustment which enables them to coordinate either bilaterally or on a multilateral basis. In other words, stakeholders participate in a vast system of reciprocal manipulation to achieve coordination.

This is how Lindblom sought to identify different forms of mutual adjustment within a decision-making process with multiple decision-makers, common in governmental action. He underscored the extent to which the synoptic model – that is, the model that relies on absolute rationality – was pegged to a model of central coordination and decision-making by a single actor. A decision-making process is thus inevitably detached given that the strategies which each actor drives are disintegrated and scattered.

Lindblom thus defends a notion which is not easy to demonstrate but which nonetheless deserves attention. Indeed, he considers that mutual adjustment develops through the strategies that stakeholders develop to resolve their problems. In other words, what is common is the difficulty they encounter to resolve complex problems. The multiple mutual adjustments they contribute to thus enable them to reduce a problem's complexity, starting with a fragmented and disjointed treatment of the problem. Following is Lindblom's conclusion which he himself qualifies as paradoxical: The more the interdependent decision makers, the easier the coordination process.[9]

Mutual adjustment is therefore a means of analysing how individuals coordinate themselves without necessarily reaching agreement on common values. However, stakeholders must agree on the solution. Lindblom takes the example of a project that sought to extend social security benefits. Although their values were different or even opposed, the stakeholders were able to come to an agreement. Ambiguity in the meaning and the values of a reform is thus an integral part in building agreements. Put differently, participants need not agree on a vast whole regrouping of a reform, its meaning, and its value; rather, agreement is needed on the effective and concrete part of the decision.

For Charles Lindblom, it is through this process that decision-making processes operate. He attempts to show that centralised decisions do not comply with democratic issues. He denounces the monopoly of power and the definition of public interest to show the importance of approaches where power is multiple and distributed and where coordination by mutual adjustment makes it possible to produce "intelligent" decisions.

Similar to the "science of muddling through", Lindblom alternates between the description of a reality in which he sees: a power that is fundamentally fragmented and a decentralised coordination device which he names partisan mutual adjustment; a normative approach which demonstrates the intelligence of these devices; and a prescriptive approach which points out that these decisions must be developed through mutual adjustment.

This normative and prescriptive pull blurs how decision-making processes are understood despite the fact that Lindblom proposes a strong hypothesis concerning the plurality of authority and the complex processes of multiple adjustments through discussion and negotiations primarily using action tools. However, it facilitates reflection on a heuristic concept intended to highlight a meso phenomenon based on multiple micro interactions. It is no longer simply a matter of reporting the existence of a network; rather it is about understanding that the network is the means through which a solution is developed and a joint statement stabilised around it.

For us, mutual adjustment primarily operates through persuasion and anticipation of the conviction imperative. As stakeholders are aware that they will be subject to publicity, they take this into account when testing the solution they defend. They anticipate the need for a joint statement that they will have to defend publicly, as well as the "solidity" of the arguments they will have to present. Consequently, we observed the manner in which the Prime Minister used the arguments received from the Minister of Economy and Finance to test the housing stimulus proposal from the Ministry of Housing. Before giving in, he tested the statement implying that boosting housing is a means of boosting the economy, and also questioned both the validity of the statement as well as its resistance to criticism when made public (Zittoun, 2000).

We can thus speak of a joint public statement and arguments that we distinguish from discourse on specific solutions, on the one hand, and, on the other, arguments which contribute to the specificity of persuasion developed within discrete interactions. Agreement is achieved both through preparing a joint public statement and constructing singular discourse. While a joint public statement does not fall within singular interaction, maintaining an individual within the coalition must be understood based on its interpretation of the often growing gap between the joint statement and specific discourse. Mutual adjustment therefore underscores the permanent friction which contributes in building a coalition around a joint public statement on policy proposal. It also makes it possible to reconcile the micro-observation of persuasion processes and the meso approach of coalition building and of statement stabilisation.

4.4 Conclusion

As no policy proposal can emerge without the support of a certain number of stakeholders, the definitional activity of a proposal cannot be dissociated from the building of agreements which enable it to gain support from a group of actors larger than its first originators. The propagation of a proposal, far from being obvious, is therefore a key issue that the promoters of a solution must resolve. For this, they must be able to persuade actors to join in their quest by being active militants in order to attract the attention and interest of/from new potential owners. This is subsequently based on their ability to produce convincing arguments, on the one hand, and on the other, their ability to redefine the solution and make it appropriable. The aggregation of actors thus presents itself as inseparable from the redefinition of the proposal solution and the consolidation of the statement which gives it meaning. The links which connect the different elements of the statement, subjected to the difficult tests of discussion, therefore find themselves consolidated.

Thus, it could be said that the gluing we evoked in the previous chapter cements itself over the course of coalition building, leading to the building of a coalition-statement. This curious assemblage is thus composed both of a joint public statement and a series of subjective and discreet statements which are like interpretations and variations of the proposal statement for each actor who has adopted it. This idea is based on the notion defended by Bruno Latour and Michel Callon that "scientific facts" consolidate themselves over the course of the construction of networks which support them (Callon, 1986; Latour, 2006). Nevertheless, our conception of networks which only associate human beings through the intermediary of discourse that supports proposals is rather different. Here, discourse is the means which makes it possible for actors to reach an agreement amongst themselves and to structure collective action – action that seeks to resolve a problem encountered by society.

5
Policy Statements to Legitimise "Decision-Makers"

In the previous chapters, we have seen that actors define solution proposals within statements that give them meaning and build coalitions in order to support them. While this process makes it possible to understand how actors come together to defend a common proposal, it is insufficient in explaining how a solution is imposed and ultimately transformed into a decision. Certain proposals supported by coalitions and possessing "solid" arguments thus stagnate continuously without turning into "decisions". Others encounter conflict or opposition, which relegates them to the cemetery of proposals that never see the light of day.

In this chapter, we would like to pursue the idea that elaborating a solution is also based on a definitional struggle of roles and positions in which individuals seek not only to impose a decision but, especially, to impose themselves as "decision-makers" with regard to a solution. Researchers notably refuse to attribute this title to actors. They consider that a decision is primarily the product of a complex, intertwined process that combines the action of multiple individuals taken within spaces with significant constraints. Nevertheless, actors can fight to take ownership of this label or distribute it. This does not imply questioning the objectification of the "decision-maker" title but rather observing the definitional struggles between actors with regard to this label. The ordered world that discursive coalitions seek to design during the policy-making process is therefore not only one of a world where problems are resolved and where public policies change but also of a world where decision-makers decide and governments govern (Zittoun, 2009a).

In general, the entire hierarchy of social positions within a topographic map is played out or replayed with each policy-making process.

Some actors attempt to show that they play a role within this hierarchical space, and have enough "weight" to influence "decision-makers". Unlike in the previous chapter, this is not simply an identity issue but also a power issue.

To address the power issue within the decision-making process, we would first like to revert to the complex relationship that links the positions' space to the position-taking space. Numerous authors consider that taking into account an asymmetric space of positions is incompatible with a discursive perspective, which seriously considers the influence of arguments and the variations of the positions taken within discussions. To overcome this difficulty, we need to consider the asymmetric space of positions, not as the result of a researcher's objectivity but rather as a representation that actors develop and attempt to share or impose with each new instance of public policymaking. Subsequently, the policy-making process appears as a central political activity that also orders the social space and organises domination through discourse.

5.1   The paradoxes of taking positions into account

Considering positions within policy-making processes that take into account discursive practices is a particularly thorny issue. Indeed, there exist two approaches that both focus on the dimension of power in discourse. The first approach considers that language is primarily a weapon that governments use to reinforce their dominant position. Executive power thus depends on the asymmetric division of power, and language is simply a tool that supports it. On the contrary, the second approach considers that power resides within language, in the strength of arguments, and the reasoning that leads to the inflection of actors' positions. Here, the actor's position is of minor importance.

As a consequence, these two approaches have often been considered as incompatible. As Hannah Arendt argues, an approach that focuses on persuasion or a practice that refers "to an equal order" is not identical to an approach based on an authoritarian order "which is always hierarchical".[1] This incompatibility leads to a paradox that must be overcome in order to explain policy-making processes.

Propaganda: political discourse to enable elites to maintain power

Many authors have focused on the role of language as a tool that nurtures actors' dominant position. Since the late 1920s, Harold Lasswell, for instance, focused on the relationship between power and language through a study on the methods of propaganda used during the Second World War (Lasswell, 1927a). Over the following decades, he enlarged his field of study to widely diverse contexts, such as India or Chicago, in order to better grasp the political significance of discourse (Lasswell, 1927b; Lasswell and Blumenstock, 1939; Smith et al., 1946; Arora and Lasswell, 1969; Namenwirth and Lasswell, 1970). In his studies, he focused in particular on the choice of words and symbols within discourse, a choice which in his opinion contributes to legitimising the elite in place.

In his book, *Who Gets What, When, How?*, Lasswell (1936) shows how the disappearance of the term "union" in presidential discourses after the Civil War, and then "United States", which replaced it after the First World War for the benefit of "America", helps disseminate and impose a certain idea of a Nation and legitimises the elite who govern it. He also insists on using emotions in discourse (e.g., aggression, guilt, affection); a tactic used by elites.[2]

In the edited volume, *Language of Politics, Studies in Quantitative Semantics* (Lasswell and Leites, 1949), Lasswell focuses on language's capacity to have a political effect in terms of legitimising elites and dividing power. Based on this type of effect, Lasswell suggests invoking the political function of language. He thus insists on all types of influence, including unexpected and unintended effects. It is not language for language's sake that interests him but rather language because of its effects. Under what conditions do words affect authority? What symbols (words and images) influence authority or the hope for authority? These are the questions underlying his studies.

Lasswell uses the example of myths to show how language is a tool that legitimises authority. For him, myths are images, formulas, diversions, and ideologies. He therefore establishes that both economic theories and scientific proposals have sometimes served as political doctrines. Beyond doctrines, political myths are also used in the elaboration of social norms, in defining what is good or bad, or what is right or wrong. They can also be used to forge symbols and identities.

However, while Lasswell argues that language is political because of its impact, his studies paradoxically focus primarily on discourse. He thus studies the content of discourse by focusing on repeated patterns. Consequently, he examines discourse and searches for patterns such as "the enemy is a menace" or "the enemy will be conquered" within the political discourse of the First World War (Lasswell and Leites, 1949).

While the author ponders the significance of repeating certain formulae, and questions the existence of a link between this repetition and its impact within or on society, he does not provide an answer neither in his book nor in the more sophisticated comparative study that he carries out in 1969 between India and the United States. This latter study focused on the analysis of the discourse of elites and its evolution in accordance with key historical events (Arora and Lasswell, 1969).

Political language as the mystification of elites to legitimise themselves

Among the wide range of studies that sees political discourse as a form of legitimisation, we would like to refer back to Murray Edelman's studies. Following Lasswell's work, Edelman insists on the importance of language and interpretation in domination processes. His studies provide a clearer vision of the political role of language based on its capacity to structure conflicts and its impact in terms of legitimising leaders and immobilising opponents.

Edelman places the production of discourse and language at the heart of political activity. In his opinion, political language "is political reality; there is no other so far as the meaning of events to actor and spectators is concerned" (Edelman, 1988, p. 104). He thus considers that what matters is not political events but rather the discourse around them.

Consequently, within a world of language marked by the ambiguity of each statement, interpretations are marked by battles and oppositions. The author therefore takes the example of government policy, such as the increase of the defence budget or the extension of social benefits, to underscore that they give rise to opposed interpretations. The extension of social benefits can be interpreted either in terms of the human dignity it brings or as encouraging laziness.

Within a political sphere characterised by differentiated battles and issues, the plurality of interpretations around a decision becomes a conflict zone adapted to their expression. Actors thus fight to impose their own interpretation. They choose their words to convince the public that their interpretation is the best even if this means making them believe that war brings about peace or that the death penalty or owning weapons decreases violence. For Edelman, interpretation corresponds to the mystification of power, which seeks to reconstruct the past and build the present by showing data that is generally unobservable.

Edelman therefore argues that politics is primarily a spectacle made up of actors pronouncing discourses which first seek to legitimise elites in dominant positions. While the issue of governmental action is central, the discourses that they study are always postliminary. Edelman is thus confronted with the same paradox as Lasswell. While he takes an interest in political discourse for its legitimising effects, he focuses his analysis only on discourse that he deconstructs and simply evokes his expected outcomes.

Technical and scientific language as another form of legitimising elites

While numerous public policy analysis authors have built their studies around a critical study of methods of rationalisation,[3] the production of a technical and/or scientific discourse began to be studied in the late 1960s in the same manner as political discourse. Put differently, it began to be studied as constructed discourse whose greatest difficulty is to legitimise the elites who defend it.

In the late 1960s, Habermas' studies on technical and scientific rationality marked a turning point with regard to the approaches that considered scientific production as an alternative to ideology (Habermas, 1973). Habermas thus defines what he calls a strategic activity; this he distinguishes from a communicative activity in which discourse seeks to influence the behaviour of others. This approach inspired many authors working on public policy who took an interest in the legitimisation process that accompanies the production of technical discourse.

From this perspective, Frank Fischer's work on *Think Tanks* is particularly revealing of this tendency. In an article entitled "Policy Discourse and the Politics of Washington Think Tanks" (Fischer and Forester, 1993), he proposed to study the strategies of public policy experts in the Johnson administration. He illustrated that the expertise of these experts was not neutral. On the contrary, this expertise provided a series of technical arguments legitimising liberal solutions that the government sought to implement.

More precisely, Fischer criticised the idea that there exists technical and neutral information capable of sustaining democratic deliberations and decision-making processes. He showed that this idea widely prevailed at the end of the war upon the creation of public policy analysis. It developed a category of experts and specialists that he qualified as the new technocratic class. According to the author, these experts largely sustained political parties over many years. During the Johnson era, they were the Planning, Programming and Budgeting System (PPBS) promoters and largely contributed to the agenda setting of a liberal policy. From the mid-1960s, public policy research became a genuine industry sustaining think-tanks, university institutes of research, and consulting agencies.

Fischer noted that in the 1970s, conservatives also took on this "battle of ideas" by multiplying the links between them and public policy experts. They favoured the emergence of some form of contra-intelligentsia which gave them legitimacy. These experts provided arguments to reinforce proposals and, by using complex and technical language, eliminate them from democratic debate. It is based on this that Fischer endeavoured to demystify technical production produced by these experts and suggested their reintegration within democratic debate.

The importance of the asymmetry of positions and speaking rights

In all these approaches, language is a domination weapon. It makes it possible to underscore to what extent the enunciation of language cannot be addressed without taking into account the effects it produces in terms of legitimisation. In his studies on the role of language within domination processes, Pierre Bourdieu enriches this perspective by insisting particularly on what he names the effects of position.

Bourdieu first develops a critique of the studies that take language seriously. He criticises Austin and Habermas in particular for overlooking what he calls the effects of position. In his opinion, language efficiency, notably in terms of authority and domination, does not fall within logical characteristic of language but rather is outside of it.[4]

To support this critique, the author evokes what he considers to be one of the key oversights of these theories: the study of the moments that precede discussion and make it possible. It is necessary to focus on the person who speaks and to take an interest in the conditions that make their speech possible. Similar to Homer's skeptron, which is held out to the person who is going to speak to signify his authority to speak, Bourdieu underscores that behind every speech act exists a reality of social positions and unequal speaking rights. Consequently, Bourdieu explains that the weakening of religious discourse has less to do with the evolution of the forms of discourse than with the entire legitimacy of religious institutions that support it.

While Bourdieu makes unequal social positions a decisive factor in social relationships, he nevertheless does not neglect the significance of discourse. Language must be considered as a weapon – a weapon that can be efficient if the position of the one who pronounces it is taken into account. The legitimacy of the situation in which the speaker pronounces it and the legitimacy conferred to the speaker by those who listen to his/her discourse must be considered as well. For Bourdieu, "symbolic power requires, as a condition of its success, that those subjected to it believe in the legitimacy of power and the legitimacy of those who wield it" (Bourdieu, 2001, p. 173).

Admittedly, Bourdieu's challenge is in knowing how to reconcile his belief that authority is "outside" language and to justify that language nevertheless plays a key role. Why would actors use language as a weapon if authority is developed outside language? Bourdieu criticises Saussure for introducing a radical divide between internal linguistics and external linguistics: "between the science of language and the science of the social uses of language" (Bourdieu, 2001, p. 159). Curiously, despite this critique, he deepens this divide: "The power of words is nothing other than the delegated power of the spokesperson, and his speech – that is, the substance of his discourse, and inseparably, his way of speaking – is no more than a testimony and one among others, of the guarantee of delegation which is vested in him" (Bourdieu, 2001, p. 161).

By seeking to combine the inequality of positions and the power of language, Bourdieu ends up depriving language of all power. Consequently, by so doing, he is no longer able to explain a phenomenon that he also identifies: why do actors place as much emphasis on language if position is exterior to language?

Persuasion and conviction: communicative or strategic activities?

However, if, as has been suggested by Bourdieu, Edelman, and Lasswell, the positions' space structures the position-taking space, does the persuasion activity that we analysed in the previous chapter really have its own efficiency or is it simply a decoy with regard to the positions held by actors? Is the weight of the arguments used by actors linked to content or rather to the position of the person who makes the statement? Put differently, taking up the distinction proposed by Habermas, should persuasion be considered as an activity that is primarily communicative or strategic?

Indeed, Habermas (1999) suggests that communicative action should be distinguished from strategic action. The first is a communicative activity in the strictest sense. It takes place when actors coordinate their action plans using linguistic communication, by taking advantage of illocutionary forces specific to speech acts. According to Habermas, interlocutors work towards establishing an agreement during discussion and are considered to be autonomous and flexible.[5] They use language to declare their intentions, understand the intentions of the other(s), and establish an agreement that is shared intersubjectively. In this model, it is within exchange that the common reason for agreement is built.

Strategic action is an activity that also uses language to make it possible for actors to understand each other. Unlike the previous action, it does not refer to equal actors who build a common understanding but rather to unequal actors who mutually influence each other. One's speech limits the free will of the other who finds himself blocked because of his language and because of the manner in which he structures his thoughts. Habermas thus speaks of the communicative activity "in the weakest sense" to indicate that as interested parties coordinate their action through their reciprocal influence on each other, language is not used in a communicational way, but rather it depends on consequences. He therefore uses Austin's concept of perlocutionary acts, which highlights the effects of a speech act to better underscore that a strategic activity is primarily characterised by the fact that actors act depending on the success they would like to obtain, but always in such a way that the illocutionary effects dominate the perlocutionary successes.

The distinction that Habermas proposes nevertheless poses a problem when it concerns applying it to the empirical activities that we described in the previous chapter. First, conviction, whereby an actor expresses a proposal publicly in order to make it legitimate to a broad public, is similar to a strategic activity. Conviction is organised primarily depending on an expected outcome – gaining adhesion – and the communicative activity remains insignificant, involves little exchange, and is one-sided. In such cases, the illocutionary act is developed primarily for perlocutionary success, but, paradoxically, as the effect cannot be perceived by the speaker, it is hypothetical and the action remains dominated by actors' intentions.

Nevertheless, conviction cannot simply be considered a strategic activity without any real communicative dimension. This dimension is the only one that takes into account the mutation of public statements that we have evoked. By means of indirect discussion, actors who present a proposal are confronted by critical arguments like objections, oppositions, and challenges, which often push the speaker to transform his statement in order to consolidate it. A pragmatic analysis of debate shows that the process is not simply unidirectional without any attempt at building agreement, and as a consequence, position-taking spaces do not solely depend on position spaces.

Persuasion, which is the second type of activity that we studied, is an even more complex case than the previous one. This activity relies on arguments, interest, and discussion which make it possible for the owner of a proposal to share it. Actors thus seek to build agreements within a process of intersubjective understanding, and this corresponds to a communicative activity in Habermas's strictest meaning.

Nevertheless, these discussions are not used in a position space in which each actor is equal. In public policy-making processes, positions such as mayor, minister, head of department, or expert cannot be considered as equal. Moreover, persuasion primarily seeks to make interlocutors adhere to the proposal. Put differently, persuasion also has many characteristics of a strategic activity.

Is it then not paradoxical to consider conviction and persuasion as both strategic and communicative activities? In order to understand the efficiency of persuasion or conviction, the aforementioned authors incite us to choose between an explanation linked to the position of actors and one centred on the content of their speech and the significance of their discursive exchanges. However, in public policy-making processes, the position as well as discursive exchange both appear to play a major and inseparable role.

Unbalanced interactions: position as an issue

To take into account both the asymmetry of positions and the impact of exchange, we can also focus on a set of approaches whose common point is considering power as an asymmetrical relationship rather than as an attribute linked to an asymmetrical position. While these approaches do not consider an asymmetrical position as the objective element, they remain vague on the status of position.

Many studies have questioned the construction of power within relationships rather than within positions. While these approaches known as relational approaches are very diverse as Braud (1985) has shown, they all consider the domination that presupposes both the action of the dominators and the acceptance of the dominated as central. As Max Weber explains, domination is an opportunity for an order to encounter docility (Weber, 1995, p. 95), and it is different from force. He defines this concept as "sociologically amorphous" because of myriad personal qualities and situational permutations that enable a person to impose their will in a given situation (Weber, 1995, p. 95).

Domination is therefore a relational concept that relies both on the intentionality of he who gives an order as well as on the one who accepts it. Weber thus insists on the fact that each genuine domination relationship includes, at minimum, a will to obey and, consequently, an external or internal interest in obeying. It is at the heart of this phenomenon that he develops his concept of legitimacy, which relies on the acknowledgement of this domination by the dominated: all domination seeks to awaken and maintain belief in its legitimacy.

Nevertheless, one of the major difficulties of these approaches is based on the ambiguous manner in which position is addressed in this relational context. How indeed, can we consider that a relationship is unbalanced without taking into account the "weight" of positions? And if we take into account the unbalanced "weight" of positions, how can we say this imbalance is relational and not positional? In other words, how can we tell whether the dominators dominate because they hold a dominant position or because they are accepted by the dominated?

This difficulty had already been identified by Weber. He sought to distinguish force, which only takes into account the intentionality of the person who gives the orders and the effects of this order, from domination, which must also take into account the intentionality of the person(s) executing the orders. However, it is not easy to identify this intentionality. Does an individual who responds to an order suggest that s/he believes in the superiority of the other? This is what Weber calls "belief in legitimacy" and he distinguishes it from "claimed" legitimacy. Is it because the other is superior, in which case, power becomes an attribute? Would s/he have responded, nonetheless, meaning power no longer exists? Is his/her response influenced by a third party such as rules, contracts, etc.?

To illustrate this difficulty, we can take Robert Dahl's famous definition of power.[6] Dahl takes the example of a road where vehicles circulate. He explains that if a policeman were to position himself and ask the vehicles to turn to the left, while the drivers' intention was to continue straight ahead, and that the vehicles follow his instructions, we can then say that the policeman had power over the drivers. In this example, power is based on a relationship; the policeman has power only if the drivers agree to his instructions. This is unbalanced between the two parties as one influences the behaviour of the other.

In this example, the policeman's position is central in grasping the imbalance. Indeed, we can imagine that if the driver had ordered the policeman to move out of the way, he would probably not have executed this order. The disparity of positions is therefore a fundamental explanation to understand the unequal "weight" of actors and the imbalance in the relationship. Consequently, in analysing the concept of power as a relation, we must focus on the "weight" of actors.

To exonerate themselves from this "weight", authors such as Michel Crozier have insisted on the importance of context, which can make this weight vary, and negotiation, which makes it possible to underscore the existence of a counterbalance. Crozier (Crozier, 1964; Crozier and Friedberg, 1977) takes the example of a rich and important person in touch with a roof repairer, that is, two actors occupying unequal positions within the social space. The author therefore shows that power is built within the relationship between the party that has a request, the important individual, and the one who has a benefit and negotiates the price in turn. To understand who has power, Crozier suggests focusing on the context and "relevant" resources. If the repairer is the only one in the region and the roof problem is urgent, Crozier argues that it is the repairer that has power. On the contrary, if many competitors exist, the relationship swings in the other direction. If these competitors have struck an agreement on their fees, the important individual no longer has power.

Crozier thus suggests that the weight of actors is relative to the context, which is capable of inversing dominant positions and making it possible to grasp a relationship as an exchange structured around the definition of the benefit, on the one hand, and its pricing, on the other. However, once the "weight" is determined by the context, Crozier does not attribute any autonomous place to exchange, discussion, and persuasion. Although relative, the weight of actors always remains objectifiable once the content is known. This "weight", once fixed, determines the relationship. However, in the persuasion activity that we have previously described, the "weight" of actors is not only relative, but it also becomes subjective and depends on how the actor sees it or tests it.

5.2 The definitional issues of a topography of positions

To surmount this impasse, we would like to consider the position of actors as the result of a definitional activity of actors themselves. Each of these constructs a contingent topography of the position of actors, which enables them to act strategically. This definitional activity is relative, as it depends on each actor and on his/her interaction. It is also contextual yet pragmatic, as it depends on the experiences that actors drive when they test these power relationships. This means separating researchers' perceived objective position, which is developed through the observation of unbalanced actors' empirical relationships, from the position perceived by the actors themselves and the manner in which this perception guides their actions. This position constitutes the third definitional issue around which the agreement of actors amongst themselves is structured.

To grasp this definitional activity, we would like to evoke three aspects of the policy-making process during which this activity is visible and identifiable. The first, which was highlighted by Pierre Bourdieu, occurs when choosing the interlocutor to persuade. This activity takes place upstream and is indispensable to actors, as it enables them to use a genuine promotion strategy. It is based on a topographic activity in which the positions of the different "important" actors are defined. The second aspect concerns the intention of the promoter who seeks to influence actors' position-taking regardless of their weight. To put it differently, those actors who are not subjected to an imperative of coherence easily entwine what researchers are unable to combine: the weight of actors and the weight of arguments. The efficiency of persuasion is therefore partly based on the capacity of actors to cement this curious combination to their proposal.

The game of labels in defining a topography of positions

The game of labels does not only concern problems or solutions; it can also apply to participants. These labels can apply to the role that an actor would like to play or that is attributed to the actor in the policy-making process. They also determine the actor's "weight", which makes it possible to situate the actor's importance with regard to others. Each actor therefore attempts to draw a topography, that is, a map highlighting the high points which ensure a dominant position and, in contrast, the low points. Although they also contribute to identity construction, we sought to distinguish this type of label from identity issues evoked in the previous chapter that do not necessarily presuppose a topographical comparison.

We would like to begin by briefly presenting the different types of position labels that exist. First, there exist labels which are the most commonly known and the most "official", which are those that indicate position within an organisation. These labels are given by organisations themselves and are particularly characterised by structures that are highly hierarchical. Within the department of a ministry, we therefore find the head of the department, deputy directors, heads of office, and project leaders. This means that there exists a hierarchy which actors can get support from at given moments in order to inflect a process. Public policy studies have often sought to show that these structures are inefficient, privileging "flat" concepts such as those of networks and coalitions. While these labels in no way imply the influence of individuals or their actual importance in policymaking, they nevertheless have a fundamental role, as we will see below.

The second type of label involves a specific position with regard to the decision-making process. The "decision-maker" label is undoubtedly the most interesting, as it characterises the high point of this topographical process. It can be sought by an actor for himself or for others. Once again, it is not for the researcher to determine whether the individual who bears the "decision-maker" label is the real decision-maker or not, but to grasp how actors fight to obtain or couple this type of label to their battles within policy-making processes.

The "decision-maker" label thus makes it possible for an actor to claim his authority and assert his dominant position during the decision-making process. This labelling process is particularly present in the public discourse of political leaders. It largely contributes to underscoring their usefulness, their ability to resolve problems, and ultimately legitimises the position they hold.

This fairly classic notion is found for instance in Edelman's studies which evoke the "construction of political leaders". Edelman (1988) focuses in particular on the language games that envelop the "leadership" concept and the significance of these games in projecting the ideal image of the decision maker. He thus emphasises that it is the ability to position himself as a representative of this ideal type that enables a leader to maintain his popularity. Edelman therefore completes the picture by insisting on the importance of the differentiation process that makes it possible for a leader to differentiate himself from his adversaries by making "good" decisions. By claiming decisions, the leader shows that he is legitimate in the position he occupies, and, moreover, that he is better than his competitors and contenders in the same position.

However, what is complex in this type of work is understanding labelling only as a process situated *a posteriori* which has no influence on the decision itself. Our only interest in labelling concerns the influence it has on the process itself. This means not only taking into account the anticipation of actors who know that the announcement *a posteriori* of a "decision-maker" is a key element in the decision-making process but also, more importantly, considering that it plays a fundamental role in the construction of actors' strategies.

The "decision-maker" label is nevertheless not the only one that plays a central role. There exists a third type of label which constitutes a topography of the decision-making process. This label makes it possible for actors to situate themselves with regard to the high point, which is the decision-maker. Actors do not therefore hesitate to claim their "weight" or claim their "influence" on the "decision-maker". This process makes it possible for them to assert their role and their importance and situate themselves with regard to other actors situated lower than them within the topographical space.

Defining a topography of positions, an indispensable prerequisite in the persuasion process

The game of labels and the topography that it illustrates plays a fundamental role in propagating a proposal. If an individual seeks to persuade another, he must, as Pierre Bourdieu suggests, be capable of responding to these questions: Who should be chosen? Why is one individual chosen to be persuaded over another? Conversely, why does the chosen individual respond and engage in a discussion?

We therefore argue that this topography of actors is a necessity that makes it possible for the actors to define their strategy by identifying not only the individual to convince, the "decision-maker", but also those who, within this topographical space that emerges, are likely to influence this person.

To propagate a solution, an actor cannot simply give it meaning and persuade the first stakeholder who comes along. Actors' actions are not random; they choose the stakeholder to persuade depending on the results they seek to obtain. In the policy-making process, where the challenge is to transform a proposal into an effective solution, actors develop their own vision of who decides, who has power and who does not, and who is influential and who is not. The issue here is in determining how this topography guides the actions of actors. In the same way that actors quickly glue a solution to a problem – even when the proposal is not the solution to the problem – they quickly produce a topography of stakeholders and define positions, thereby situating themselves to act. We therefore seek to understand how this topography makes it possible for actors to come up with a strategy and give meaning to their actions.

Indeed, one need only observe the manner in which actors empirically structure their persuasion activity to understand that this does not depend on random encounters but rather on their representation of the key stakeholders who could influence the success of their project. Encounter, discussion, and persuasion are not trivial phenomena; they are costly in time and energy. An actor who seeks to propagate a solution must develop a genuine strategy as their time is limited. The researcher must therefore understand that it is the definition of this cartography at a given time t, which enables the actor to select the individual that the actor would like to persuade.

Considering actors' representation of power to understand their action is an issue that has been repeatedly addressed. However, as Braud

(1985) highlighted, this notion has primarily been used to explain certain specific phenomena, such as the phenomena of anticipation and submission. He thus evokes the notion that actors sometimes comply to an order even when it has not been expressed. We would also like to focus on this notion. In particular, we would like to focus on the capacity to formalise a strategic thought for action by the actor who seeks to persuade. If we take the example of the noise policy in Paris that we analysed (Zittoun, 2009b), it is particularly interesting to observe the extent to which most actors seek to persuade the mayor, in particular, to implement speed limits and the extent to which the mayor, conscious that he lacks the decision-making power to make a decision in this issue by himself, seeks to persuade other actors that he considers to be "important". Knowing whether the mayor has power is of little importance; rather we need to understand the subtle game of the selection of relevant interlocutors.

This idea of the strategic selection of actors is also present in studies that were carried out on the cross-regulation system in France during the 1970s by Jean-Claude Thoenig and Michel Crozier (Crozier and Thoenig, 1975; Crozier and Friedberg, 1977). Their studies made it possible to underscore the extent to which the reality of actors' practices has little to do with the assumed models of comprehension of their official positions. In this particular case, it is the centralised model of the French political system which is empirically observed through concrete practices.

Without focusing on persuasion in particular, Thoenig and Crozier show how the game of influence is constructed depending on a cartography that associates assumed powers and attainable relations. All citizens in the same city are likely to call on the mayor, either in solicitation or in protest, as they consider him as the key figure in decision making. However, although this might not be the case in this highly centralised era in France, calling on the mayor reinforces his legitimacy when he constructs his strategy to convince other relevant actors' to adopt his project. To reach government leadership that he considers to be the influential level, he uses a crossed strategy that makes it possible for him to find allies. The road engineer, a civil servant who is a technical expert, is the first ally in this process.

Thoenig and Crozier do not focus on the conditions that make it possible for the mayor/road engineer coalition to come into being and on how each one persuades the different levels in concrete terms. They consider this association as evidence and thus overlook the conditions of success or failure of such a coalition depending on projects and situations. They thus enable us to underscore the importance of actors' strategies of selection in influencing the decision-making process.

The strategic capacities of an actor and his competence in elaborating complex thought are revealed here. Their perceived asymmetry is thus not merely a flat hierarchical pyramid. On the contrary, actors' thoughts are complex and perceive the plurality of the sources of power. They thus construct their strategic action on the basis of this complex perception.

In Neustadt's (1960) study, he notes the extent to which the President of the United States selects "key" senators he considers important and thus structures a topography of the senators to persuade in order to put a bill through. In other words, even the President of the United States uses a strategic process to select the actors he considers valuable. This therefore means that the strategies that actors use need to be analysed during persuasion, as well as when the actor selects the person(s) to persuade. The subjective topography of an actor is therefore the manner in which he constructs his own model of the asymmetric distribution of power to develop his strategy that then enables him to act.

For discussion to take place, there is nevertheless a second condition that we have not evoked as of yet. This involves accepting the encounter. Accepting or refusing to meet someone also expresses one's intention, although this is much more complex to grasp. Indeed, complexity results from having to understand the process that leads to acceptance or rejection. A mayor or minister rarely manages his own agenda. The agenda is structured around multiple selections and diversions by those who manage it and this can complicate the task of the individual who requests a meeting. This makes it particularly difficult to understand refusal or acceptance. This is an issue that undoubtedly requires further empirical study.

In any case, when an encounter takes place, there exists a prior agreement marked by the intentionality of the person who requested it and the acceptance of the receiver. According to Bourdieu, this prior agreement is generally overlooked by those who are merely interested in the discussion itself. We consider that it is during the making of this agreement that power issues are partly developed.

We can equally evoke the encounters that take place within the administration and that are based on a topographical protocol that a department head can only meet with another department head, an unwritten rule which nevertheless structures administrative practices. The only exception to the rule, but one which also structures this cartography of positions, is that which links a department head to an office head (a level that is hierarchically inferior) when the latter belongs to the budget department.

Persuading an "important" stakeholder: the combined influence of position and argument

During the persuasion process, actors seek to address "important" stakeholders whose power they recognise, with the intention of influencing their position-taking through persuasion. Put differently, they acknowledge the power that comes with position but at the same time use arguments in order to exercise power over them. An actor's activities cannot determine the outcome of the exchange in advance. These activities are thus structured by combining an asymmetrical conception of positions, which enables them to determine who should be persuaded. Moreover, belief in the power of arguments enables them to inflect the position-taking of the latter.

While we have observed the difficulty that a researcher faces in combining an asymmetrical definition of the position of actors and persuasion, this difficulty does not appear to exist empirically for the actors themselves. Indeed, they have no difficulty relying on a subjective construction of a topography of stakeholders, thus acknowledging the dominant position of those they address, while refusing to consider that this domination hinders all influence. On the contrary, actors who approach stakeholders they consider to be positioned above them hope to inflect their position-taking through their arguments.

To understand the complexity of this double process, one must take into account that the choice of the interlocutor does not only reveal the existence of a subjective topography of positions, but defines it as well. By choosing the stakeholder to persuade, the proposal bearer accords importance to his interlocutor and positions him as one who "must be persuaded". In so doing he gives him a status, which he contributes in defining or stabilising.

Persuasion activities not only contribute to defining the position of others, they also participate in defining the position of the promoter who carries them out. First, his commitment to these activities is marked by his belief in their possible efficiency. The actor who seeks to persuade thus defines himself as being capable of having influence and, therefore, as an "important" actor. Why engage in such an activity if this leads inevitably to failure, given the gap between positions? Promoters who seek to persuade "decision-makers" consider the encounter both as the acknowledgment of respective positions – being received by a decision maker is already a form of acknowledgement – and, in parallel, their results are filled with uncertainty as position-taking does not depend on position alone.

This complex process between acknowledging the asymmetry of positions and the uncertainty of the relationship can be explained using an analogy that we can make with a boxing match between a challenger and a world champion. For the encounter to take place, each boxer must have acquired the label which permits him to participate in the fight. The challenger chooses to encounter the champion precisely because he acknowledges this asymmetrical position. If all the boxers would like to encounter the champion, on the contrary, part of the champion's power is linked to his choice concerning the challenger that he accepts to encounter. Defining the asymmetrical position not only constitutes a necessary precondition for the encounter but rather is reinforced by the acceptance of the two fighters to be in the same ring. This is particularly true for the challenger who is only genuinely considered as a challenger from the moment when the encounter is programmed.

However, while the boxing match takes place only within the reciprocal acknowledgement of the position of each boxer, it is also necessary to understand the motivation of the two fighters based on the uncertainty of battle. It is because the challenger can take the place of the champion that he commits to the relationship. Conversely, it is because the champion can reinforce his position that he accepts this commitment. Thus our boxers illustrate not only how a topographic approach of power can be combined with relationship uncertainty but also how the two associate in order to understand the motivation and the strategy of actors.

In public policymaking, many situations far more diverse than that of a boxing match exist. There is therefore no federation that regulates fights and declares the winner. Nothing prevents several stakeholders considering themselves as "decision-makers" either because they hold a position towards which those who want to defend a new proposal turn, or because they have been able to persuade a stakeholder bearing an official "decision-maker" label. Moreover, the topographic space has multiple positions, not only with regard to "decision-makers" but also individuals who consider themselves, or who are considered to be "important", be they "experts", "advisors", or "specialists".

Defining a position as legitimising arguments

While the topography of positions plays a role upstream, it can also have an impact during discussion. During discussion, a stakeholder does not only expose an argument to establish a statement; he uses his position explicitly or implicitly to provide reinforcement. The definition of the topography of positions thus becomes an argument that intertwines with others to facilitate persuasion.

Defining a position can reinforce an argument without making it indispensable. A technical argument, for example, will be more efficient if its spokesperson explains to his interlocutor that he is a recognised specialist in the domain in question. Stakeholders thus define themselves to their interlocutor by situating themselves in a topographic space where their domination is unchallenged.

Evidently, this does not mean that defending a single dominant position is sufficient to impose an argument. Rather, it is about grasping the complexity of the topographical space which is not a one-dimensional space – with those who dominate and those who are dominated placed on the same line – but a space with several dimensions that make it possible for actors to superimpose plans through which they can project their position.

During discussion, actors can thus use an argument which reiterates their own definition of their position with regard to their interlocutor or that of other actors whose advice it is important to consider. In these position arguments, we have included all that seeks to reinforce a statement through the legitimacy of he who bears it.

This legitimacy can result from specific knowledge or competency for which the stakeholder claims mastery. For an economist, this argument could be something like "you know, I got my degree in economics" or "I am a recognised specialist" or "all economists will tell you the same". For a housing policy expert, this can involve seeking recognition owing to his role in the community of experts or to the institutional positions that he occupies. Legitimisation can also come from the institutional position that one occupies. This makes it possible to use a hierarchical label when stakeholders belong to the same organisation. Using the label can be more or less explicitly accompanied by a reminder about "who has the last word". Finally, legitimisation can be channelled through the supporters that the actor claims to represent. Asserting to be a "representative" stakeholder of a profession, an interest group, or a category of individuals who are more or less numerous also means presenting oneself as the "leader" or the "spokesman" in order to establish one's arguments.

The argumentative activity is not organised around one source of legitimacy but rather is established on distinct forms of legitimacy, some claiming knowledge and the others hierarchy, for example. By taking into account the plurality of the sources of power, it becomes possible to understand that a conflict unfolds during interactions, not only with regard to power relationships but also to the selection of the forces which confront each other.

Persuasion through force

Arguments on position thus play a fundamental role in persuasion. They serve to remind us that, while arguments on truth must be taken seriously, those on authority should not be overlooked. While in most cases it is difficult to disentangle arguments on position from arguments on position-taking, as the two are entwined, we would like to address particular occasions when a stakeholder agrees to a statement compelled by arguments on position without seeking other arguments.

We can identify two different situations. The first is based on the idea that the actor is persuaded of the validity of a proposal's content given the dominant position of its promoter. The promoter thus uses his dominant position within a sector to share his perspective. To illustrate this type of situation, we can take the ideal-typical example that Herbert Simon proposes. He describes "suggestion" as an exchange where conviction often results from the social transmission of a statement of facts, even in the absence of proof (Simon, 1945). Put differently, actors succeed in persuading their interlocutor without using arguments and this makes it possible to attest that position plays a fundamental role.

Simon cites the example of a doctor who proposes medication to a patient without needing to prove the pertinence of his choice or the effectiveness of the medication. In this case, the doctor transmits to his patient a statement which cements a solution – medication – to a problem, disease. In the absence of argument, it is the actor's position which reinforces the statement and makes it legitimate. For this process to take place, the patient must have made an appointment with the doctor, that is, he must have acknowledged the doctor's dominant position.

The concept of suggestion that Simon highlights interests us less for the phenomena it shows – as the absence of argumentation is less usual in public policy – but rather because it also underscores the significance of position during statement transmission. Simon therefore insists in particular on the phenomenon of suggestion and on the social status of the individual suggesting. The importance of status and its acknowledgement, as in the case with experts, is essential. This example makes it possible to highlight that the strength of an argument also varies depending on the position of he who bears it.

The second situation is where stakeholders disagree on the statement but seek to reach agreement on the asymmetry of positions in order to determine who gets the last word. Consequently, the challenge is no longer persuading interlocutors of the validity of the statement but rather of one's relative position. This is rather common in public policymaking. It exists for example within internal administration battles when two administration directorates fight over a proposal.

The challenge for both of them is to first determine the conditions of agreement depending on their respective force. This can be achieved by the joint identification of an arbitrator, of a procedure to resolve the contentious issues between them, and/or via the exchange of arguments on the definition of the respective positions.

The budgetary procedure is a classic example during which the budget department clashes with new costly proposals of ministries it calls "spenders". Stakeholders find themselves in opposition with regard to proposals and are hardly interested in convincing each other of the validity of their position. Their argumentation is first based on their capacity to mobilise arbitrators who will make it possible to define a cyclic power relationship and determine their respective positions as well as their proposal or opposition.

The effectiveness of persuasion in testing defined positions

While an encounter contributes to the definitional activity, its outcome tests these definitions. We have evoked the testing of the content of statements and identities. We would also like to take the testing of defined positions into account.

When propagating a proposal statement, promoters argue depending on their position. A stakeholder who claims to be "influential" sees the definition of his position tested during the process that unfolds. Should he accept to adopt the statement proposed by his interlocutor, his position, as he defines it, is subjected to testing. This therefore involves distinguishing the illocutionary discourse of actors, which defines a topography of positions, from their perlocutionary effect which makes it possible to question the impact of persuasion.

Let's go back to the previous doctor and patient example proposed by Simon. The actors mutually acknowledge their position even as they make the appointment. When the doctor proposes medicine to the patient, his position of authority is put to the test. After the appointment, if the patient goes to a pharmacy and buys the medicine, the doctor's position is strengthened. However, if the patient prefers to consult another doctor or decides against taking any medication, their relative position changes. The efficiency of the illocutionary act thus tests the doctor's position.

During the policy-making process, actors do not simply define a topography of positions constituting a "decision-maker" and "important" stakeholders capable of influencing the decision-maker. An actor tests his strategy depending on the efficiency of his encounters. To put it differently, an actor who seeks to propagate his idea begins meeting stakeholders one by one depending on the position he grants them. Nevertheless, the topography he designs is rarely rigid. On the contrary, he knocks on several doors and hopes that one of them will open. The topographic activity therefore often falls within a pragmatic approach of testing which makes it possible for stakeholders to grope, try, attempt, refine, or even modify the topography of their position with each experience. The definition of positions is therefore not fixed but rather tested with each encounter. Persuasion must thus be understood as an illocutionary discourse awaiting a perlocutionary effect that is able to stabilise or strengthen it.

Take the example of noise. It is interesting to note that the promoters of solutions, such as enacting speed limits, often knock on many doors in order to sell their proposal. They do this depending on the topographical definition they have constructed with regard to the positions of the "decision-makers" but explore many options to boost their chances. Testing positions therefore enables them to readjust their topography. If an "important" stakeholder capable of inflecting the mayor's position-taking is unable to achieve his objective, he risks losing his label as an important stakeholder.

5.3   The "decision" to fix topographies within statements

As we have previously observed, the topography of positions is a representation which largely contributes to structuring actors' strategies and the power games in which they seek to blend. This topography acts upstream in persuasion processes, during the selection of the choice of interlocutors and based on the weight of arguments. These positions are nevertheless subjective, contingent, and relatively unstable.

During policymaking, the stabilisation of these unequal positions is thus a major challenge in making it possible for an actor to receive recognition for his position and even make it visible. To achieve this, actors often include their position within the statement itself as well as when fixing the statement as it transitions from the "proposal" phase to the "decision" phase. Decisions must therefore be understood not only as the means through which actors transform a proposal into a solution but also register their position sustainably.

Consequently, while a policy proposal statement can be shared and makes it possible for numerous stakeholders to claim ownership, inscription within a topography of positions that identifies "decision-makers", "experts", and "important" stakeholders is not widely shared and pushes them to fight in order to impose their own definition. Conviction and persuasion thus make way for battles and/or negotiation.

Twisting proposal statements under the weight of labels

The definitional activity does not only have an impact on the interaction between actors, but it can also influence the proposal itself. As a proposal statement can reflect a topography of positions, one must focus on the manner in which stakeholders attempt to modify a proposal to make it reflect their own position. The twisting of proposal statements that we previously evoked during the cementing with problems and identities can similarly be found in the defining of positions. Statements are also the tracers of this topography and can therefore falter depending on the weight of the position labels. Nevertheless, unlike the two other forms of twisting, faltering under the weight of stakeholders' positions is generally the result of a battle linked to an exclusive process.

A policy-making process therefore generally passes through a phase of conflict during which a coalition built around a statement can be confronted by a stakeholder or an entire coalition supporting an alternative proposal statement. In such a case, conflict lasts even longer as the statements that reflect position are mutually incompatible. It is often a question of "contrasting" or "deciding" between alternatives that have become immeasurable. This does not mean that it is not possible to associate the two solutions or find a compromise but rather to understand that semantic debate does not only take place with regard to the proposal itself but also to the position.

The conflict in imposing a solution is also a positional challenge, often interactive, in which stakeholders develop complex strategies that make it possible to differentiate themselves from each other. This conflict is present in most public policy processes, as it is especially rare that a proposal does not require the mobilisation of stakeholders with "equivalent" positions for whom differentiation is at stake.

This conflict obviously exists between the defenders and opponents of a policy proposal that defines a new position. However, even more often, the conflict involves a particular aspect of the proposal that stakeholders determine using a range of several incompatible alternatives. The most frequent case is the budget dimension of a proposal, which gives rise to conflicts that we have already evoked between the budget and "spending" ministries, but it is not the only one. We have defined the position tracer as the site in which stakeholders confront each other.

Let us take a few examples to illustrate this process. The conflict around speed limits in Paris that we evoked earlier is a particularly revealing example with regard to this process. As we explained, this proposal opposed two deputy mayors when developing the speed limit. Beyond the conflict around ownership, we would also like to grasp conflict as topographic. In this example, stakeholders did not seek to persuade each other or develop a joint statement but, by making their statement incompatible, they established the conditions of a definitional challenge with regard to position which then made it possible for one party to claim victory.

Let's take as a second example, the Grenoble and Marseille tramway (Demongeot, 2011). We highlighted ownership stakes earlier and how these stakes are translated in the curving of layouts. However, the layouts remain unique and, when they are validated, they not only fix a "good" layout, but they also fix stakeholders' positions. These positions differentiate between important mayors, who have succeeded in having the tramway, and those who are not important, as well as between experts with a straight layout and mayors with a more curved layout. The layout thus makes it possible to fix positions and power relationships at a given moment. The tramway layout, genuine tracer of asymmetric positions, is therefore the principal object around which stakeholders battled.

These two examples show how stakeholders analyse their proposal in order to identify the tracers of their position, enabling them to battle it out. In the tramway case it is primarily the layout; in speed reduction, it is the perimeter and the procedure. While no rule in this area has been set to identify the tracer of positions, this is often linked to stakeholders' ownership spaces.

Decision as a myth or chronicle of a death foretold

The integration of topographic positions within a statement is a complex and competitive process. This competitive process is not resolved simply through persuasion and assembling actors around statements but also notably through the transformation of either of these statements into a "decision". A decision can thus be considered as the moment when stakeholders fix a statement. Before we go any further on the role of decisions within policy-making processes, we need to revert to this particularly controversial concept that poses many problems.

The decision concept is a concept that has been examined by researchers who have questioned whether it matches reality. Highly popular in the 1950s and the 1960s, decision as a research theme progressively disappeared in the 1970s and the 1980s. Associated to the notion that there is a specific moment when a specific stakeholder makes a decision, the concept was highly criticised by authors who showed that this did not correspond at all to the empirical reality that it was expected to describe. In addition, it was victim to a surge of public policy analyses that were increasingly process-based, and this overly synchronic concept drowned with time. The gap between real phenomenon and the concept as it was defined is thus behind the disappearance of these studies on decision. To effectively grasp the problems that this concept of decision tackles, we must briefly revert to the criteria addressed by these authors.

Critics of the decision concept share a common reasoning that is relatively analogue. Authors first define the decision concept by showing the reality it is expected to highlight, then by observing the reality and the absence of a match with the model in question. For researchers, this implies that the model does not arrive bare but rather is charged with content and that the role of the researcher is defined in the unveiling of an unbalanced reality and the demystification of the concept that stakeholders use. In France, one of the authors who has significantly contributed to the demystification of decisions is Lucien Sfez (Sfez, 1992). His studies interest us as they reveal the movement which brought decision to an end and, furthermore, they open up rather interesting alternative avenues to his own criticism.

In his book, Sfez takes a critical view of classic theories of decision in order to show the limits and errors, and he frequently sweeps away the absence of solidity of these theories (Sfez, 1992). The author explains that a decision corresponds in no way to what researchers and stakeholders say of it. He therefore criticises both the decision-makers who think they decide, and the authors who also believe that the decision-makers decide.

The critique of decision is therefore primarily a critique of what Sfez considers a dogma and illusion. In his book, *L'Enfer et le Paradis*, Sfez "crosses swords with the producers of truth who are political representatives" (Sfez, 1978, p. 15). In this book, he strives to disclose what lies behind the use of the decision concept by the decision-makers themselves, thereby lifting the illusions of such a dogma.

Moreover, the author draws a parallel between the knowledge available on the "decisions" concept and decision-makers' practices supported by this myth. Decision disappears at the same time as a certain conception of centralised and rationalised political power, common in the 1970s. According to Sfez, decision exists but is not grasped with the knowledge that we possess. He thus carries out a dichotomy between knowledge and phenomena, all the while criticising such a dichotomy. This is why his criticism sometimes deals with a phenomenon that we misunderstand, and at other times, of a concept that we poorly define, without clearly differentiating the two.

The function of myths in the decision-making phenomenon

If decision as a concept is a myth, does this mean that the concept plays no role in the decision-making process? It must be noted that actors who promote a policy proposal generally use discourse on decision-making processes. While this discourse does not describe the phenomenon as it really is, we cannot neglect this ongoing process. By inquiring about the decision-making process, we clearly observe that actors do not only have a subjective representation of how the decision-making process functions, but also use it to build their strategy and choose the interlocutor to persuade. How can an actor, convinced that decision making is primarily a fragmented process driven by the institutional constraints rather than by the incentive of a decision-maker, be motivated to act on the decision-making process? Stakeholders promoting a policy proposal therefore believe that their activity could be efficient. This belief stems from the idea that decision-makers exist, and that they can modify decision-making.

This therefore means focusing on these stakeholders' discourse on the decision-making process in order to grasp their role in transforming a proposal into a "decision". Like many other researchers, Sfez has shown that decision, understood as the moment when an individual makes a choice between several alternatives thereby fixing his situation, is a myth. However, these researchers have often distanced themselves from the concept and risked losing the significant role that this represents for actors. In this critical movement, Sfez nevertheless stands apart as he sought to go beyond a critical analysis and questioned not only the gap between myth and reality but also the role that this myth plays in the decision-making process.

First, when he questions the functions of a decision, Sfez considers that "a decision's function is to make it possible for a stakeholder to act. If indeed decision-makers have to remember the weight of determinisms and structures at every moment of an action, their momentum towards action would be broken (...) A decision is the fantastic intermediary between self and the world" (Sfez, 1992, p. 24). Decision as a concept is undoubtedly an illusion according to the author, but it is indeed what makes action possible.

According to him, the belief in decisions is not only a force for action, it is also a means of giving reassuring order to the world: "Torn between the awareness of determinisms and the voluptuousness of his liberty, the common man wants to passionately believe in decisions, ideological lifesavers, gatekeepers between liberty and determinism, an opposition that is itself ideological" (Sfez, 1992, p. 25).

Finally, for Sfez, a decision highlights a fragmented space in which decision is possible as well as the liberty of an individual to choose. He explains this as "fragment to create a counter-weight, fragment to enable liberty in order" (ibid., p. 26). Decision is therefore the concept that enables reconciliation of order which must be maintained and liberty which must be preserved. "A decision therefore quite frankly plays its custodian role; it is what makes it possible for the system to avoid entropy whilst maintaining most of the existent order" (ibid., p. 11).

To understand decision as a phenomenon, Sfez proposes to approach modern linguistics and use concepts such as code and overcode. Overcode is the translation and transfer of codes that could be fixed. We will not get into the details or the critique of such a theory, which draws more from a linguistic analysis that dissociates language from its use, meaning from the social practices in which it plays a role. Although Sfez's study has undoubtedly been excessively orientated towards a critique of stakeholders to denounce the illusions they create, it has opened up elaborate avenues which deserve to be taken into consideration.

Discourse on the decision to fight against the instability of links within statements

Our objective is to understand the role that discourses play in "decision" during policymaking and during the building of discursive coalitions. This issue is all the more interesting as even those who attack myths all justify themselves by criticising the excessive use of this concept in governmental or local life.

As in all discourse, we consider that discourse on decisions is primarily an action which makes it possible to observe an intentionality, that of the stakeholder who uses it. It also has consequences on those it targets, which are not necessarily those intended. It is therefore less the descriptive dimension of discourse that should be tested but rather more its prescriptive dimension as well as its outcomes.

Discourse on decision is primarily what makes it possible to show that the consistently unstable links that envelop a solution can harden and become rigid. A proposal statement is constructed depending on language games which give meaning to a solution by becoming the link which cements the relationship between the stakeholders. However, as we have evoked, it is the nature of a statement to always be feasible. Put differently, it always presents weaknesses that opponents can use to contest or propose an alternative. It is therefore always unstable and fragile.

A "decision" therefore presents itself as a solution to this instability, a means through which to close a statement that has been up to this point overly exposed to criticism. To resolve a problem and thus restore order in society, actors stabilise the link that connects to a solution by assembling stakeholders and calling on a decision that promises to cement the link.

It is interesting to note that the cementing promise often contributes to cementing in advance. In other words, evoking a future decision that makes it possible to shift from propositional discourse to execution and therefore to the resolution of the problem contributes in reinforcing the links that associate a problem and a solution. If actors did not believe that their action proposals could one day be implemented and enable a solution to unfold in order to eradicate a problem, they would not waste their time proposing solutions to a problem.

Discourse on decisions to freeze time

Discourse on decisions is not simply a means through which to fix the links of a solution, it is also – and this is its second characteristic – a means through which to freeze a solution in time, thereby transforming it into a stable policy change statement.

For a stakeholder, a decision signals the end of a struggle; it is the moment when the winner is declared. Calling on decisions therefore shows that there is an avenue to accomplish the battle undertaken. Using this concept is of considerable importance for the individual who wishes to persuade stakeholders to share his solution and his struggle because it shows everyone that the struggle has an outcome.

A decision is rather like the "end" of a film or a race. It is impossible to persuade individuals to go to see a film that has no end or to take part in a race which has no finishing line. Knowing if this "end" exists is of little importance. Rather, the issue is in understanding that belief in its existence persuades stakeholders to commit to the process.

Philippe Urfalino argues that a decision should be seen as the end of discussions and debates, a fact that would enable stakeholders to stop the deliberative processes in which they were engaged (Urfalino, 2007).

On the contrary, we would like to consider that the discourse of a decision makes it possible to express the expectations of a stop and an end; it is therefore a concept that has to do with temporality.

Evoking the existence of a forthcoming decision therefore means structuring the sequencing of time, thus somewhat restoring order within time that is always in disorder. As Bachelard (1932) has highlighted, while the intuition of the instant reveals the chaos and discontinuity of time, using a concept such as the length or the construction of measurement instruments restores order. A decision works as a measurement tool that structures meaning with regard to temporality.

In our opinion, this temporal dimension applies when the stakeholder appeals to a future decision as well as when he evokes a past decision. In the latter case, he gives life to the past in order to show in the present that it is not legitimate to reopen debate. We therefore focus on the decision concept to evoke the future or past which makes it possible to put order into the present.

Nevertheless, a decision does not mean the end of debate or discussion; it only expresses a discursive strategy to stop combat. It is not because the word "end" appears that the film has no follow-up. If shareholders do not share the "decision" claimed, nothing prevents them from continuing their struggle.

Discourse on the decision to politicise the topography of positions

Discourse on decision is also the means through which the topography of asymmetrical positions is fixed and politicised. We have already evoked the importance of labelling and of defining positions in the policy-making process. Here, we would like to insist further on decision theories that the discourse bearing these proposals conveys and their significance in stabilising and politicising these positions.

Whether evoked upstream or exploited downstream of the decision itself, by indicating who should or who has decided, discourse on decision defines the hierarchy of positions as well as a decision theory where varying constraints do not prevent "decision makers" from making a decision. Tested within the decision-making process, this discourse consolidates, transforms, and fixes this topography of positions which, up to this point, was relatively unstable and multi-fold.

The theory of decision is primarily based on political will and promotes the idea that society can change under the influence of these decisions and its decision-makers. As Sfez argues, if actors were to spend their time wondering who decides or whether the decision-maker really decides, then they would not act or they would rebel. Put differently, identifying a genuine theory of decision in which people play a role contributes in turning actors' attention towards soliciting a decision rather than towards opposition or revolt against social order.

By proposing a genuine theory of decision, actors also attempt to overcome topographies that are partial, subjective, contingent, and fragile in order to shape an objective topography that is more stable. It does not only involve evoking "decision-makers" but also proposing a genuine theory on government and on the forms of governance.

It is within this theoretical framework that the contradictory approaches to power that we have evoked are generally reconciled. Actors develop discourse on the government that governs by making decisions that are able to impact society as well as discourse on the ability of actors who do not necessarily occupy the peak of these topographies to influence them. Discourse on decision therefore believes in the existence of political order, able to regulate and inflect social order, as well as in the ability of individuals to interact in creating this order. However, this double belief does not simply propagate the idea of political order, it also contributes in constructing it by regulating behaviour, structuring actions, and canalising revolt. Through discourse on decision, actors contribute in producing political order.

To understand this process, we can borrow from Thoenig's study which, through the discovery of the crossed legitimisation processes that we previously evoked, insists on the mayor's specific role (Thoenig, 1976). Thoenig shows how the multiple stakeholders in a village develop a theory of decision in which the mayor is the decision-maker. This notion primarily structures the activity of those who support and seek it in order to act in one direction or another. However, this also contributes to regulating the actions of opponents. By opposing the mayor, opponents also recognise him as a decision-maker and contribute to his legitimisation. In other words, as opposed to actors located outside the village who do not consider the mayor as a decision-maker, those who oppose contribute, through their conception of decision, to putting order into their actions and transforming the mayor into the producer of political order.

Political decisions or the impossible activity of closing policy change statements

Defining a theory of decision based on the idea that decision exists, that the decision-maker can be identified, and that the decision-making moment is detectable, contributes to a final phenomenon, that of the closure of debate. While a policy statement is constructed based on its capacity to make existing public policies debatable, expecting a decision is a characteristic of stakeholders' will to close debate, and thereby the statement, by making it indisputable.

By closure, we refer to the process which transforms likelihood into truth, a weak bond into a strong one, a statement into proof. We focus on closure here to underscore its importance as well as to show its impossible completion. This closure concerns the link connecting a statement to its "decision-maker". It also concerns the link connecting the solution to elements that give it meaning, to the coalition that supports it, and to the topography of the asymmetric repartition of power that it illustrates.

With regard to the link between a problem and a solution, we primarily find two types of closure. They are both problematic in their own way and cannot succeed. The first type of closure is based on the objectification and rationalisation of the statement. This consists of transforming "likelihood" into certainty. It is one thing to emphasise that an action *can* contribute to resolving a problem; it is quite another to say that it *is* the solution to a problem. To make this transformation possible, stakeholders eliminate all traces of bricolage, which enabled them to construct this coupling by using a discourse of restoring order among scattered elements. Moreover, they can also eliminate all traces of subjectivity within the statement in order to reinforce rationalisation. It is the latter process that makes it possible to construct an "objective" discourse of rationalising a solution.

When a stakeholder demonstrates that there is only one solution to resolve a given problem, he reinforces the rationality of the link between the problem and solution by erasing the idea of subjective choice or even choice in general. It is a process we come across frequently during crisis periods for example. When a leader explains that no other solution can resolve the issue of pensions other than increasing retirement age, he tries to make the solution unquestionable and objective.

Paradoxically, this type of closure contributes to depoliticising the statement. Indeed, it eliminates conflict by relegating all contestation to irrationality and political will. The stakeholder is subjected to the rationality that his solution imposes. The objectification of a statement is therefore a major problem for stakeholders who need to assert the topography of statements. There is, therefore, no expression of political will evident, as the actor presents himself as one who is confronted by, rather than one who acts on, society. In such a case, order completely eliminates disorder, which it must feed on nonetheless.

This type of closure thus leads to a paradox. It is both the assertion of putting a society into order which tends to construct the uniqueness of the decision taken and the absolute resolution of problems – that is eliminating the two major causes of disorder. It is also the reason behind the disappearance of the decision-maker who draws his legitimacy solely from the continuous existence of problems to resolve and contenders to fend off. When a subject is uncontested, it also leaves the political scene. Closure is therefore a permanent movement which repeats itself endlessly.

A second type of closure establishes a connection to "values" or "ideologies" incompatible with those of opponents. It thus structures a divided space of debate closure based on a fixation of opposed position-taking. Here, the adversary is no longer the one with whom we debate given that his values are different. Unlike the previous one, this strategy does not erase the subjectivism of choice; underlying this subjectivism is a space to assert the willpower of actors. Paradoxically, however, it does not really eliminate debate but rather transforms it into a political confrontation between the positions taken, which have become incompatible. As it has become incompatible, the proposal is not declared the "best" proposal but rather a proposal driven by the decision-maker.

Consequently, debate is structured around the processes through which power can be accessed to stress that the decision-maker's position is both fragile and uncertain. This type of debate is observed in particular when it concerns public debate, such as gay marriage, for example. In this process, debate is nonexistent and transforms itself into a power relationship. Opponents do not only stress their position-taking; they also take advantage by stressing the government's contingency.

The illocutionary activity of closure, which seeks to interrupt debate, should not be confused with closure itself characterised by the success of this activity. Closure can therefore never succeed as opponents do not only seek to exploit the multiple flaws necessary for the impossible resolution of social problems that bricolage generates, but also because governments need to support their flaws which alone reveal their political willpower.

In sum, we can say that while the policy-making process undergoes a phase of statement elaboration and propagation, its transformation into a decision requires specific politicisation involving the ability of its spokespersons to make plausible its capacity to absorb societal disorder as well as the decision-making capacity of the leaders who establish it. To transform a statement into a decidable solution, it must therefore somewhat become the proof that the government, capable of restoring order within society, is legitimate.

The legitimisation of a solution is thus inseparable from the definition of positions of those who become "decision-makers". To stabilise a proposal, actors therefore define a topography of positions and distribute a series of labels, starting with the "decision-maker" label. As a result, generating solutions always incorporates a reconfiguration of the power stakes which accompany it. In the words of Habermas, generating a solution is therefore both a communicative activity developed through persuasion and a strategic activity which also structures the asymmetric issues of position. It is two sides of the same process which defines both, and tries to make compatible, actors' positions and their position-taking.

Combining these two contradictory sides is thus possible. Moreover, it is the actual principle of the antinomial dialectics we evoked in our introduction to define political activity. Indeed, the decision-making phase, which is based on the politicisation of solutions, makes it possible for the decision to respond to a contradictory requirement: making a statement into a policing tool, in the sense of Rancière (1998), or a commanding tool, in the sense of Freund. In other words, a statement marked by its capacity to transform a proposal into an unquestionable solution driven by a legitimate "decision-maker" and a controversial political tool. It is this tool which makes debate and opposition possible and legitimises the existence of disorder, which therefore makes restoring order possible.

Far from the garbage can model, which discerns change in public policy based on the almost random drawing[7] by actors from a garbage can in order to find problems to solutions they have in hand, the elaboration of a policy proposal assumes a complex recycling activity for the actors who drive them. This activity includes coupling with a problem through argumentation, with a coalition through persuasion as well as with a "decision-maker" through imposition.

5.4 An empirical example of decision: political decision making of the Paris tramway

To illustrate the manner in which the approach mentioned earlier makes it possible to grasp the political process of policymaking, we would like to implement it around the study of a specific empirical situation – the installation of the first tramway line in Paris. Presented during its inauguration in December 2006 by the Mayor of Paris as the symbol of genuine public policy change, this tramway was the result of a complex decision-making process, comprising twists and turns, transformations, abandon, and relaunch. This section proposes to follow the career of this tramway, from the moment it emerged as a proposal up to its decision as a new public policy and to highlight what can be grasped more effectively through a pragmatic approach.

Although it refers to a specific French situation, the tramway project reflects the path of numerous public policy proposals. We chose this project because of its ability to be a situation "like any other". Moreover, we chose it because it has the merit, through certain characteristics in its history, of making the career of a proposal more visible. It was not only under debate for close to 15 years, giving rise to multiple variations of meaning, forms, and alliances, but was also developed through two distinct and competing proposals each driven by a different coalition.

In order for its exemplary character to work, we chose not to layout the process in detail (Zittoun, 2013b), but focus instead on three specific episodes which illustrate each in its own way the last three chapters of this book: the definition of the tramway and the difficulty of successful coupling to give it meaning; the propagation of a solution; decision and the definitional stakes of a topography of positions.

Methodological considerations

The section below is based on a survey conducted on the Paris tramway between 2007 and 2010. This survey was carried out on the basis of a substantial collection of documents comprising a press review; the transcription of municipal council of Paris debates; technical dossiers elaborated by the RATP,[8] APUR,[9] the Mayor of Paris, and STIF[10]; and documents developed by associations (users' or inhabitants' associations, etc.). In addition, 17 interviews were carried out with political, technical, or associative stakeholders involved in the project.

The interviews, which lasted between 1.5 and 4 hours, sought to reconstitute the key moments during which the tramway was discussed and decided on. They thus took a specific non-directive form which transformed the interviewee into a "witness" of the scenes that had taken place and the discursive exchanges that had unfolded. These interviews only took into account the "analyses" of the interviewee when these were recontextualised, that is, when they were viewed within the real past context of statements. Our methodological choice during these interviews was to push the actor to reconstitute the debates in which he had participated by evoking, in particular, the oppositions and agreements achieved, the arguments exchanged, and succesive mutations of the project driven by these discussions. This interest in discursive interactions made it possible to grasp the experienced social situations that the actor tried to recall during the interview. The underlying assumption in a method such as this is that reflection on the project as well as coalitions between actors are primarily shaped during actual interactions.

Admittedly, the risk of deformation linked to reconstitution *a posteriori* is quite significant and we sought to reduce its effects by chronologically positioning elements, making confrontation possible during the interviews (via the use of press articles, reports, and other testimonies). We also attempted to overlap the testimonies relating a similar meeting or the same important encounter. In addition, we made the assumption that the moments stakeholders remember are primarily those where the project takes a significant step forward, which is an assumption that undoubtedly merits a long discussion.

The three meanings of the Paris tramway

To acknowledge the defining of a solution that we evoked in Chapter 2, we would like to highlight how the meaning of the Paris tramway varied. Indeed, while the tramway proposal was seriously evoked thrice by stakeholders in the 1980s, in 1993, and in 1995, each time, it was defined differently by the actors behind it. First, it was the solution to a circularity problem of users in Paris; second, it was an exit problem of users from the Paris suburbs; and finally it became a solution to the pollution problem of the capital's inhabitants. Here, it is not only the problem that is modified but also the solution which, to stick to the problem, sees its path revisited by its bearers.

The tramway project appeared in Paris in the 1980s – several reports by experts make reference to it. It is the result of the reflection of a few technicians belonging to different concerned organisations, such as RATP, STP, APUR, and SNCF, which all specialise in transport. Each time they proposed a tramway on undeveloped land, the *Petite Ceinture Ferroviaire*,[11] to first resolve the problem of users who sought to travel circularly.

To give their proposal meaning, the experts first identified in their reports a major problem encountered by a specific public. This public was unable to travel circularly without passing through the centre of Paris and losing a considerable amount of time. Having defined this problem, the actors tagged it with both a cause – the "starry" policy[12] of transport driven over the years, and a solution – the implementaton of a circular mode of transport on the *Petite Ceinture Ferroviaire*.

In other words, the experts not only defined a problem, cause, public, public policy, and solution in their reports but also proposed chaining these elements and restoring order among them. The solutions proposed were therefore first presented as the means through which to resolve problems by correcting the consequences of public policy.

At this stage of the proposal statement, the report evoked four possible modes of transport but a single layout, that of the *Petite Ceinture Ferroviaire*. The four solutions considered by the authors to resolve the circularity problem of transport and fill undeveloped urban land were the tramway, the RER,[13] the metro, and the VAL.[14] In other words, by reducing layouts to a single possibility and possible solutions to one mode of rail transport able to fit on the PCF, the statement left open four possible modes of transport. However, there was no follow-up on these reports which ended up on administrations' shelves.

In 1993, the Paris tramway was back on the agenda but with a new meaning and a new layout. Taking advantage of the debate on the extension of the T2 tramway that was under construction,[15] the defenders of the Paris tramway project proposed to push this extension by entering Paris and borrowing the *Petite Ceinture Ferroviaire*. Assigned to carry out the study were the actors who had carried out the first studies and they glued their solution, the tramway, to a new problem, the exit of commuters using the T2. Consequently, the meaning of the tramway project, which was no longer responsible for resolving the same problem, was modified by this new association.

Far from being simply a change in meaning, the tramway project changed arguments and forms. By including the project in the extension of the existing tramway, the spokespersons eliminated all alternative modes of transport. It was no longer a question of the metro or the RER, as in the previous statement, but of the tramway alone. Moreover, it was not only the problem of circularity of passengers in Paris, which disappeared from the statement, but the circular layout itself, which henceforth looked more like a coil from the outside. Ultimately, the Paris tramway proposal was no longer the means through which its protagonists could change a transport policy that was too "starry" but rather the means through which they could modify a transport policy which forced commuters to pass through the centre of Paris.

During this brief episode when the tramway project came out of the closet, the project's promoters did not simply couple it with the new problem on the agenda – the extension of the T2. They redefined the public concerned, the layout considered, and the public policy to change, in order to better support their statement. While this redefinition made it possible to put the Paris tramway project back in the spotlight, it was insufficient to move the project forward.

It was not until 1995 that the tramway project regained its importance. This time around, the problem was not linked to the extension of the T2 tramway but rather to the pollution problem in Paris during the summer of 1995. Taking advantage of this new problem on the agenda, the promoters of the tramway recycled their project by coupling it with a new problem. This new coupling not only modified the meaning of the tramway for the third time but modified the terms of debate, the public concerned, the layout identified, and the public policy to be modified as well.

The re-emergence of the tramway project thus began by the alert raised by *Airparif* – the organisation that measures air quality in Paris – in the summer of 1995. For the first time in the capital city, the prefect of Paris echoed the alert and "called on the inhabitants of Ile de France to avoid multiple journeys by car until the evening of Sunday, 16 July.[16] Pollution therefore made newspaper headlines and became an unacceptable problem requiring the mayor's response.

Taking advantage of this new opportunity, the spokespersons of the tramway succeeded in including their project on the list of solutions proposed by the mayor during his press conference a few days later. The tramway was thus no longer a solution to the PCF's problem of undeveloped land or the extension of the T2 but rather was primarily a solution to pollution. However, once again, the coupling's meaning had to be redefined. It was also necessary to redefine the layout, tramway, and pollution problem.

By identifying traffic as the main culprit of pollution,[17] the stakeholders not only simplified the problem by eliminating the other possible causes, but, in this way, they transformed the problem to address. It was no longer about addressing pollution, which is a rather complex phenomenon that can challenge non-measurable variables such as weather, wind strength, or the topography of an area, but rather of tackling city traffic, which shows the drivers on whom it is possible to act.

In other words, selection among possible causes to highlight a specific cause contributed to shifting the pollution problem to that of traffic. It is this shifting that made the problem "treatable". For its part, the tramway was no longer there to resolve the PCF's undeveloped land or extend the T2 but rather to fight against traffic. Its transporting "performance" was here replaced by its "efficiency" in fighting cars.

Here, the statement establishes a link between the instrument – the tramway – and the expected outcomes – reduction in traffic. This link also made it possible to shift an instrument towards the outcomes making the solution "compatible" with the "treatable" problem.

It is this double shift from the problem towards its cause and from the solution towards the outcomes which made the coupling of the problem and its solution possible. This association and shift modified the meaning of the tramway, which consequently fought pollution; of its public, "Parisians", victims of pollution and no longer travellers and commuters; of the culprit, traffic and no longer a "starry" policy; and also a new way of establishing the terms of debate on its layout.

Indeed, from September onward, the mayor no longer spoke of a tramway on the *Petite Ceinture Ferroviaire* but on the "southern bypass", which covers a larger perimeter. Through this new designation of location, he indicated that there were now two potential competitive layouts to fight against pollution, that of the PCF and that of the *Boulevard des Maréchaux*.

It is not a matter of identifying a new layout within the perimeter introduced but rather of considering that it exists in the field of possible layouts. In other words, for as long as the problem to address is the PCF's undeveloped urban land or the extension of the T2 layout, there is no longer room for an alternative layout. The statement somewhat locks possibilities by making meaning an imperative. On the contrary, as soon as the problem becomes a pollution problem, the choice of the layout is no longer locked in the same manner and leaves an opportunity for those supporting an alternative layout to defend their own statement.

The production of a statement thus appears as a means through which meaning can be given to a proposal. It makes assembling with a problem possible provided that there is a specific redefinition of the scattered elements which make them up in order to enable their assembling. While this assembling thus functions as a "language game", it remains clear that this game has its rules, thus opening and closing the field of possible competitors, and generally obliges the redefinition of the problem and the solution.

Convince and Persuade to propagate the two layouts: the challenges of argumentative struggles

To understand a proposal statement's career, we must also focus on how it propagates itself among stakeholders beyond its prime promoters. Indeed, no decision results from a limited number of actors but rather supposes a complex collective process made up of aggregations and agreements. Rather than considering this aggregation process as "natural", a result of a pre-existent network of actors, or of a community of values, we would like to consider it as a problem that the prime promoters must resolve by persuading stakeholders who do not necessarily have an opinion at the beginning.

To grasp this process, we would like to focus on how the promoters of each layout in competition practically try to persuade certain actors of the pertinence of their choice, of the arguments that they use, and the interlocutors they choose. Under what conditions and at what cost for the tramway do stakeholders accept to support a project? Why do they choose one layout over another? To understand this process, we would like to go back to three key moments of the propagation of the tramway. All three make it possible to grasp the significance of persuasion.

The first moment concerns the mayor who in July 1995 took a position in favour of the tramway as a solution to resolve the pollution problem. This makes it possible to better grasp the coupling process which made it possible for the tramway proposal to take advantage of the fact that pollution was put on the agenda. To understand his position-taking in favour of the tramway, we must analyse all the discussions which took place around the mayor just before he addressed the press conference. During the pollution "crisis", he convened his advisers to ask them for a list of measures to announce.[18] Discussions therefore took place within the municipality in the presence of the members of the team, the head of administration, and a few elected officials. During these meetings, the promotion activity behind the solutions was essential as the solutions available and candidates to resolve the pollution problem were numerous.

It is during these meetings that actors attempted to propose solutions and argue in their favour. Three actors thus jointly suggested the construction of a tramway as pollution problem solving. Up until then, this proposal was absent from the political sphere.[19] During discussion, these actors argued not only on the tramway's capacity to be a "good" solution to the pollution problem but also in the interest of the mayor owning a "modern" and "innovative" mode of transport. Put differently, the arguments concerned the solidity of statements on the tramway to solve the pollution problem as well as the identity this tramway proposal could attribute to the mayor if he took such a position. This qualification process is all the more interesting because it refers to a major characteristic of the discursive process – the inseparable link between the statement and its enunciator. It also refers to the resulting specificity – the strong relationship that links the qualities of a proposal and those of its spokesperson.

When these three actors put forward the tramway, they linked through their statement the modernity of this mode of transport and their own identity which they defined as "progressive".[20] The question is less in knowing whether they are "progressive' because they propose a "modern" solution or whether it is because their solution is "modern" that they can claim to be "progressive". Rather, it is about grasping the inseparable character that unfolds between the qualities of the tramway and the identity of its spokespersons. Consequently, persuading the mayor is not simply making him see that the tramway is a convincing solution to resolve the pollution problem, that is, a proposal statement which can resist public criticism on its capacity to become a pollution problem solver, but also that this statement also confers on him the qualities of the object he defends, those of a "modern" mayor who distinguishes himself from his predecessor.

From this point of view, the transfer of identity between a proposal and its owner appears as a fundamental quality of public policy, as it is rather difficult for an actor to qualify himself as "innovative" or "progressive" within the political sphere. On the contrary, the mayor can do this through his capacity to propose "innovative" solutions which mark a significant change; at least this is the argument that his advisers will use to convince him. These arguments seem to have worked because following these discussions, Jean Tibéri, the Mayor of Paris, adopted the tramway as a possible proposal. Nevertheless, far from being a simple absorber of ideas, he refused to make it THE solution as had been recommended by his advisers and integrated it within a broader plan of measures.

The second key moment took place two months later, in September 1995, when the Mayor of Paris launched studies on the tramway on the "southern bypass" of Paris and not on the *Petite Ceinture Ferroviaire*. This moment showed that the redenomination of the perimeter, far from being a simple change in labelling, is the result of argumentation destined to put the two layouts into competition.

Indeed, while only one layout was considered in July during the press conference on pollution, a second layout emerged immediately after an informal meeting between the mayor and the chairman of the RATP,[21] who persuaded him. While it has not been possible to accurately trace this discussion, it has been possible to reconstitute the preparatory discussion which took place three days earlier between the chairman of the RATP and his close advisers. Before persuading the mayor, the chairman was also persuaded by a series of arguments supported by his advisers.[22]

During this preparatory discussion, two groups opposed each other using arguments. These groups show the internal departmental divisions at the RATP. On the one hand were the "bus" specialists joined by a new generation of transport[23] experts who paid more attention to the inter-action between transport and urban planning. On the other hand were "metro"[24] specialists. While their positions within the organisation are not equal, as those who defend the metro are often seen as all powerful within the RATP, the arguments defended by those who defend buses seem to have counterbalanced this unbalanced weight.

By highlighting the saturation problem of the PC bus line, the bus specialists defended the idea that the tramway could advantageously replace it on the *Boulevard des Maréchaux*, thereby responding similarly to the pollution problem that the mayor sought to address. To put it differently, by positioning the tramway on the *Boulevard des Maréchaux*, the stakeholders proposed to make the tramway the solution to two problems rather than to a single one.

While these arguments influenced the position-taking of the RATP chairman, it appears that the argument that the tramway on the *Boulevard des Maréchaux* would be the most visible, urban, modern, and less of a "disguised metro" had the most decisive impact.[25] In other words, the argument that the layout on the *Boulevard des Maréchaux* makes the "innovative" and "modern" character of the tramway less disputable and facilitates its transfer on the identity of its owner seems to have been a determining factor in the position taken by the RATP chairman. It should also be noted that for the RATP chairman, it is less about having an argument which persuades him but rather having an argument that he can use to persuade the mayor. The determining argument thus has an impact for its anticipation of future testing rather than for its immediate impact.

Similarly, this argument was able to persuade the mayor because it provided him with an exportable argument which enabled him to convince his fellow citizens, rather than because it influenced his own position. Put differently, the influence of arguments is all the more important as the position-taking of actors varies more when they know that once the choice is made, they will have to argue out the position taken less for justification purposes than to persuade other stakeholders. Ultimately, the mayor adopted this idea that the second layout was cred-ible and deserved to be in competition with the first layout. By indi-cating that the tramway would be on the southern bypass, he proposed that both layouts should be studied and posed himself as the judge of this choice.

The third moment we focus on is actually a period of three years during which the stakeholders involved in one or the other layouts attempt to persuade the mayor who had positioned himself as judge. This period interests us because, on the one hand, it makes it possible to analyse the stabilisation of the two proposal statements, each with a specific meaning, a different layout, and a series of arguments which make it the "best" solution, and on the other, their propagation, which unfolds around two distinct discursive coalitions.

As pollution was no longer at the centre of the agenda and experts were consulted to state their position between the two layouts, debate took a slower and diffuse pace. During this more discreet period, more actors joined the debate and took a position for one layout or the other. The propagation of the tramway as a solution took place for both the *Maréchaux* and the *Petite Ceinture Ferroviaire* layout. This led to the building of two coalitions structured around discourse on one or the other layout.

In the studies on networks and coalitions, the stakeholders involved are often considered to have established links amongst them in advance. These links explain their capacity to come together around a same policy proposal. In the Paris tramway example, it is rather difficult to establish a common link on a specific matter between the mobilised actors other than their adhesion to one or the other layout, as stakeholders are spread throughout all the organisations. Whether we analyse the RATP, STP, Mayor of Paris, APUR, or FNAUT,[26] we find within each organisation and at all hierarchical levels those who defend the tramway on the *Petite Ceinture Ferroviaire* and those who defend it on the *Boulevard des Maréchaux*. We thus witness the building of two coalitions; the discourse that becomes richer and institutionalised forms the cement.

The statement and arguments that accompany each layout stabilise it into the "best" solution to address the problems to be resolved. For the first layout – that of the *Petite Ceinture*, its promoter explained that it was the best project to resolve transport problems in the south of the capital city and reduce traffic by proposing a rapid mode of transport. It was primarily defended by transport experts at the RATP, STP, City Hall of Paris, and APUR.

These specialised experts in transportation engineering were notably mobilised to draw up a comparison report between the two layouts through a joint commission. In this commission, which was chaired by an STP member who favoured the PCF, experts used their knowledge and know-how to show that, with regard to classical indicators of transport, the *Petite Ceinture Ferroviaire* layout clearly appeared to be the most "efficient". Going twice as fast and therefore twice as attractive, it made it possible to transport many more people and thereby better satisfy the general interest of those transported. This coalition also brought together the important elected officials of Paris such as the Mayor of the 13th district, Jacques Toubon; the deputy mayor's finance assistant considered to be "close to the mayor", Jean Legaret; elected officials from the opposition belonging to the Socialist, Green and Communist parties; and important directors from the municipal administration and highly involved representatives of charitable organisations including FNAUT.

The second layout – the *Maréchaux* – became the "best" project for its promoters to develop an innovative way to design the city by taking the place of cars and proposing a mode which enabled the rehabilitation of an entire neighbourhood. Actors defending the *Maréchaux* layout were numerous as well. There was the RATP chairman and some important members of his services, the Vice President of the STP, Georges Dobias, members of APUR, and of the City Hall of Paris. These experts insisted in particular on the importance of the spatial significance of the layout which physically took the place of cars. They also stressed the importance of urban integration stakes, which made the tramway a part of the city. This coalition was defended by Gally de Jean, Mayor of the 15th district; several elected officials of the RPR, Socialist, and Green parties; and several charitable organisations including some leaders of FNAUT.

There were the "undecided" in the midst of these two coalitions, starting with the Mayor of Paris himself, who did not take any position between 1995 and 1998, and who became the target of the persuasion strategies of each of the competitive coalitions. He was not alone; when we read the official position of the spokespersons of the groups belonging to the Green and Socialist parties and even the FNAUT, indecision reigns. This indecision prevented the splitting of the structures that were quite divided. Moreover, it made it possible for the undecided to position themselves at the centre of persuasion strategies.

Choosing the layout: twisting the layout depending on actors' "weight"

By enabling the consolidation of a convincing public statement and its propagation through ownership within a coalition that bears it, persuasion makes it possible to place two serious solutions on the repertoire of available solutions in the transformation of transport policies. This process somewhat works as a filter eliminating or transforming any candidate unable to resist the testing of arguments and criticism which seeks to verify the solidity of the statement or the quality of the identity it provides. However, it says nothing of what happens when several proposals attain the repertoire.

In the tramway case, although the mayor announced that he would state his position from 1996, he prolonged his indecision up to 1998 as both layouts seemed convincing. The tramway example is even more interesting as, when the mayor made his decision, there was a major political crisis during which his legitimacy was strongly challenged. This reveals the necessity to take into account another aspect of discourse – discourse as a tool for legitimising authority and defining unequal positions.

To grasp the significance of the inseparable link which associates the definition of a genuine topography of positions unequally associated to those of position-taking, we would like to go back to two key events in the choosing of the tramway which each illustrate in their own way the importance of the "weight" of actors in the decision-making process.

The first event concerns the conception of a third layout in 1997 called the "mixed layout". This layout situated partly on the *Boulevard des Maréchaux* and partly on the *Petite Ceinture* reveals how some actors sought to have a layout which took into account its ability to solve not only pollution and identity problems but also political problems.

These actors who were primarily technicians,[27] conceived a new layout that attempted to reconcile the viewpoint of the Mayor of the 13th district, Jacques Toubon (former minister of Culture, close to Jacques Chirac, and defender of the *Petite Ceinture Ferroviaire* layout), with that of the Mayor of the 15th district, Gally de Jean, close to Jean Tibéri, who was a staunch defender of the *Maréchaux* layout. This was a "mixed" layout as it passed through the 13th district on the *Petite Ceinture Ferroviaire* and changed the layout when it arrived in the 15th district to position itself on the *Boulevard des Maréchaux*.

This layout that reconciled the two positions taken by the two district mayors was primarily the result of the strategic analysis by the two stakeholders who considered that the Mayor of Paris was unable to make a decision as he sought to avoid trouble vis-à-vis these elected officials who "weighed" heavily. It was therefore the technical means which made it possible for the two political stakeholders to reach a compromise. More so, this new twisted layout was the receptacle of the "weight" of stakeholders who thus left their impact.

This mixed layout sheds light on the inseparable character of the link between position and position-taking. From the moment the two district mayors take up a strong position in favour of one of the two layouts, they make the ultimate choice of layout a yardstick enabling the measurement of their respective "weight". Favouring one or the other layout for the Mayor of Paris inevitably means finding himself under the yoke of interpreting the respective "weights" of these two elected officials. It does not mean simply considering that the asymmetry of positions imposes the choice of the layout or that, on the contrary, the choice of the layout structures the new asymmetrical space of positions; rather, it means that once the position taken is adopted, the layout, its spokesperson, and his weight are inseparable.

From this point of view, the mixed layout physically expresses these "weights" and proposes to find a common ground to prevent a tug of war; at least, this is how its designer interprets it. The question is therefore less in knowing whether their analysis of weight is objectively relevant, but rather, understanding that taking into account these "weights" subjectively impacts the new layout by deforming it. The mixed layout is somewhat what proves the existence of these "weights", which are the principal cause of deformation. No other explanation can justify such a twisted layout.

A second event deserves our attention as well as it enriches and complicates this question of the "weight" of stakeholders. This concerns the mayor's position-taking in favour of the *Maréchaux* layout. Indeed, this took place in the midst of a major political crisis during which the legitimacy and authority of the mayor were challenged. Position-taking clearly appeared as a means for the mayor to assert his authority by underscoring that he is not under the influence of elected officials, such as Jacques Toubon, thereby minimising his "weight". From this perspective, the choice of the layout did not only reflect the mayor's "weight", but was also a tool that shaped and modified it, increasing his weight and reducing that of his opponent.

It is important to first locate the moment that the mayor took his position in order to grasp what took place. On the day following the regional elections[28] in 1998, Jacques Toubon accused Jean Tibéri of being responsible for the defeat of the Paris right-wing party and created his own group from the split RPR and UDF groups[29], comprising 30 members (there are 92 in the municipal majority). Jacques Toubon not only challenged the mayor's reputation concerning matters that had deteriorated but also his lack of projects and his inability to govern.[30]

The standoff between the two men lasted three months[31] and was particularly brutal.[32] Jean Tibéri rejected all negotiation despite the strong involvement of the RPR and even the President of the Republic.[33] This came to an end at the end of July when Jacques Toubon gave up;

he dissolved his group and returned to the fold. This was titled "Toubon surrenders" by the *Libération* newspaper.[34]

Beyond this political event, what interests us here is the manner in which the position taken by the mayor in the midst of this crisis is primarily an act intended to prove that he is indeed the mayor – that he has the authority to govern. It is within the dynamics of action that this legitimacy and "weight" were constructed and not within a rigid photography of positions.

Toubon considered the mayor's indecision as proof of his incapacity to govern. As a consequence, the mayor's position-taking during a stormy Municipal Council meeting is the means for the mayor to assert that he has the necessary authority to be mayor. In other words, it is not because he is the mayor that he chose – otherwise why had he not chosen before? He chose to assert that he was the mayor and that his new opponent, Jacques Toubon, who questioned his legitimacy, lacked the "weight" given to him. "Weight" is thus played out in this new tug of war.

During this period, numerous discussions are carried out internally between Jean Tibéri and those close to him. These discussions deal specifically with the real "weight" of Jacques Toubon and whether it is necessary to negotiate with him or not. "Weight" was debated here, with no element enabling its clear measurement. From this perspective, Tibéri's strategy was very clear. By considering that Toubon did not have the "weight" to overthrow him, he refused to negotiate with him. He thus explicitly rejected the mixed layout which was not only the result of Toubon's "weight" but also had the effect of recognising this weight as it was the proof of its existence.[35]

The political crisis triggered by Toubon around the legitimacy of the mayor, and which was based in particular on the absence of progress on dossiers, paradoxically contributed to strengthening Mayor Jean Tibéri and pushed him to take a position and advance the dossiers on the tramway. In some ways, the problems that Toubon highlighted, and which were conveyed internally by his team, made it possible to assert solutions in terms of dossiers and a new organisation.[36] Once the crisis was overcome, the mayor publicly and conclusively took a position in favour of the *Maréchaux* layout.

These two events reinforced the need to take the "weight" issue seriously in order to understand policymaking. However, it must be understood that far from being an objective value of positions, "weight" forms discourse that is intersubjective, as it depends on the mutual interpretation of he who has "weight" and he who takes it into account. "Weight" is also pragmatic as it can be built within action and the testing of strength. The statement bearing the proposal thus finds its stability in its capacity to respond to problems, produce identities, and support the topography of positions.

5.5 Conclusion

When we closely study the tramway's statement-making that the mayor uses during its inauguration, we notice that the mayor's discourse is far from being a transitory discourse of justification that is pronounced *a posteriori* without influence on the decision. His discourse is primarily the result of a complex and tortuous discursive process that largely contributed to its implementation. A solid, convincing, and shared public proposal statement is indeed produced over time, both by anticipating the justification activity necessary *a posteriori* and by the necessity to give meaning to action in order to share it.

The making of a proposal statement is grasped through the analysis of the discursive practices of actors. These practices are definitional, argumentative, and analytical. During the practices, actors test the action proposals that they would like to see implemented. The statement thus takes shape based on its capacity to overcome testing, which evaluates its robustness when faced with criticism on its capacity to resolve problems and to account for the identity and weight of its owners. The success of the *Maréchaux* tramway therefore resulted from its capacity to integrate itself within a resistant statement in which it was transformed into a convincing solution with regard to the air pollution problem. It also transforms those who bear it into "progressive" stakeholders and legitimises its principal owner, Jean Tibéri.

Studies on problems had already highlighted the significance of discursive practices. During agenda setting, these practices make it possible to make a situation an unacceptable problem, identify a cause, and designate the responsible party. This had been summarised by Felstiner, Abel, and Serat[37] as "Naming, Blaming, Claiming". Attentively analysing the policy-making phase makes it possible to show the importance of discursive practices in the elaboration of a repertoire of "credible" solutions. This time, however, it is not about making a situation unacceptable but, on the contrary, making the solutions able to resolve problems, convincing; the proposals able to accumulate support, persuasive; and legitimate the decisions able to establish a hierarchy of positions. We can summarise this by an equivalent formula: "Solving, Persuading, Empowering".

Rather than to continue interrogating whether public policy proposes solutions that really resolve problems, actions which really change public policy, and changes that leaders have really decided, that is, on the descriptive validity of discourse, we must first grasp the role and the effects of a proposal statement that participates in the necessary enchantment of the activity of putting into order the disorder left by problems and those who bear them.

6
Conclusion: How Public Policy Shapes Politics

According to George Burdeau, politics is what love is to reproduction; a necessary enchantment that responds to an imperative, summoning neither sarcasm nor ridicule (Burdeau, 1979). In the path we have described, public policymaking appears as a necessary political activity which enchants the world by showing that social problems are soluble; that culprits will be punished; that public policies are in place; and that those in authority have the power to decide. Public policymaking thus proposes to restore order that problems, conflicts, and all sorts of disillusions have disordered. As Julien Freund explained, public policymaking is a political activity which reconciles the antinomial dialectics of order and disorder, agreement and conflict, enchantment and disillusionment.

Undoubtedly, researchers have often felt uncomfortable with enchantment. In somewhat exaggerated terms, we find policymaking studies, the work of which consists of identifying the disillusioned and disorderly reality of the bricolages that actors carry out, on the one hand – decisions which lack a decision-maker, incoherent public policies, solutions without problems, and changes for which nobody is responsible. On the other hand are semiologists, who focus on political discourse to show enchanting characters far removed from reality. They all consider that it is the frontier between discourse and practices that distinguishes enchantment and disillusionment.

In this book, we sought to show that both have been faced with multiple dilemmas that they have been able to overcome only by leaving the artificial opposition between the world of discourse and that of practice. First and foremost, discourse is a social practice which marks intentionality; it unfolds within a relationship and has practical consequences. Discursive practices should therefore not be analysed based on their content in order to judge their scientific validity, reveal their camouflaged normativity, or underscore their illusory or mythical character but rather in light of the intentionality that they express, of the relationships they create, and the concrete consequences they provoke. During the policy-making process, discursive practices assign meaning, construct identities, distribute power, propagate proposals, convince and persuade, build agreements and disagreements, map powers, and legitimise Power.

We therefore chose to consider discursive activities as significant social practices within all public policymaking processes. What are tramways, laws, houses, and speed limits if not discourse that actors bring to life through their proposal statements? Let there be no misunderstanding – in no way do we consider here that the materialisation or the implementation of these proposals anchored in discourse has in itself no real interest, but we have chosen to focus on the public policymaking space which corresponds to a particular scene where political stakeholders, experts, a specific part of administration, interest groups, etc. intermingle. We therefore focused on the tramway proposal career, up to its construction, and on speed limits, up to the putting up of the road sign. In other words, we focused on the intentionality of those who decide that a sign or a tramway should be implemented. This therefore implies understanding policymaking as a political activity of those who govern.

At the outset, we argued that discursive practices are significant activities in all kinds of empirical public policymaking. Nevertheless, this should not be seen as a theoretical choice made in advance but rather as the result of repeated empirical analyses. Each time we tackled a terrain, we met stakeholders whose principal activity was to produce knowledge, arguments, and criticism to shape or block a proposal and persuade other stakeholders of the relevance, accuracy, or efficiency of the proposal. However, the observation tools that policymaking studies propose did not make it possible to take this into account except within interpretive and deliberative approaches. Unfortunately these have focused too often on applied policy analysis rather than on understanding empirical policy-making processes.

It is primarily to address this empirical issue that we have shaped public policy statements; a heuristic concept that enables us to grasp discursive practices as empirical activities which contribute in shaping proposals. We subsequently started on this journey, which resulted in this book, to give it a more theoretical foundation. It was not about losing actors' games and the power struggles whose significance had been shown by public policy studies. Neither was it about getting rid of all the cognitive bricolages and inconsistencies that studies had clearly shown. First and foremost, it was about finding a means to reproduce these contributions by integrating a third dimension – language games – which not only combined with actors' games and power games but also shaped them by defining identity and position and by cementing interaction and coalition.

A public policy statement is thus a concept which enables us to analyse the manner in which these three games combine. A magnifying and distorting mirror, this concept makes it possible to focus on all the bricolages and power games that previous studies had identified, as well as include the activity of making meaning and putting into order that is an essential and difficult activity in which actors indulge. A statement is therefore a knowledge device which enables us to analyse the manner in which actors give meaning to a tool, use this meaning to persuade themselves, and persuade other actors of the pertinence of adopting the proposal. Based on this meaning, they build a coalition which supports the proposal and structures a topography of power with, at its head, a legitimate decision-maker. By underscoring that persuasion is a fundamental activity for the propagation of a policy proposal, and propagation indispensable to impose it, we sought to show that meaning in action also falls within a practical and strategic dimension that neither the actors nor the researchers interested in actors' strategies can ignore.

Based on this heuristic concept, we proposed to orient the researcher's study towards the reconstitution of concrete scenes through which a statement is empirically discussed, criticised, and propagated. First and foremost, it consists in identifying these moments based on the principle that each actor shapes his own idea during the encounters and discussions he has with regard to this proposal. Moreover, the appropriation of such a proposal is a costly process, notably in terms of identity, which leaves traces in the mutation of a statement.

For the political scientist, propagation is a process which involves real contact, making it possible to identify these moments and reconstitute the exchanges which have taken place there. Admittedly, reconstitution is a process that is methodologically difficult; it is based on the memory of actors that is always selective and the always deformed speech that they use to restore it. Nevertheless, it is less costly than the use of concepts such as ideas or interests which enable researchers to think on behalf of actors.

It is interesting to note that this methodological question has always been something of a grey zone in public policymaking studies. It must be said that a paradox exists between the excessive use of interviews in classic studies and the lack of interest in discourse and debate on the processes themselves. What credit can be given to words if these words are not taken seriously within the activities themselves? The interview situation is a situation of exchanges which, although particular, is based on discourse which we cannot attribute a different epistemological status from that in other situations of exchange.

We would like to consider the interview and analysis as means through which to follow or reconstitute real scenes of discussion between actors. Moreover, it is through these discussions that the testing of a proposal statement is identified, both with regard to validity as well as the identity dimension and power relations.

Each of these methods poses numerous problems. As discursive practices, we need to consider interviews as discursive activities between two individuals, activities which have their own logic and autonomy, and which cannot be considered neutral in terms of content. As discourse is structured notably on the basis of the person to whom it is addressed, it is not possible to consider that actors' words are not partly shaped by the actor as well as by the researcher he addresses. While taking into account the distorted aspect of the interview, we would like to consider here that the deformation level becomes more important when the actor persuades the researcher of the relevance of his analysis than when he retraces the persuasion process that he used with regard to the other actors. Admittedly, memory and the putting into words to report a past event poses numerous problems. Nevertheless, the weakness of memory is also an asset to sort and select moments that the actor himself considers to be important.

Observation as a method does not present such a difficulty in reconstituting a more or less distant past as it involves directly observing the present. However, this observation poses two major problems. First, the presence of the researcher in the discussions cannot be seen as neutral. As actors construct their speech based on their interlocutor, the presence of the researcher can only deform the speech of the individual who knows he is under observation. Observation poses another problem: how can one select among the multiple discussions those that will be important for the propagation of the statement? In processes that are spread over several years, it is not possible. Only approximate and distorting methods therefore deserve to be analysed each time researchers use them.

Reconstituting statement making, proposal careers, and the building of coalitions is always a methodologically sensitive activity for the researcher. However, while he cannot reconstitute propagation accurately, he must be able to find the essential steps around adhesion or the appropriation of the new actors and the successive mutation of the statement. Identifying, selecting, sorting, and reconstituting are therefore steps which make it possible for the researcher to give a process intelligibility.

The interest of such work relies less on the specific and contingent policy-making history that it shows than on the description of a propagation process which makes it possible to compare it to other processes in order to understand how political order is constructed. Statement making thus shows the putting into political order. Faced with unacceptable problems in society, actors start proposing instruments which they graft onto problems. The proposed action indicates the response to the disorder and highlights the power that makes it possible. Its production is, first and foremost, a political activity and this is what interests us.

Actors are faced with multiple uncertainties which envelop public policy. These uncertainties are based on a public policy's capacity to resolve problems, on who decides, and on the consequences that are always unexpected from the moment public policy is implemented. However, it is the manner in which persuasion and conviction are used to address uncertainty which forms the political priority.

For the political science researcher, knowing whether policy change is real, desperately searching for explanatory variables of a phenomenon of change, or finding a new way to analyse public policy and to solve problems are all activities that neglect political and power activities. Focus should be placed on how policymakers judge, analyse, criticise, suggest, persuade, propose, reach agreement, convince, or oppose each other on public policy issues.

Indeed, it is at the heart of these activities that this key political activity of putting disorder into order resides. The key challenge for the researcher is to analyse and reveal the role of this political activity around public policy which constantly repeats itself in society – a political activity which consists of making actions and transforming them into solutions.

We have placed the study of statement making as a political phenomenon at the centre of our work. Easton outlined this idea by considering output as a political response to social disruption generated by an input but he stopped at the famous black box. Unfortunately, the authors who opened the black box ignored the political landscape in which Easton had placed it.

Although fundamentally opposed to rational choice theories, Deborah Stone also proposed to continue on this path through an innovative book

Policy Paradox, (Stone, 2002). Stone focused in particular on showing to what extent politics should not be distinguished from public policy as policy refers to facts or reason and public policy to values or emotions. She built on the idea that the analysis of public policy is a political activity where the frontiers of the feasible and the unfeasible, and order and disorder are drawn. Nevertheless, the ability to construct a public policy analysis that integrates the political dimension and improves public policy was once again evoked as an afterthought. Subsequently, this is the reason that prevented these authors from proposing a real alternative.

By fully assuming the intricate relationship between politics and public policy, we propose to more strongly assert the anchoring of public policy studies in political science. We also propose a political science which considers the analytical production of public policy knowledge and discursive activities to establish agreements and disagreements around it as a major political activity. Through the analysis of public policymaking, this political scientist makes it possible to understand contemporary society and its political transformations. It is no longer a question of analysing public policy by producing knowledge that is always partial with regard to the content or the processes without taking actors into account. Neither is it a question of carrying out a political science of public policy by highlighting policymakers' games without any real concern in the specificity of the object around which actors mobilise themselves.

First of all, it is a question of understanding the role of knowledge production, of the construction of meaning, and of language games on actual policymaking based on the study of the discursive practices of actors in interaction. It is through production, stabilisation, and the rarefaction of policy proposal statements that we can understand policymaking as a political activity. In other words, political activity is an activity through which discourse "in action" attempts to maintain order in the face of a reality that is always disorganised, discontinuous, and elusive. It is also the restoring of order that enables contestation and triggers further disorder. Policymaking thus integrates antinomial dialectics of order and disorder to become a political process in its own right.

Notes

Introduction: The Political Process of Policymaking

* The English version of this book was translated by Eunice Sanya Pelini with the help of the author.

1. "For the actions of a new prince are more narrowly observed than those of a hereditary one, and when they are seen to be able they gain more men and bind far tighter than ancient blood" (Machiavelli, 2005, p. 287). Machiavelli stresses the importance of winning the esteem of one's subjects through "great enterprises" not only in military affairs but also in the internal affairs of state.

2. Pierre Favre borrows this expression from Canguilhem.

3. "The raison d'être of politics is human plurality. (...) Politics deals with the community and the reciprocity of different human beings. Men organise themselves politically according to certain essential commonalities found within or abstracted from an absolute chaos of differences (...) From the outset, politics organises completely different human beings by considering their relative equality and disregarding their relative diversity" (Freund, 1986, p. 21).

2   Creating Social Disorder: Constructing, Propagating and Policitising Social Problems

1. Followers of the Chicago school of political sciences, such as Harold Lasswell or Herbert Simon, strongly affirm his influence on their own thoughts. He is also often cited by authors such as Charles Lindblom, Charles Jones, and David Smith. Nevertheless, one of the historians of political sciences is more subtle on Dewey's influence and stresses in particular the complex and ambiguous relationships that he maintained with political sciences and politicists (Farr, 1988, 1999). While he does not deny his direct influence among some authors, Farr points out the relatively low number of references to Dewey in the two major journals of Political Sciences, the *American Political Science Review (APSR)* and the *Political Science Quarterly* during the 20th century. He further explains John Dewey's aversion to political sciences as was developed then. Dewey considered political sciences, but also all social sciences in general, as immature and far from genuine scientific approaches.

2. Some attribute it to Layme Hoppe "Agenda-setting strategies: the case of pollution problems". Unpublished papers, annual meeting APSA, 1970.

3. "Underlying our work in this book is an understanding of political decision making that is firmly based in bounded rationality. (...) We argue in *The Politics of Attention* that policy is a function of two distinct sources. The first is "friction" in the "rules of the games" that make it difficult for any action to take place in a political system. (...) The second source of stability may be found in the cognitive and emotional constraints of political actors – the bounds of their rationality."

4. "Long periods of stability are interrupted by bursts of frenetic policy activity" (Baumgartner and Jones, 2005, p. XVII).

3 Defining Solution: A Complex Bricolage to Solve Public Problems

1. "As if discourse, far from being a *transparent* or *neutral* element where *sexuality* is disarmed and politics is pacified, is in fact one of the places where sexuality and politics exercise in a privileged way some of their most formidable powers" (Foucault, 1971, pp. 11–12).
2. "[Discourses] are to be treated as ensembles of discursive events; (...) [where an event] is not immaterial; it takes effect, becomes effect, always on the level of materiality: events have their place; they consist in relation to, coexistence with, dispersion of, the cross checking accumulation and the selection of material elements" (Foucault, 1971, p. 55).
3. "What confuses us in the uniform appearance of words when we hear them spoken or meet them in script and print. For their application is not presented to us so clearly. Especially when we are doing philosophy (...) *Philosophy* may in no way interfere with the actual use of language; it *can* in the end *only describe it*. For it cannot give it any foundation either. It leaves everything as it is. (...) Every sign by itself seems dead. What gives it life? In use it is alive (...) One cannot guess how a word functions. One has to look at its use and learn from that" (Wittgenstein, 1958).
4. "Commentary limited the hazards of discourse (...) [it] limited the hazards of discourse through the action of an identity taking the form repetition and sameness. The author principle limits this same chance element through the action of an identity whose form is that of individuality and the I" (Foucault, 1971, p. 31).
5. http://www.whitehouse.gov/the-press-office/remarks-president-education-reform-national-urban-league-centennial-conference
6. The 9/11 commission report: Final report of the national commission on terrorist attacks upon the United States. US Independent Agencies and Commissions, 2011. http://govinfo.library.unt.edu/911/report/911Report.pdf
7. "Some couplings are more likely than others. Everything cannot interact with everything else. For one thing, the timing of an item's arrival in its stream affects its ability to be joined to items in other streams" (Kingdon, 1995, p. 207).

4 Propagating Solution: Argumentative Strategies to Cement Coalitions

1. Ricoeur makes reference here to Balzac's *Peau de chagrin* where the leather talisman shrinks each time it grants a wish.
2. "The task of the mayor and the Development Administrator was to persuade them that a particular proposal satisfied their own criteria of judgement, whether these were primarily the criteria of businessmen concerned with traffic and retail sales, trade union leaders concerned with employment and local prosperity, or political liberals concerned with slums, housing, and race relations" Dahl, pp. 1965, 136).

3. "Thus the men who were most influential in redevelopment constantly struggled to shape their proposals to fall within what they conceived to be the limits imposed by the attitudes and interests of various elements in the community" (Dahl, 1965, p. 138).
4. "The play of power is not a substitute for policy analysis, simply resolving those issues unsettled by analysis, policy analysis is incorporated as an instrument or weapon into the play of power, changing the character of analysis as a result" (Lindblom, 1968, p. 30).
5. "As politicians know only too well but social scientists too often forget, public policy is made of language. Whether in written or oral form, argument is central in all stages of the policy process. Discussion goes on in any organization, private or public, and in any political system, even a dictatorship; but it is so much at the heart of democratic politics and policy that democracy has been called a system of government by discussion. Political parties, the electorate, the legislature, the executive, the courts, the media, interests groups and independent experts all engage in a continuous process of debate and reciprocal persuasion" (Majone, 1989, p. 1).
6. "In sum, the argumentative turn in policy analysis and planning represents practical, theoretical and political advances in the field. Practically, the focus on argumentation allows us to examine closely the communicative and rhetorical strategies that planners and analysts use to direct attention to the problems and options they are assessing. Theoretically, the focus on argumentation allows us to recognize the complex ways analysts not only solve but formulate problems, the ways their arguments express or resist broader relations of power and belief, and the ways their practical arguments are inescapably both normative and descriptive. Finally our focus on argumentation reveals both the micro-politics of planners' and analysts' agenda setting, selective representations, and claims, and the macro-politics of analysts' participation in large discourses, whether those are articulated in relatively organized discourse coalitions or through more diffuse, if perhaps more subtly influential, ideologies and systems of political belief." (Fischer and Forester, 1993, p.14).
7. Interview with the Director of Construction of the Housing Ministry, conducted in 1998.
8. Authors such as Heclo and Wildavsky (1974), Lowi (1972), Richardson, Gustafson and Jordan (1982), Kingdon (1995), Sabatier and Jenkins-Smith (1993) come to mind.
9. "We conclude that partisan mutual adjustment is a method for coordinating decisions of strategic problem solvers. (...) There is a paradoxical quality to this argument. One ordinarily assumes that the more numerous the decision makers, the more difficult the process of coordination. We are instead suggesting that given that decision making is incremental and disjointed, more rather than fewer decision makers can facilitate coordination" (Lindblom, 1965, p. 148).

5   Policy Statements to Legitimise "Decision-Makers"

1. "Authority, on the other hand, is incompatible with persuasion, which presupposes equality and works through a process of argumentation. Where arguments are used, authority is left in abeyance. Against the egalitarian order

of persuasion stands the authoritarian order, which is always hierarchical. If authority is to be defined at all, then it must be in contradistinction to both coercion by force and persuasion through arguments. (The authoritarian relation between the one who commands and the one who obeys rests neither on common reason nor on the power of the one who commands; what they have in common is the hierarchy itself, whose rightness and legitimacy both recognise and where both have their predetermined stable place)," Arendt, 1958, p. 82).

2. "When elite resort to propaganda, the tactical problem is to select symbols and channels capable of eliciting the desired concerted acts. There is incessant resort to repetition or distraction. (...) Propaganda, when successful, is astute in handling: Aggressiveness, Guilt, Weakness, Affection. (...) Propaganda, then, is conducted with symbols which are utilized as far as possible by elite and counter-elite; but the intensity of collective emotions and the broad direction and distribution of collective acts are matters of the changing total context" (Lasswell, 1936, p. 37).

3. Herbert Simon questions objective rationality; Charles Lindblom is against the synoptic method and Aaron Wildavsky criticises Planning Programming Budgeting System (PPBS) methods denying the role of values.

4. "This is the principle of error whose most accomplished expression is provided by Austin (or Habermas following him)...when he thinks he has found in discourse itself – in the linguistic substance of speech as it were – the key to the efficacy of speech. To try to understand linguistically the power of linguistic manifestations, to search within language for the principle of the logic and efficacy of the institution, is to forget that authority comes to language from outside, a fact concretely exemplified by the *skeptron* that, in Homer, is passed to the orator who is about to speak. Language at most represents this authority, manifests and symbolises it" (Bourdieu, 2001, p. 161).

5. According to Habermas, in such a case, not only do we assume free will, but autonomy as well (by autonomy he means the capacity to engage one's own free will depending on normative awareness).

6. Drawing from Simon's definition where it is "the power to make decisions which guides the actions of others" (March and Simon, 1958; Simon, 1983 [1945]), as well as from discussions with March and Lasswell's studies, Dahl produces a definition that he qualifies more as intuition rather than rigorous construction (Dahl, 1957): "A has power over B to the extent that he can get B to do something that B would not otherwise do" (p. 202–203).

7. Here, "almost" stresses that John Kingdon does not support the random character of encounter but has difficulty providing an alternative explanation.

8. The *Régie Autonome des Transports Parisiens* is the company which manages public transport in Paris.

9. *Agence Parisienne d'Urbanisme* is the agency in charge of large urban development projects in the city of Paris.

10. *Le Syndicat des Transports d'Île de France* is the company which defines the general trends of public transport policies within the Paris area at the regional level. It is composed of different institutions: Mayor of Paris, Ile-de-France region, and the State.

11. PCF is a 23 kilometres long railway line that was constructed between 1852 and 1867 and encircled Paris. It was intended at the time to link eight Paris

stations each belonging to a different private company. While in 1900, the year of the universal exhibition, almost 40 million passengers used PCF, in 1934, only 6 million did. A victim of the metro, the PCF was principally replaced during that year by a bus, the PC bus which, although the name evoked the *Petite Ceinture*, circulated on another circular track parallel to it: the *boulevard des Maréchaux*. The final section for passengers was closed in 1988 to leave room for 3 kilometres of the RER C, and that for goods in 1993.

12. The "starry" policy means that all the tracks depart from the centre of Paris and go towards the suburbs, somewhat designing a star.
13. The RER is a rapid metro destined for the suburbs.
14. The VAL is a hybrid mode of transport between the metro and the tramway.
15. The T2 tramway was introduced in the 1990s in the Paris suburbs.
16. "The use of cars within Paris is not recommended" *Le Monde*, 14 July 1995.
17. "One thing is clear: the levels of air pollution that we are experiencing pose a more general problem of the evolution of traffic within cities, as, without a doubt, while industrial pollution has been effectively addressed for years, air pollution is today very largely due to traffic", (transcription of the debates of the Municipal Council of Paris, session held on 24 July 1995. 10–1995 – D1082).
18. "We were looking for a list of measures..." (Interview with one head of administration of Paris).
19. "At a political level, the project was not ready. It was not in people's minds. It was in the moment. Honestly, in 1995, constructing a tramway in Paris was as crazy as constructing bicycles. (...)" (Interview with a member of Jean Tibéri's team).
20. "It's the somewhat 'progressive' streak around Tibéri (...), I also found myself there, pushed to new ideas and to a break with the former administration. In all the domains: there are fewer offices than with Chirac, there are more bicycles than with Chirac. We were renovating. Chirac had built the city like a Ministry. Tibéri was something else. We were becoming a local community. With new ideas. We said to ourselves a tramway, that's new", (Interview with a member of Jean Tibéri's team).
21. "Very rapidly, when they begin speaking about it in the papers, it's the SNCF project which holds the lead. Not the RATP. Then, it is at that moment that Bailly sees Jean Tibéri and he tells him there's an alternative project on the Maréchaux", (Interview with a member of Jean Tibéri's team).
22. "It was just before this meeting [with Tibéri] where Jean-Paul brought us together but quite briefly. He said 'what card shall we play?' Not as a company but as a Paris community. What are the forces involved? The elements for, the elements against. How should we position ourselves? (...) The CEO of the RATP was a very important actor" (...), (Interview with an RATP manager).
23. "It's those who consider that the tramway can be urban? Absolutely. Look where I place them. They are those who convince the RATP chairman. Without difficulty." (...) "I remember the meeting in his office where we followed through with arguments and got him convinced." (...) "No difficulty convincing Jean-Paul Bailly during a meeting which is still fresh in our minds", (Interview with an RATP manager).

24. "PZ: because there is a bus expert and a metro expert? Of course. There are metro experts, bus experts and general experts. Generalists are the experts who say that one mode of transport does not exist per se. A mode of transport is an urban system designed in interaction with its urban environment. In this regard, the metro is not an urban system, it is a transport system. Regardless of whether it passes under the yard or a little further, what is important is the stations that emerge on the surface" (Interview with an RATP manager).

25. "And it's him. The arguments, civilised path, uncivilised path and we're not going to make the 14th metro line, he is the one who formalised them like that" (Interview with a RATP manager).

26. Fédération Nationale des Associations des Usagers de Transport (National Transport Users' Federation).

27. "We proposed a third solution to Tibéri. I personally went for the occasion. Why? I thought it was a solution that was technically feasible, it gave satisfactory results (...). PZ: where is the mixed solution from? It's from Lambolay's imagination who wakes up one morning and comes to see me and tells me. He felt that the project was not progressing, that it was trailing. The deliberations started terribly late even though the decision had already been taken in advance. In people's minds. We were unable to present our baby as we didn't know if we would obtain a majority. Then Lambolay comes to see me. He must have discussed with Toubon. Toubon rather liked Lambolay besides, he tried to ensure that it was put on the PC. Lambolay comes to see me with the dossier" (Interview with an administrative official of the City of Paris).

28. "It is a question of learning from the two and a half failures because the last municipal elections in Paris were not good for the UDF–RPR majority" explained one of the dissidents, Claude Goasguen, general secretary of the UDF on France Inter, (Reuters, 7 April 1998).

29. RPR and UDF were the two main right political parties in France.

30. "We want to remobilise the municipal majority, create conditions for its victory during the next (municipal) elections in 2001, to promote a democratic and transparent government of City Hall by our existence and our actions" (quotation from Jacques Toubon, Reuters communiqué, 6 April 1998).

31. "Chirac's advisors say that 'Tibéri always starts a meeting by saying "we are not going to make a decision today".' This is not true. The coup showed that he was capable of rapidly making a decision. I speak of a coup as we are the ones who used the word coup, on purpose, voluntarily, to break the system; besides, that turned out well", (Interview with a member of Jean Tibéri's team).

32. "Institutional chaos at City Hall; Jean Tibéri close to a political knock out. An all-out war initiated since Monday morning within RPR between the Mayor of Paris and Jacques Toubon continues to wreak havoc" (*Libération*, 9 April 1998).

33. The Toubon Tibéri conflict going nowhere (*Le Monde*, 25 May 1998).

34. *Libération*, 28 July 1998.

35. "We arrived at Jean Tibéri's; we were done in less than half an hour. He practically blamed us for proposing a solution to please Toubon. I don't think he had said no because of Toubon, I think he had said no because in his mind,

the problem was already sorted. There were many choices which had not been made; technical, lateral and axial choices, all that"... (Interview with an administrative official of the City of Paris).

36. "The putsch is both a terrible thing which led to other disappointments which led to 2001. But at the same time, it is clear that it's Tibéri who's ahead, he fulfilled the requirements. That's what the press said after the putsch. There was the courage to go, he imposed sanctions. He's not the small Mayor that has been described. It's the putsch that led to the reorganisation of the administration. This is the problem that Toubon rightly pointed out. And how do we respond to that? The response is that delegations withdraw [of deputy Mayors]. But it is also necessary for the Mayor to respond. His political response is "I'm going to reform my administration". Elected officials will be listened to. Projects will progress more rapidly", (Interview with a team member).

37. W. L. F. Felstiner, R. L. Abel and A. Sarat, "Emergence and Transformation of Disputes: Naming, Blaming, Claiming..., The", *Law & Society Review*, 15, 1980, p. 631.

Bibliography

ALLISON (Graham) and ZELIKOW (Philip) (1999), *Essence of Decision, Explaining the Cuban Missile Crisis*, New York (NY): Longman.

AMOSSY (Ruth) (2006), *L'argumentation dans le discours*, Paris: Armand Colin.

ANDERSON (James) (1975), *Public Policy-Making*, New York (NY): Praeger.

ARENDT (Hannah) (1958), "What is *authority?*", in C. Friedrich (ed.), Nomos I: *Authority*, Cambridge, MA: Harvard University Press, pp. 81–112.

ARENDT (Hannah) (2006), *Between Past and Future*, New York: Penguin Classics.

ARON (Raymond) (1967), *Les étapes de la pensée sociologique*, Paris: Gallimard.

ARORA (Satish) and LASSWELL (Harold) (1969), *Political Communication; The Public Language of Political Elites in India and the United States*, New York (NY): Holt.

ARROW (Kenneth) (2004), "Is Bounded Rationality Unboundedly Rational? Some Ruminations", in Mie Augier and James March (eds), *Models of a Man: Essays in Memory of Herbert A. Simon*, Cambridge (MA): The MIT Press, pp. 47–55.

AUGIER (Mie) and MARCH (James) (2004) (eds), *Models of a Man: Essays in Memory of Herbert A. Simon*, Cambridge (MA): The MIT Press.

AUSTIN (John) (1962), "How to do Things with Words", Oxford: Oxford University Press.

Bachelard, G. (1932), *L'Intuition de l'instant*, Paris, Stock.

BACHRACH (Peter) and BARATZ (Morton) (1962), "Two Faces of Power", *The American Political Science Review*, 56(4): 947–952.

BACHRACH (Peter) and BARATZ (Morton) (1963), "Decisions and Nondecisions: An Analytical Framework", *The American Political Science Review*, 57(3): 632–642.

BALANDIER (Georges) (1967), *Anthropologie politique*, Paris: PUF.

BALANDIER (Georges) (1992), *Le pouvoir sur scènes*, Paris: Balland.

BANFIELD (Edward C.) (1961), *Political influence*, Glencoe (Ill.), The Free Press.

BAREL (Yves) (1984), *La société du vide*, Paris: Seuil.

BAUMGARTNER (Frank) and JONES (Bryan D.) (2005), *The Politics of Attention: How Government Prioritizes Problems*, Chicago (IL): University of Chicago Press.

BECKER (Howard) (1985), *Outsiders*, Paris: Métailié.

BENTLEY (Arthur F.) (1908), *The Process of Government: A Study of Social Pressures*, Chicago (IL): The University of Chicago Press.

BERNSTEIN (Richard J.) (1992), "The Resurgence of Pragmatism", *Social Research*, 59(4): 813–840.

Bevir, M. and R. A. W. Rhodes (2003). Interpreting British Governance, London, Routledge

BOLTANSKI (Luc) (2009), *De la critique: Précis de sociologie de l'émancipation*, Paris: Gallimard.

BOLTANSKI (Luc) and THÉVENOT (Laurent) (1991), *De la justification: les économies de la grandeur*, Paris: Gallimard.

BOUDON (Raymond) (1995), *Le juste et le vrai*, Paris: Fayard.

BOURDIEU (Pierre) (2001), *Langage et pouvoir symbolique*, Paris: Seuil.

Bourdieu, P. and R. Christin (1990). "La construction du marché; le champ administratif et la production de la "politique du logement"." *Actes de la recherche en sciences sociales* 81–82: 65–85

BRAUD (Philippe) (1985), "Du pouvoir en général au pouvoir politique", in Madeleine Frawitz, Jean Leca (eds), *Traité de science politique, tome 1: La Science politique, Science sociale, l'Ordre politique*, Paris: Presses Universitaires de France.

BRAYBROOKE (David) and LINDBLOM (Charles) (1963), *A Strategy of Decision: Policy Evaluation as a Social Process*, New York (NY), Free Press of Glencoe.

BURDEAU (Georges) (1979), *La politique au pays des merveilles*, Paris: Presses Universitaires de France.

CALLON (Michel) (1986), "Éléments pour une sociologie de la traduction. La domestication des coquilles Saint-Jacques et des marins-pêcheurs dans la baie de Saint-Brieuc", *L'année sociologique*, 36, 169–208.

CEFAÏ (Daniel) (2007), *Pourquoi se mobilise-t-on?: les théories de l'action collective*, Paris: La Découverte.

CHATEAURAYNAUD (Francis) (2011), *Argumenter dans un champ de force, Essai de balistique sociologique*, Paris: Petra.

CHEBBAH-MALICET (Laure), GUILLALOT (Elsa) and ZITTOUN (Philippe) (2005), *Les SDF, vers une politiques de l'urgence sociale?* Paris: PUCA Recherche.

CHOMSKY (Noam) (2002), *Understanding Power*, New York: New Press.

COBB (Roger W.) and ELDER (Charles D.) (1971) "The Politics of Agenda-Building: An Alternative Perspective for Modern Democratic Theory", *The Journal of Politics*, 33(4): 892–915.

COHEN (Daniel) and LINDBLOM (Charles) (1979), *Usable Knowledge: Social Science and Social Problem Solving*, New Haven (CT): Yale University Press.

COHEN (Michaël), MARCH (James G.) and OLSEN (Johan) (1972) "A Garbage Can Model of Organisational Choice", *Administration Science Quarterly*, 17(1): 1–25.

CORCUFF (Philippe) (2006), *Les nouvelles sociologies: Entre le collectif et l'individuel*, Paris: Armand Colin.

COUGHLAN (Neil) (1975), *John Dewey: An Essay in American Intellectual History*, Chicago (IL): University of Chicago Press.

CROZIER (Michel) (1964), *Le phénomène bureaucratique*, Paris: Seuil.

CROZIER (Michel) and FRIEDBERG (Erhard) (1977), *L'acteur et le Système*, Paris: Seuil.

CROZIER (Michel) and THOENIG, (Jean-Claude) (1975), "La Régulation des systèmes organisés complexes: le cas du système de décision politico-administratif local en France", *Revue française de sociologie*, 16(1): 3–32.

CYERT (Robert M.) and MARCH (John G.) (1963), *A Behavioral Theory of the Firm*, Englewood Cliffs (NJ): Prentice-Hall.

DAHL (Robert A.) (1949), *Congress and Foreign Policy*, New Haven (CT): Yale Institute of International Studies.

DAHL (Robert A.) (1957), "The Concept of Power", *Behavioral Science*, 2(3): 201–215.

DAHL (Robert A.) (1965), *Who Governs ?*, New Haven (CT): Yale University Press.

DAHL (Robert A.) (1971), *Polyarchy: Participation and Opposition*, New Haven (CT): Yale University Press.

DAHL (Robert A.) and LINDBLOM (Charles E.) (1953), *Politics, Economics, and Welfare: Planning and Politico-Economic Systems Resolved into Basic Social Processes*, New York (NY): Harper.

DEBAISE, D. (2007), *Vie et Expérimentation. Peirce, James, Dewey*, Librairie Philosophique Vrin, Paris.

DELEUZE (Gilles) (1986), *Foucault*, Paris: Les éditions de minuit.

DEMONGEOT (Benoit) (2011), *Discuter, politiser, impose, une solution d'action publique, l'exemple du tramway*, Grenoble: Doctorat de Science Politique.

DE SAUSSURE (Ferdinand), BALLY (Charles) and SECHEHAYE, (Albert) (1986), *Course in General Linguistics*, New York (NY): McGraw-Hill.

DEWEY (John) (1927), *The Public and Its Problems*, New York (NY): H. Holt and Company.

DEWEY (John) (1938), *Logic – The Theory of Inquiry*, Henri Holt,

DEWEY (John) (2003), *Le public et ses problèmes*, Pau: Publications de l'université de Pau/Editions Léo Sheer.

DEWEY (John) and BENTLEY (Arthur F.) (1949), *Knowing and the Known*, Boston (MA), Beacon Press.

DOSSE (François) (1995), *L'empire du sens: l'humanisation des sciences humaines*, Paris: La Découverte.

DOUGLAS (Mary) (1986), *How Institutions Think*, Syracuse (NY), Syracuse University Press.

Durnova, A. and P. Zittoun (2013). "Les approches discursives des politiques publiques." *Revue Française de Science Politique* 63(3): 569–577

DYE (Thomas R.) (1972), *Understanding Public Policy*, Englewood Cliffs (NJ): Prentice-Hall.

EASTON (David) (1965a), *A Framework for Political Analysis*, Englewood Cliffs (NJ): Prentice-Hall.

EASTON (David) (1965b), *A System Analysis of Political Life*, Chicago: University of Chicago Press.

EDELMAN (Murray) (1988), *Constructing the Political Spectacle*, Chicago: University of Chicago Press.

ELIAS (Normae) (1991), *Qu'est-ce que la sociologie?*, La Tour d'Aigues, Editions de l'Aube.

FARR (James) (1988), "The History of Political Science", *American Journal of Political Science*, 32(4): 1175–1195.

FARR (James) (1999), "John Dewey and American Political Science", *American Journal of Political Science*, 43(2): 520–541.

FAVRE (Pierre) (2005), *Comprendre le monde pour en changer: épistémologie du politique*, Paris: Presses de Science Po.

FAVRE (Pierre) (2007), "La question de l'objet de la science politique a-t-elle un sens?", in Pierre Favre, Olivier Filleule and Fabien Jobard (eds), *L'atelier du politiste, théories, actions, représentations*, Paris: La découverte.

FAVRE (Pierre) (2008), "Ce que les *science studies* font à la science politique", *Revue Française de Science Politique*, 58(5): 817–829.

FELSTINER (William), ABEL (Richard) and SARAT (Austin) (1980), "Emergence and Transformation of Disputes: Naming, Blaming, Claiming", *The Law & Society Review*, 15(3–4): 631–654.

FISCHER (Frank) and FORESTER (John) (1993), *The Argumentative Turn in Policy Analysis and Planning*, Durham (NC): Duke University Press.

FOUCAULT (Michel) (1966), Les mots et les choses, Paris, Gallimard.

FOUCAULT (Michel) (1971) *L'ordre du discours*, Paris: Gallimard.

FOUCAULT (Michel) (2008), *L'archéologie du savoir*, Paris: Gallimard.

FREGA (Roberto) (2006), *John Dewey et la philosophie comme épistémologie de la pratique*, Paris: L'Harmattan.

FREUND (Julien) (1986), *L'essence du politique*, Paris: Dalloz.

FRIEDRICH (Carl J.) (1963), *Man and his Government: An Empirical Theory of Politics*, New York (NY): McGraw-Hill.

GARFINKEL (Harold) (1984), *Studies in Ethnomethodology*, New York (NY): Wiley.

GILBERT (Claude) and HENRY (Emmanuel) (2009), *Comment se construisent les problèmes de santé publique*, Paris: La découverte.

GOFFMAN (Erving) (1967), *Interaction Ritual*, New Jersey; Transaction Publishers.

GRAWITZ (Madeleine) and LECA (Jean) (1985), *Traité de science politique, tome 1: La Science politique, Science sociale, l'Ordre politique*, Paris: Presses Universitaires de France.

GUSFIELD (Joseph) (1981), *The Culture of Public Problem*, Chicago (IL): Chicago University of Chicago Press.

HABERMAS (Jürgen) (1973), *La technique et la science comme "idéologie"*, Paris: Gallimard.

HABERMAS (Jürgen) (1999), *Vérité et Justification*, Paris: Gallimard.

HAJER (Marteen) and LAWS (David) (2006), "Ordering Through Discourse", in Robert Goodin, Martin Rein and Michael Moran (eds), *The Oxford Handbook of Public Policy*, Oxford: Oxford University Press, pp. 251–268.

HALL (Peter) (1986), *Governing the Economy: The Politics of State Intervention in Britain and France*, Cambridge (IL): Polity Press, B. Blackwell.

HALL (Peter) (1993), "Policy Paradigms, Social Learning and the State: The Case of Economic Policymaking in Britain", *Comparative Politics*, 25(3): 275–296.

HALL (Peter) and TAYLOR (Rose) (1996), "Political Science and the Three New Institutionalisms", *Political Studies*, 44(5): 936–957.

HECLO (Hugh) and WILDAVSKY (Aaron) (1974), *Private Government of Public Money*, London: Macmillan.

JAMES (William) (1890), "The Principles of Psychology", New York (NY): Holt.

JAMES (William) (1909), *A Pluralistic Universe*, London: Longmans, Green and Co.

JAMES (William) (1995), *Pragmatism: New Name for Some Old Ways of Thinking*, Mineola, (NY), Courier Dover Publications.

JOBERT (Bruno) (1994), *Le tournant néo-libéral en Europe*, Paris: L'Harmattan.

JOBERT (Bruno) and MULLER (Pierre) (1987), *L'État en action, politiques publiques et corporatismes*, Paris: PUF.

JONES (Charles O.) (1970), *An Introduction to the Study of Public Policy*, Belmont (CA): Wadsworth Publishing Company.

KINGDON (John) (1995), *Agendas, Alternatives and Public Policies*, New York (NY): Longman.

KUHN (Thomas) (1962), *The Structure of Scientific Revolutions*, Chicago: The University of Chicago Press.

LAGROYE (Jacques) (2003), "Les processus de politisation", in Jacques Lagroye (ed.), *La politisation*, Paris: Belin, pp. 359–372.

LASCOUMES (Pierre) and SIMARD (Louis) (2011), "L'action publique au prisme de ses instruments", *Revue Française de Science Politique*, 61(1): 5–22.

LASSWELL (Harold) (1927a), *Propaganda Technique in the World War*, London: Kegan Paul, Trench, Trubner and Co. Ltd.

LASSWELL (Harold) (1927b) "The Theory of Political Propaganda", *The American Political Science Review*, 21(3): 627–631.

LASSWELL (Harold) (1936), *Politics: Who Gets What, When, How*, New York (NY): Whittlesey House McGraw-Hill Book Company.

Lasswell, H. (1942a) "The developping science of democracy". dans L. White (ed) *The future of Government in the united states. Essays in honour of Charles E. Merriam*. Chicago.

LASSWELL (Harold) (1942b), "The Relation of Ideological Intelligence to Public Policy", *Ethics*, 53(1): 25–34.

LASSWELL (Harold) (1971), *A Pre-View of Policy Sciences*, New York (NY): American Elsevier Publishing Co.

LASSWELL (Harold) (2003), "On The Policy Sciences in 1943", *Policy Sciences*, 36(1): 71–98.

LASSWELL (Harold) and BLUMENSTOCK (Dorothy) (1939), *World Revolutionary Propaganda. A Chicago Study*, New York (NY): A. A. Knopf.

LASSWELL (Harold) and KAPLAN (Abraham) (1952), *Power and Society: A Framework for Political Inquiry*, London: Routledge and Kegan Paul.

LASSWELL (Harold) and LEITES (Nathan) (1949), *Language of Politics: Studies in Quantitative Semantics*, New York (NY): G. W. Stewart.

LATOUR (Bruno) (1993), *Aramis ou l'amour des techniques*, Paris: La découverte.

LATOUR (Bruno) (2006), *Changer de société – refaire de la sociologie*, Paris: La découverte.

LATOUR (Bruno) (2008), "Pour un dialogue entre science politique et 'science studies'". *Revue Française de Science Politique*, 58(4): 657–678.

LERNER (Daniel) and LASSWELL (Harold) (1951), *The Policy Sciences: Recent Developments in Scope and Method*, Stanford (CA): Stanford University Press.

LINDBLOM (Charles) (1958), "The Science of Muddling Through", *Public Administration Review*, 19(2): 78–88.

LINDBLOM (Charles) (1965), *The Intelligence of Democracy: Decision Making Through Mutual Adjustment*, New York (NY): Free Press.

LINDBLOM (Charles) (1968) *The Policy-Making Process*, Englewood Cliffs (NJ): Prentice-Hall.

LINDBLOM (Charles) (1979), "Still Muddling, Not Yet Through", *Public Administration Review*, 39(6): 517–526.

LINDBLOM (Charles) (1990), *Inquiry and Change: The Troubled Attempt to Understand and Shape Society*, New Haven (CT): Yale University Press.

LIPPMANN (Walter) (1922), *Public Opinion*, New York (NY): Harcourt, Brace and Co.

LIPPMANN (Walter) (1925), *The Phantom Public*, New York (NY): Harcourt, New York University Press.

LOWI (Theodore) (1972), "Four Systems of Policy, Politics, and Choice", *Public Administration Review*, 32(4): 298–310.

MACHIAVEL, (Nicolas) (2005), *The Art of War and The Prince*, Special Edition.

MAJONE (Giandomenico) (1989), *Evidence, Argument, and Persuasion in the Policy Process*, New Haven (CT): Yale University Press.

MARCH (James G.) and SIMON (Herbert A.) (1958), *Organizations*, New York (NY): Wiley.

MEAD (GEORGES) (1934). *Mind, Self, and Society*. Chicago(IL): University of Chicago Press.

MEAD (GEORGES) (2009), *Mind, Self and Society from the Standpoint of a Social Behaviorist*, Chicago (IL): University of Chicago Press.

MERRIAM (Charles E.) (1925), *New Aspects of Politics*, Chicago (IL): The University of Chicago Press.

MERTON (Robert K.) (1965), *Eléments de théorie et de méthodes sociologiques*, Paris: Plon.

MEYER (Michel) (2004), *Perelman: le renouveau de la rhétorique*, Paris: Presses Universitaires de France.

MULLER (Pierre) (2000), "L'analyse cognitive des politiques publiques: vers une sociologie politique de l'action publique", *Revue Française de Science Politique*, 50(2): 189–207.

NAMENWIRTH (J. Zvi) and LASSWELL (Harold) (1970), *The Changing Language of American Values: a Computer Study of Selected Party Platforms*, Beverly Hills (CA): SAGE Publications.

NEUSTADT (Richard) (1960), *Presidential Power: The Politics of Leadership*, New York (NY): Wiley.

NEWELL (Alex) and SIMON (Herbert) (1972), *Human Problem Solving*, Englewood Cliffs (NJ): Prentice-Hall.

OFFNER (Jean-Marc) (1998), "Le tramway Saint-Denis-Bobigny entre enjeux et usages", *Les Annales de la Recherche Urbaine*, 80–81: 137–144.

PADIOLEAU (Jean G.) (1982), *L'État au concret*, Paris: PUF.

PEIRCE (Charles S.) (1868a), "Questions Concerning Certain Faculties Claimed for Man", *Journal of Speculative Philosophy*, 2: 103–114.

PEIRCE (Charles S.) (1868b), "Some Consequences of Four Incapacities Claimed for Man", *Journal of Speculative Philosophy*, 2: 140–157.

PEIRCE (Charles S.) (1878), "How to Make Our Ideas Clear", *Popular Science Monthly*, 12: 286–302.

PERELMAN (Chaïm) and OLBRECHTS-TYTECA (Lucie) (1958), *La Nouvelle Rhétorique: Traité de l'Argumentation*, Paris: Presses Universitaires de France.

PIERSON (Paul) (2000) "Increasing returns, path dependence and the study of politics", *American Political Science Review*, 94(2): 251–267.

POPPER (Karl) (1945), *The Open Society and its Enemies*, London: Routledge and Sons.

RADAELLI (Claudio) (1999), "Harmful Tax Competition in the EU: Policy Narratives and Advocacy Coalitions", *Journal of Common Market Studies*, 37(4): 661–682.

RADAELLI (Claudio) (2004), "Récits (policy narrative)", in Laurie Boussaguet, Sophie Jacquot and Pauline Ravinet (eds), *Dictionnaire des Politiques Publiques*, Paris: Presses de Science Po, pp. 364–370.

RADAELLI (Claudio) and SCHMIDT (Vivien) (2005), *Policy Change And Discourse In Europe*, London: Routledge.

RADIN (Beryl) (2000), *Beyond Machiavelli: Policy Analysis Comes of Age*, Washington (DC): Georgetown University Press.

RANCIERE (Jacques) (1998), *Aux Bords du Politique*, Paris: Gallimard.

REBOUL (Olivier) (1991), *Introduction à la Rhétorique: Théorie et Pratique*, Paris: Presses Universitaires de France.

RICHARDSON (Jeremy), GUSTAFSSON (Gunnel) and JORDAN (Grant) (1982), "The Concept of Policy Style", in Jeremy RICHARDSON (ed.), *Policy Styles in Western Europe*, London: Allen and Unwin, pp. 1–16.

RICOEUR (Paul) (1976), "La métaphore vive", *Religious Studies Review*, 2(1): 23–30.

RICOEUR (Paul) (1984), *Temps et récit, tome 2. La configuration dans le récit de fiction*, Paris: Seuil.

RIDLEY (Clarence) and SIMON (Herbert) (1943), *Measuring Municipal Activities: A Survey of Suggested Criteria for Appraising Administration*, Chicago (IL): The International City Managers' Association.

ROE (Eymerie) (1994), *Narrative Policy Analysis*, Durham: Duke University Press.

RORTY (Richard) (1982), *Consequences of Pragmatism: Essays, 1972–1980*, Minneapolis (MN): University of Minnesota Press.

ROSE (Richard) (1969), *Policy-Making in Britain: A Reader in Government*, London: Macmillan.

ROSS (Dorothy) (1991), *The Origins of American Social Science*, Cambridge (IL), Cambridge University Press.

SABATIER (Paul A.) and JENKINS-SMITH (Hank C.) (1993), *Policy Change and Learning: An Advocacy Coalition Approach*, Boulder (CO): Westview Press.

SCHATTSCHNEIDER (Elmer Eric) (1935), *Politics, Pressures, and the Tariff: A Study of Free Private Enterprise in Pressure Politics*, Upper Saddle River (NJ): Prentice Hall.

SCHATTSCHNEIDER (Elmer Eric) (1975), *The Semisovereign People: A Realist's View of Democracy in America*, Fort Worth (TN): Harcourt Brace College Publishers.

SCHMIDT (Vivien) (1999), "La France entre l'Europe et le monde Le cas des politiques économiques nationales", *Revue Française de Science Politique*, 49(1): 51–78.

Schmidt, V. A. et Radaelli, C. M. (2004) "Policy change and discourse in Europe : conceptual and methodological issues", *West European Politics*, 27.

SCHUDSON (Michael) (2008), "The "Lippmann-Dewey Debate" and the Invention of Walter Lippmann as an Anti-Democrat 1986–1996", *International Journal of Communication*, 2(1): 1031–1042.

SETBON (Michel) (1993), *Pouvoirs contre SIDA de la transfusion sanguine au dépistage, décisions et pratiques en France, Grande-Bretagne et Suède*, Paris: Seuil.

Sfez (Lucien) (1978), L'enfer et le Paradis, Paris, Presses Universitaires de France

SFEZ (Lucien) (1992), *Critique de la Décision*, Paris: Presses de la Fondation Nationale des Sciences Politiques.

SIMMEL, G. (1991) *Sociologie et épistémologie*, Paris: PUF.

SIMON (Herbert A.) (1945), *Administration Behavior*, New York (NY): Free Press.

SIMON (Herbert A.) (1947). Administrative Behavior: A study of Decision-making Processes in Administrative Organization. 4th ed. in 1997, The Free Press.

SIMON (Herbert A.) (1959), "Theories of Decision-Making in Economics and Behavioral Science", *The American Economic Review*, 49(3): 253–283.

SIMON (Herbert A.) (1969), *The Sciences of the Artificial*, Cambridge (MA): MIT Press.

SIMON (Herbert A.) (1982), *Models of Bounded Rationality*, Cambridge (MA), MIT Press.

SIMON (Herbert A.) (1983), *Administration et Processus de Décision*, Paris: Economica.

SIMON (Herbert A.) (1988) "Nobel Laureate Simon 'Mook Back': A Low Frequency Mode", *Public Administration Quarterly*, 12: 275–300.

SKOCPOL (Theda) (1979), *States and Social Revolutions: A Comparative Analysis of France, Russia, and China*, Cambridge (MA): Cambridge University Press.

Smith, B. L., Lasswell, H. D. et Casey, R. D. (1946) *Propaganda, communication, and public opinion; a comprehensive reference guide*, Princeton,, Princeton university press

SPECTOR (Malcom) and KITSUSE (John I.) (1977), *Constructing Social Problems*, Menlo Park (CA): Cummings.

STONE (Deborah) (1989), "Causal Stories and the Formation of Policy Agendas", *Political Science Quarterly*, 104(2): 281–300.

STONE (Deborah) (2002), *Policy Paradox: The Art of Political Decision Making*, New York (NY): Norton.

TARDE (Gabriel) (1901), *L'Opinion et la Foule*, Paris: F. Alcan.

THOENIG (Jean-Claude) (1976), *L'ère des technocrates*, Paris: L'Harmattan.

THOENIG (Jean-Claude) (2004), "Politique Publique", in Laurie Boussaguet, Sophie Jacquot and Pauline Ravalet (eds), *Dictionnaire des Politiques Publiques*, Paris: Presses de Science Po, pp. 326–333.

THOENIG (Jean-Claude) (2005), "Pour une épistémologie des recherches sur l'action publique", in Daniel Filâtre and Gilbert De Tersac (eds), *Les Dynamiques Intermédiaires au Coeur de l'action Publique*, Toulouse: Octares, pp. 285–306.

TIERCELIN (Claudine) (1993), *C.S. Peirce et le Pragmatisme*, Paris: PUF.

TRUMAN (David) (1951), *The Governmental Process: Political Interests and Public Opinion*, New York (NY): Alfred A. Knopf.

URFALINO (Philippe) (2007), La décision par consensus apparent. Nature et propriétés", *Revue Européenne des Sciences Sociales*, 45(1): 47–70.

VEYNE (Paul) (1971), *Comment on écrit l'histoire*, Paris: Editions du Seuil.

VEYNE (Paul) (2008), *Foucault, sa pensée, sa personne*, Paris: Albin Michel.

WALLAS (Graham) (1908), *Human Nature in Politics*, London: A. Constable and Co.

WALZER (Michael) and MILLER (David L.) (2007), *Thinking Politically: Essays in Political Theory*, New Haven (CT): Yale University Press.

WEBER (Max) (1995, *Economie et Société, tome 2*, Paris: Plon.

WEBER (Max) (2000) *Le savant et le politique*, Paris: Plon.

WILDAVSKY (Aaron) (1964) *Politics of the Budgetary Process*, Boston (MA): Little Brown.

WILDAVSKY (Aaron) (1969), "Rescuing Policy Analysis from PPBS", *Public Administration Review*, 29(2): 189–202.

WILDAVSKY (Aaron) (1987), *Speaking Truth to Power: The Art and Craft of Policy Analysis*, New Brunswick (NJ): Transaction Publishers.

WITTGENSTEIN (Ludwig) (1958), *Philosophical Investigations*, trans. G. E. M. Anscombe, New York: Macmillan.

WITTGENSTEIN (Ludwig) (1996), *Le Cahier bleu et le Cahier brun*, Paris: Gallimard.

YANOW (Dvora) and SCHWARTZ-SHEA (Peregrine) (eds) (2006), *Interpretation and Method: Empirical Research Methods and the Interpretive Turn*, Armonk (NY): M. E. Sharpe.

ZITTOUN (Philippe) (2000), *La politique du logement, 1981–1995*, Paris: L'Harmattan.

ZITTOUN (Philippe) (2001), "Partis politiques et politiques du logement, échange de ressource entre dons et dettes politiques", *Revue Française de Science Politique*, 51(5): 683–706.

ZITTOUN (Philippe) (2007), "La carte parisienne du bruit, la fabrique d'un nouvel énoncé de politique publique", *Politix*, 78(2): 157–178.

ZITTOUN (Philippe) (2008), "Référentiels et énoncés de politiques publiques: les idées en action", in Olivier Giraud and Philippe Warin (eds), *Politiques Publiques et démocratie*, Paris: Seuil, pp. 73–92.

ZITTOUN (Philippe) (2009a). "Understanding policy change as a discursive problem." *Journal of Comparative Policy Analysis* 11(1): 65–82.

ZITTOUN (Philippe) (2009b), *Des indicateurs pour gouverner: boussoles ou miroirs déformants?*, Paris: PUCA, coll. Recherche.

ZITTOUN (Philippe) (2013a). "Entre définition et propagation des énoncés de solution." *Revue Française de Science Politique* 63(3): 625–646

ZITTOUN (Philippe) (2013b), La fabrique des politiques publiques, Paris, Presses de Science Po.

The 9/11 commission report: Final report of the national commission on terrorist attacks upon the United States. US Independent Agencies and Commissions, 2011, http://govinfo.library.unt.edu/911/report/911Report.pdf

Index

Printed and bound by CPI Group (UK) Ltd, Croydon, CR0 4YY